HISTORY AND RENEWAL OF LABRADOR'S INUIT-MÉTIS

HISTORY AND RENEWAL
of Labrador's Inuit-Métis

edited by JOHN C. KENNEDY

ISER

**Institute of Social and
Economic Research**

© 2014 by John C. Kennedy

Library and Archives Canada Cataloguing in Publication
History and renewal of Labrador's Inuit-Métis / edited by John C. Kennedy.

(Social and economic papers ; no. 32)
Includes bibliographical references and index.
ISBN 978-1-894725-15-6 (pbk.)

1. Métis--Newfoundland and Labrador--Labrador--History. I. Kennedy, John C., 1943-, editor II. Series: Social and economic papers ; no. 32

E99.M47H58 2014   971.8'200497   C2014-905522-6

Social and economic papers; 32)

Design and typesetting: Alison Carr
Copy editing: Richard Tallman
Cover photograph: Mr. Brown, his family and house, Fox Harbour, 13 October 1893. Courtesy of The Rooms Provincial Archives Division, VA 152-93 / E. Curwen

Published by ISER Books — Faculty of Arts Publications
Institute of Social and Economic Research
Memorial University of Newfoundland
297 Mount Scio Road
St. John's, NL A1C 5S7
www.arts.mun.ca/iserbooks/
Printed and bound in Canada

Contents

List of Figures and Tables

Acknowledgements

Our Community–University Research Alliance (CURA) researchers in the project "Understanding the Past to Build the Future" thank the Social Sciences and Humanities Research Council of Canada (SSHRC) for its generous support of the project; the NunatuKavut Community Council and other partners; the two anonymous reviewers who offered many helpful suggestions to earlier drafts; ISER Books Academic Editor Sharon Roseman and Managing Editor Alison Carr; and the Labrador people who kindly shared with us their time and knowledge. In thanking the above, the editor accepts responsibility for any errors of fact or omission. Individual authors, listed alphabetically, wish to thank the following:

AMANDA CROMPTON thanks the CURA project researchers and, specifically, Dr. Lisa Rankin for encouraging her interest in French Labrador. Amanda also thanks the anonymous reviewers for drawing her attention to sources that substantially enhanced her chapter.

AMELIA FAY thanks Lindsay Swinarton (Université Laval) for sharing her Ph.D. dissertation data from Oakes Bay, Jim Woollett (Université Laval) for allowing access to his collections at Laval and helping throughout her fieldwork, and Peter Ramsden for producing the maps.

LAURA KELVIN thanks Lisa Rankin, the Archaeology Department at Memorial University, the Northern Science Training Program, the Newfoundland and Labrador Provincial Archaeology Office, the town of Cartwright, and the Elders who participated in her project.

JOHN C. KENNEDY thanks Amanda Crompton, second CURA Coordinator, who generously agreed to help read, format, and discuss the chapters. Amanda's scholarship is obvious in her chapter and her help was very much appreciated. John gratefully acknowledges the exemplary leadership of Lisa Rankin, our team's Principal Investigator, who generously provided editorial assistance on her students' papers. John thanks his wife and former Grenfell nurse, Karen Olsson, who offered emotional support and patiently provided assistance throughout the editorial process. He also thanks Peter Ramsden for the creation of two maps. Finally, Kennedy thanks the people of southeastern Labrador who once again allowed him into their homes and generously shared their knowledge.

GREG MITCHELL acknowledges the constant encouragement and patience of the book's editor. Greg thanks all the Inuit-Métis participants in the endless surveys and map biographies since 1979 and Mr. George Russell who, over the past few years, has coaxed and cajoled him into continuing his work. Greg thanks his wife, Lynn Mitchell, for tolerating his numerous absences while in the field and while cloistered with his computer. Greg thanks NunatuKavut Community Council and two presidents, one past, Mr. Chris Montague, and one present, Mr. Todd Russell. They not only encouraged this research but also solved administrative and political problems so that this important research could be completed.

PHOEBE MURPHY thanks Lisa Rankin for all of her support, John C. Kennedy for his leadership and dedication to this project, and the community of Cartwright.

LISA RANKIN acknowledges the hard work of all the archaeological crews involved in this research between 2003 and 2012. Without their efforts this story could not be told. Thanks also to Doris and Lewis Davis, Peyton and George Barrett, and our friends at the Cartwright Hotel and Brenda's B&B who took such great care of us. Finally, thanks to Peter Ramsden, John C. Kennedy, and the two anonymous reviewers who kindly offered valuable direction. All your efforts are appreciated.

HANS ROLLMANN is especially grateful for the perceptive comments on drafts of the paper in this volume by John C. Kennedy, and to Patty Way for sharing generously from her vast genealogical knowledge of Labrador families. I am also grateful to the Unity Archives, Herrnhut, Germany; the Moravian Church House Library and Archives in London, England; the Moravian Historical Society in Nazareth, Pennsylvania, U.S.A.; and the Moravian Archives in Bethlehem, Pennsylvania, for help and for permission to use their rich archival materials.

MARIANNE STOPP is grateful to Labrador genealogist Patty Way, whose research on Lydia Campbell, 10 years ago now, was central to formulating the paper she prepared for the Historic Sites and Monuments Board of Canada. Gordon Fulton, director (retired) of the former Historical Research Branch, carefully guided the nomination through the several stages that led to Campbell's designation.

PATRICIA (PATTY) WAY would like to thank Hans Rollmann, John C. Kennedy, and Jason Curl for sharing data, and also, posthumously, Bernard Heard, Sr. Credit especially goes to Lisa Rankin for unfailing support and to Peter Ramsden for creation of the map and genealogy chart. Thanks go as well to my husband, Gary (Stig) Bird, for his patience and to the rest of my family for understanding about "family treeing." Thanks will always be due to the people of Labrador who continually inspire me to continue this work.

Contributors

DR. AMANDA CROMPTON is a historical archaeologist. Amanda served as CURA Project Coordinator until December 2013 and is currently completing post-doctoral research at Memorial University.

AMELIA FAY, Ph.D. candidate, conducted archaeological research in the Nain area for her dissertation under the supervision of Dr. Lisa Rankin and is now Curator of the Hudson's Bay Company collection at the Manitoba Museum.

LAURA KELVIN, M.A., conducted oral history research and an archaeological survey of Sandwich Bay while a student of Dr. Lisa Rankin. She is now a Ph.D. student at Western University.

DR. JOHN C. KENNEDY taught Anthropology at Memorial University between 1973 and 2004.

GREG MITCHELL is Senior Researcher with NunatuKavut Community Council.

PHOEBE MURPHY, M.A., was a student of Dr. Rankin's and conducted archaeological research in Sandwich Bay while attending Memorial University; she is now a consulting archaeologist in Kamloops, British Columbia.

DR. LISA RANKIN is an Associate Professor of Archaeology in the Department of Archaeology at Memorial University. Since 2001 she has conducted research in coastal Labrador and served as the Principal Investigator of our SSHRC project, "Understanding the Past to Build the Future."

DR. HANS ROLLMANN is Professor of Religious Studies, Memorial University.

DR. MARIANNE STOPP has worked as an archaeologist in Labrador for over 30 years and is a historian in the Heritage Conservation and Commemoration Directorate, Parks Canada.

PATRICIA WAY is a retired educator and life-long genealogist who divides her time between Goose Bay and Cartwright, Labrador.

CHAPTER 1

Introduction

John C. Kennedy

This book presents new research on the archaeology, history, and contemporary adaptations of the people of central and southeastern Labrador, that is, the coast and interior from Lake Melville south to Chateau Bay. Our project is entitled "Understanding the Past to Build the Future," a five-year Community–University Research Alliance (CURA) funded by the Social Sciences and Humanities Research Council of Canada (SSHRC). Our team is largely composed of academic researchers (and students) who have worked in central or southeastern Labrador for some years, ensuring a level of familiarity with previous research that we hope eliminates duplication.[1] Our findings challenge long-standing assumptions about Labrador's Aboriginal history.

As with current inconsistent practice, some authors in the volume refer to the coast south of Groswater Bay as southern Labrador, others as southeastern Labrador, and we have not attempted to standardize this descriptor. Most people living in south/central Labrador are of hybrid or dual European and Inuit ancestry.[2] These mixed peoples organized politically as Métis in 1986 and their current organization, NunatuKavut Community Council (NCC), has made remarkable progress towards recognition of Inuit-Métis rights in the face of stiff opposition. The Inuttitut word NunatuKavut means "our ancient land" and needs to be distinguished from the similar neologism, Nunatsiavut, meaning "our beautiful land," the name for the autonomous Inuit self-government in northern Labrador.[3]

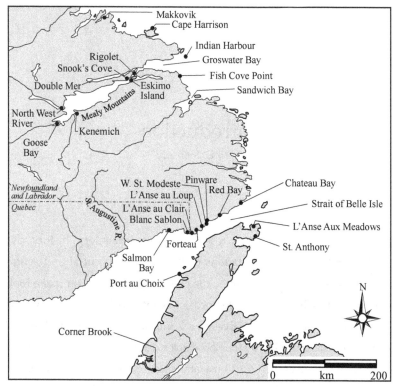

Figure 1. Newfoundland and Labrador. (John C. Kennedy Map; created by Peter Ramsden, 2014)

For understandable reasons linked to the recent history of northern Labrador, leaders of NunatuKavut refer to their membership as "southern Inuit." However, NCC members interviewed by Pace (2008), by Kelvin (2011), and by me in 2013 appear more comfortable calling themselves Métis (Kennedy, chapter 11). In this rapidly changing political landscape we are opting here for a middle ground between the "southern Inuit" preferred by the NCC leadership and Métis, the name most "rank-and-file" members self-identify as. Our use of Inuit-Métis acknowledges both their mixed origins and Inuit ancestry.

A fact generally understood within Labrador but less known beyond the region is that both historically and today, the degree of what I shall call "Inuitness" occurs along a gradient or continuum that increases

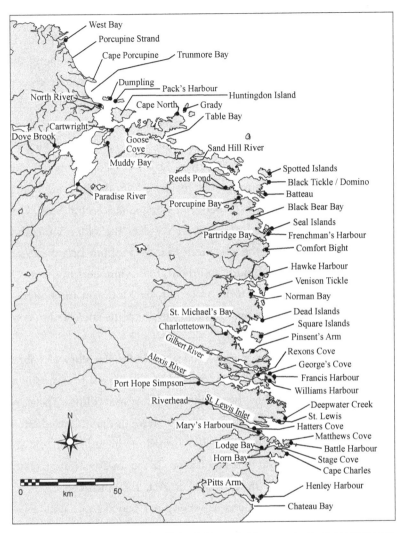

Figure 2. Southeastern Labrador. (John C. Kennedy Map; created by Peter Ramsden, 2014)

as we go north along the Labrador coast. "Inuitness" refers to the use and knowledge of Inuttitut (the Inuit language) and to a range of cultural practices and beliefs people of Inuit ancestry believe to be their own. Even within the Inuit self-government of Nunatsiavut, we find that Inuttitut is less spoken in the communities of Makkovik, Postville, and Rigolet[4] than further north in Hopedale and Nain. For example, 300 of the approximately 500 Inuit whose mother tongue is Inuttitut live in Nain, with the other 200 divided between Hopedale and Makkovik (Clarke et al. 1999). A similar gradient of Inuitness occurs along the southeastern coast where elements of the Inuit origin of Inuit-Métis culture generally increase as we move north from the Lodge Bay–Mary's Harbour area. Like any generalization, mine has exceptions. In northern Labrador, for example, Rigolet and Tuchialic have a greater Inuit legacy than Makkovik further north, much as St. Lewis (Fox Harbour) had more "Inuitness" than communities further north. But overall, "Inuitness" increases as one moves between Cape Charles and Nain. Our archaeological and historical research corrects the older view that northern Labrador was the sole Inuit homeland. Inuit occupied and used much of coastal Labrador and their greater numbers in the north are the direct result of historic protection by Moravian missionaries whom British and later Newfoundland governments entrusted to contain and protect Labrador Inuit.

The story we tell is not well known. Globally, the story of Labrador's Inuit-Métis is one of identity politics, that is, the political mobilization of communities defined by a common history and culture. The story is part of the broader resurgence of Canadian Métis that followed effective lobbying by the Native Council of Canada to include Métis as Aboriginal Canadians in the 1982 repatriated Canadian Constitution (Dahl 2013:105). Significantly, the Constitution Act, 1982 included Métis together with Inuit and Indians as Aboriginal peoples of Canada but failed to define what Métis meant or to say whether their inclusion applied to all Canadian communities who self-identified as Métis. The story of Labrador's Inuit-Métis is also part of the recent political history of Labrador, of the way Labrador's "Aboriginal map" was created before and after Newfoundland and Labrador became Canada's tenth province in 1949, and even of scholarly opinions of where particular peoples—some only known archaeologically—lived in Labrador.

Relevant Jurisdictional History

By the late fifteenth century, Europeans had the capacity and ambition to sail westward, where in Labrador they encountered two distinct Aboriginal peoples. Both had names for themselves that meant "the humans," or "the people." The first people were "Indians" who called themselves "Innu" and whose hunting culture had evolved in Labrador from earlier peoples. We learn more about the second people, the Inuit (formerly called "Eskimos"), below. Basque whalers, French fishers and sealers, Dutch explorers, and other Europeans visited Labrador and exploited seals, whales, and fish before the beginning of the British era, in 1763.

Aboriginal rights within what was once called British North America relate primarily to lands ("hunting grounds") used since "time immemorial" by specific Aboriginal groups, as first recognized in the Royal Proclamation of 1763. The Royal Proclamation did not create new rights but, instead, recognized and respected existing Aboriginal rights to lands (Cumming and Mickenberg 1972:30–31). The Royal Proclamation was the basis for making treaties with the original inhabitants of North America so as to enable development under the new British regime. Although waves of westward-bound Euro-American settlers would ignore the Proclamation and numerous court cases would weigh its implications, the Royal Proclamation's acknowledgement that Aboriginal peoples have existing rights explains why it remains the contractual model for treaty rights in the United States and Canada.

In its 2010 land claim, the NCC describes a forgotten treaty between Labrador Inuit and the British government concluded at Chateau Bay on August 21, 1765. Elsewhere (Kennedy, 2015) I maintain that the British government considered the 1765 treaty the linchpin leading to the first Moravian land grant, in 1769. But where would the Moravians locate their Labrador mission? Based on several exploratory expeditions, the missionaries preferred Esquimaux Bay (Lake Melville) where "southern" Inuit commonly wintered, whereas the Inuit whom the missionaries asked suggested Kikertet (today's Island of Ponds/Spotted

Island) (Handcock 2008:28–29). Governor Palliser, however, did not want Inuit interfering with his plans for a fishery from southeastern Labrador west to Quebec, and decreed that any mission to the Inuit must be in northern Labrador (Hiller 1977:83). In 1771, the Moravians established their first of an eventual chain of mission stations along Labrador's northern coast, providing spiritual and economic services to the Inuit and, later, to the growing category of mixed Inuit-European "Settlers" emerging during the nineteenth century (Kleivan 1966; Fay, chapter 4; Rollmann 2009, 2010, chapter 9). From the mid-nineteenth century on, "Settlers" and Inuit would increasingly see themselves as separate peoples (Ben-Dor 1966; Kleivan 1966; Kennedy 1988), although distant administrators were unaware of such local distinctions. Indeed, the Newfoundland government would come to associate northern Labrador with the Moravians, and they with Inuit, and by the twentieth century the government referred to both "Settlers" and Inuit as "Natives," providing

Figure 3. Richard Blomfield [Broomfield], wife and children, Long Bight, 1893. (Eliot Curwen fonds, The Rooms Provincial Archives Division, VA 152-150 / E. Curwen)

the template for membership used in the late twentieth century by the Labrador Inuit Association (Rollmann, chapter 9; Kennedy, 2015).

Beginning in the 1830s, the Hudson's Bay Company (HBC) began to trade in Labrador, taking over Moravian trading stores in 1926 only to suddenly abandon its Labrador trade in 1942, to be replaced by a Newfoundland government trading operation that would eventually become the most visible agency of government in northern Labrador.

Newfoundland's late entry into the Canadian federation created uncertainty over who would have responsibility for Newfoundland's Aboriginal peoples, whose jurisdictional history differed from Aboriginal peoples elsewhere in Canada. During the Newfoundland National Convention (1947–1948) contemplating Newfoundland's political future, the question arose: If Newfoundland joined Canada, would the federal government be constitutionally and financially responsible for Newfoundland and Labrador's Aboriginal peoples? This question was discussed during the Convention (Budgel 1984; Tompkins 1988; Neary 2012a, 2012b), but there was no reference to Aboriginal peoples in the Terms of Union signed in 1948. The reasons for this omission are complex and some believe that Ottawa may have simply considered the costs too high. Yet it also appears that Newfoundland believed that extending the Indian Act to Newfoundland Aboriginal peoples would be a "retrograde step" insofar as they were allowed to vote, unlike Canadian status Indians at the time. Newfoundland Aboriginal peoples were "penciled out" of final drafts of the Terms of Union because the federal government thought them to be enfranchised, few in number, and without the reserves assumed under the Indian Act (Tompkins 1988:17, 25–26).

Following Confederation in 1949, both governments negotiated a series of agreements in which the new province maintained its jurisdiction over Aboriginal peoples, providing services funded primarily by Ottawa. Much has been written about these federal–provincial agreements (e.g., Newfoundland 1974; Budgel 1984; Tompkins 1988; Moss 1988) but the important point here is that they applied originally and primarily to Aboriginal peoples in northern Labrador. At least at first,

Newfoundland bureaucrats and politicians associated "Native" with Eskimo, and Eskimos with the Moravians and northern Labrador.

Documentation pertaining to the development of the first federal–provincial agreement in 1954 only mentions "northern Labrador" (Tompkins 1988:37–45), as is the case in documents relating to Confederation examined by Neary (2012a, 2012b). Although the federal–provincial agreements included northern (and later central) Labrador Innu (formerly called Naskapi and Montagnais Indians), and later Goose Bay Inuit, and during the 1970s the people of Black Tickle, conventional

Figure 4. Mrs. Pawlo, wife of a successful fisherman at Fox Harbour, 1893. One of her grandparents was an Englishman; the other three were Esquimaux. (Eliot Curwen fonds, The Rooms Provincial Archives Division, VA 152-82 / E. Curwen)

wisdom of the time associated Aboriginal peoples with "the Moravian Coast" from Cape Harrison north to Killinek, inhibiting any claim to Aboriginality further south.

The federal–provincial agreements funded northern Labrador people according to *where* they lived, so-called "designated communities," rather than their cultural identity. Why? Historically, in northern Labrador (and, as we now know, most of coastal Labrador) European men such as those described by Rollmann (chapter 9), Way (chapter 7), and Stopp (chapter 8) married Inuit women. These unions produced the hybrid category, Kablunângajuit, meaning "partly white," the Inuit name the Moravians recorded in 1908 (Kleivan 1966:91; Kennedy, chapter 11). Within northern communities, everyone knew who was and was not Inuit (Ben-Dor 1966), but such determinations were more difficult for distant administrators. Consequently, the federal–provincial agreements funded people geographically, according to where they lived, rather than by their identity as Inuit or Settlers. And while these agreements directed unprecedented resources to improve conditions in the primarily Inuit/Settler communities of northern Labrador, the mixed European–Inuit peoples further south were overlooked. To be fair, though, at the time the stigma associated with Aboriginality probably meant that the parents of today's Inuit-Métis would have preferred to call themselves "White" or "Liveyeres" (Duncan 1902), or "Labradorians" rather than be numbered among the "Skimos," the derogatory term then used for Inuit or persons of strong Inuit ancestry (see Kennedy, chapter 11). This would change.

The Canadian government assumed legal jurisdiction over Indians (and, after 1939, Inuit) under section 92(24) of the 1867 British North America Act, and this fiduciary or guardianship responsibility in which the Crown promises to safeguard Aboriginal interests was reaffirmed under section 35 of the 1982 Constitution Act and extended to include Métis (Elliot 1985:85). The inclusion of Métis as "Aboriginal peoples of Canada," without defining what "Métis" meant, created both problems (Boisvert and Turnbull 1985:142–143; Sawchuck 2001) and opportunities. As with previous declarations, including the Royal Proclamation, the inclusion of Métis under section 35 brought court challenges, such as *R. v. Powley* (2003), by persons claiming Aboriginal rights as Métis under the Constitution Act. While the Supreme Court of Canada concluded that the Powleys, a father and son who were hunters, had the constitutionally protected Aboriginal right to hunt moose for food under section 35, their Aboriginal rights as Métis were confined to their Métis community of Sault Ste. Marie, Ontario. Put differently, under *Powley*, the category "Métis" applies to persons belonging to specific Métis communities, not to all persons of mixed Aboriginal and European ancestry. Being Métis requires *belonging* to a Métis community.[5] The *Powley* "test" modified the pre-contact *Van der Peet* (1996) determination of Aboriginal rights to take into account that Métis communities are, by definition, post-contact. The ethnogenesis of particular Métis communities must precede the establishment of "effective European control." Ethnogenesis (discussed more below) is the state of social self-consciousness causing actors to acknowledge that "we" are not like "them" (e.g. Brown 1985:1125; Kennedy, chapter 11; Stopp, chapter 8). Another consequence of the *Powley* case is that Métis communities "can potentially be found anywhere in Canada" (Dahl 2013:118), as opposed to simply western Canada.

On January 8, 2013, the federal court in Ottawa ruled in *Daniels v. Canada* that Canada's Métis and non-status Indians are "Indians" under the Indian Act, and thus the responsibility of the federal government. The federal government has appealed *Daniels* to the Supreme Court, making it impossible here to speculate on its consequences for Labrador's Inuit-Métis.

The Political Mobilization of Inuit-Métis

Revisions to the Indian Act in 1951, the extension of the right of Canadian Indians to vote in 1960, and the contentious "White Paper" in 1969 led to the birth of Aboriginal organizations across Canada in the 1970s and 1980s. Newfoundland and Labrador's first Aboriginal organization, the Native Association of Newfoundland and Labrador (NANL), was founded at Gander by Newfoundland Mi'kmaq *and* Labrador Innu in February 1973 (NANL 1973a).[6] NANL's executive, especially its energetic executive director, realized that most Aboriginal peoples lived in Labrador, and launched a housing program directed at Inuit and Settler members, mainly from northern Labrador. The appeal of NANL's housing program lay in its practicality: the redirection of existing federal and provincial programs (e.g., LEAP, ARDA, CMHC, DREE, etc.) to train and employ Aboriginal people for the construction or renovation of their homes (NANL 1973b; Anger 1983:219–220).[7]

Just as NANL was gaining popularity in Labrador, a second Aboriginal organization, the Labrador Inuit Association (LIA), was formed in September 1973 as a regional affiliate of the Inuit Tapirisat of Canada (ITC). For a short time, NANL and LIA co-operated, presenting a joint development proposal to the Federal–Provincial Native Affairs Committee on November 28, 1973. But relations eventually soured and confusion, rivalry, and distrust replaced the initial co-operation between the two groups. Both groups courted northern Labrador Settlers, who, as I observed during fieldwork and later described (Kennedy 1982:104–108), initially favoured the Indian "strangers" of NANL to their Inuit neighbours. In the end, federal pressures convinced Inuit to ignore ITC's recommendation that all LIA members speak Inuttitut and, in the face of vigorous competition from NANL, to offer the Settlers of northern Labrador, many with Inuit ancestors, full membership in October 1974 (Brantenberg 1977:397–398).[8]

In June 1975, questions about the meaning of the word "Native" led NANL to change its name to the Indian and Metis Association of Newfoundland and Labrador (IMANL) and to open an office in Goose Bay (Kennedy 1987:16). The unaccented "Metis" in IMANL appears to have referred to northern Labrador Settlers who continued to mull over their invitation to join LIA. By the fall of 1975, Labrador Innu withdrew from the IMANL to form the Naskapi–Montagnais Innu Association, becoming in 1990 the Innu Nation. The IMANL, still with Settler members, struggled to remain in Labrador, receiving federal funding in June 1975 for land claims research and, in November of the same year, funding to renovate 182 Labrador homes (Kennedy 1987:17). But eventually all northern (and later, eligible central and southeastern) Labrador Settlers joined LIA and/or became Nunatsiavut beneficiaries.[9]

In the early 1980s, coastal people residing in the Goose Bay area discussed forming an Aboriginal organization. Evidence of this appears in the handwritten notes from a lively meeting held in Happy Valley on February 13, 1981. The 20 or more people present debated the definitions of "Métis" and "Labradorian" and whether people "south of Cartwright would accept to be known as Métis." After 35 minutes of opinion and rebuttal, the majority preferred Labradorian to Métis and this appears to have led to the short-lived Native Labradorian Association of Labrador.[10] However, a year later the repatriated Constitution's inclusion of Métis as "Aboriginal Canadians" provided a new possibility, enabling Labrador peoples of mixed ancestry ineligible to join the LIA because they lacked "connection" to the Labrador Inuit land claims area to organize as Aboriginal people.[11] The Labrador Inuit land claims area includes the approximately 72,520 km[2] of land, adjacent waters, and islands that the LIA claimed and stretches from Killinek south to Fish Cove Point (see LIA 2003:51).

The earliest use of the term "Métis" in Labrador comes from Father Charles Arnaud's 1872 (see Tremblay 1977) description of Esquimaux and Métis at Rigolet (Labrèche and Kennedy 2007:49), although visitors to the southeastern coast recorded a population of mixed European–Inuit as early as 1824 (Kennedy 1995:84; Rollmann 2008). Father Arnaud had difficulty differentiating between the two groups at Rigolet. Both spoke Inuttitut, but appeared ashamed to do so in front of "outsiders" (Tremblay 1977). Important as Arnaud's observations are, the term "Métis" was not used again in Labrador for over a century. Richling (1978:50) referred to the "Metis-like genetic amalgam of [Hopedale] Settlers," while Mailhot (1997:27) describes the late nineteenth-century expansion of "Métis trappers of European and Inuit descent" along the Churchill River.

Formal registration of the Labrador Metis Association (LMA) occurred on September 4, 1986. The group's Articles of Association defined "Métis" as persons of Indian or Inuit *and* "White" ancestry and their descendants. The executive signatories to these documents resided in the Goose Bay area and were employed, middle-class "Labradorians." The Labrador Metis Association gave voice to a "forgotten people" excluded from the federal–provincial Aboriginal agreements and ineligible to join the LIA less because of ancestry or culture than as a consequence of where they were born.

Following its formation in the Goose Bay area, LMA membership drives along the southeastern coast to Pinware River increased membership. In 1998, the LMA changed its name to the Labrador Métis Nation (LMN), and in 2010 the LMN took the Inuttitut word, Nunatu-Kavut, meaning "our ancient land," as its new name. People eligible to join the LMN or today's NCC joined for many reasons. Inuit-Métis share an identity, memory, and a sense of belonging to local landscapes, based on generations of making a living on the land and sea (Pace 2008). By the 1980s, Inuit-Métis were aware that the Innu and Inuit had land claims to portions of Labrador and that soon they could be left out. There were other instrumental reasons as well, which are discussed later on. Today, NunatuKavut Community Council has around 6,000 members. The organization's accomplishments are too numerous to list but include the filing of a comprehensive land claim in 1991 (supplemented in 1995, 2002, 2003, and 2010); a food fishery program beginning in 1994; post-secondary educational funding for Métis youth; and forestry agreements with the province since 2003. The LMN used funding from the so-called Powley Initiative to fund research on Inuit-Métis resource harvesting. In the wake of reduced federal funding, the NCC is increasingly funded through co-operation agreements with mining companies, such as Search Minerals, Labrador Iron Mines, and Tata Steel.

Canadian Métis: A Few Words on Context

Ever since the first European men set foot in North America, their unions with Aboriginal women or *métissage* produced biracial or hybrid offspring, even though the socio-political relevance of this new category varied tremendously according to timing and local circumstances.[12] The HBC initially prohibited its male servants from having relations with Aboriginal women, but later reversed this position, allowing such unions by the end of the eighteenth century, as did its rival, the Montreal-based North West Company (1779–1821). French, English, and Scots traders, trappers, and hunters worked for or supplied one or both companies. In Labrador, as elsewhere in Canada, many (if not most) European males who would later marry Aboriginal women initially came to work for the HBC (Stopp, chapter 8). Jennifer Brown (1985:1125) writes that biological mixing, or *métissage*, should not, ipso facto, be equated with ethnogenesis, the state of social self-consciousness causing actors to acknowledge that "we" are not like "them," which in turn requires a vocabulary of distinctiveness used both internally and externally by some other group (Stopp, chapter 8; Kennedy, chapter 11). The development of a distinct identity among the first generation of hybrid offspring, or ethnogenesis, is often a socially constructed and reflexive response to intrusive events or developments that either threaten a pre-existing way of life or offer people new opportunities. Métis ethnogenesis occurred at various times for different Métis communities and may occur in several phases, each with different social and political consequences within the same group. Writing generally about Canadian Métis, Brown (1985) observes that this awareness, and the vocabulary to describe it (i.e., Métis, *"bois-brûlé,"* and later "half-breed"), did not arise until after 1763. Citing Giraud, Andersen (2008:349) summarizes the genesis of the Red River Métis in 1869, and a sense of self-consciousness bolstered by language, laws, dress, and the like. *Métissage* followed the history of Canada westward, as a social consequence first of the fur trade and then, by the nineteenth century, the slaughter of American bison on the Plains of what became the provinces of Manitoba and Saskatchewan.

Historian John E. Foster (2001) argues that Plains Métis ethnogenesis began when French servants or *engagés* employed by eastern-based fur companies overwintered with Indian bands, married Indian women, and apprenticed with their in-laws to learn the hunting and trapping skills essential for survival. Eventually, some *engagés* opted to become *les hommes libre* (freemen), with the final stage of ethnogenesis coming when freeman families interacted and their children married other Métis. By the nineteenth century some Métis families travelled the Plains in the distinctive and ingenious Red River carts in search of bison, overwintering as *hivernants* in sheltered locations, such as the Cypress Hills. Archaeological excavations of several *hivernant* overwintering sites by David Burley et al. (1988) conclude that the archaeological footprint of Saskatchewan Métis overwintering sites is distinct from coeval Euro-Canadian settler sites, a finding similar to those of Beaudoin (2008) and Kelvin and Rankin (chapter 6).

As mixed peoples strongly attached to the land and sea (Mitchell, chapter 10), Labrador's Inuit-Métis share some similarities with other Canadians self-identifying as Métis but likely are also in many ways very different from these other groups. Like the Métis of the Plains, the Labrador Métis sense of community builds on ties of kinship and family that endured despite physical and social mobility. Inuit-Métis families moved seasonally. Trappers spent long winters on distant traplines, and, beginning in the twentieth century, some Inuit-Métis travelled to work away from home. Despite mobility, Inuit-Métis returned to and found meaning in kith and kin. Like their western counterparts, Inuit-Métis "lived and thrived at the intersection of mobility and fixedness" (Macdougall et al. 2012:9).

Western Métis fought to defend their lands and way of life. Métis defended their interests in military skirmishes at Seven Oaks (near today's Winnipeg) in 1816 (Ens 2012). Followed by pressure from Britain, the HBC sold Rupert's Land[13] to the new Dominion of Canada in 1869, which quickly moved to populate and develop the new lands (Andersen 2008:349–350). These and other developments led to the Red River

Rebellion of 1869–1870, the formation in 1870 of the province of Manitoba, and to some Métis relocating to establish a settlement at Batoche in present-day central Saskatchewan, culminating in the Northwest Rebellion of 1885. Métis defeated at Batoche dispersed after 1885, surfacing again politically in the more favourable climate of the mid-1960s (Sawchuck 1978). There were no Labrador equivalents to these military skirmishes and political solutions.

Some western Métis speak Michif, a mixed French–Cree language that may have emerged with ethnogenesis (Bakker 2012), whereas Labrador Métis speak English. Political organization of Labrador's Inuit-Métis dates from the 1980s, as opposed to western Métis, whose organization in some cases dates to the late nineteenth century (Sawchuk 1998). The Métis National Council (MNC) represents Métis from Ontario west whereas the NunatuKavut Community Council is an affiliate of the Congress of Aboriginal Peoples (CAP).

Figure 5. Joe Goudie, wife, and nine children, ca. 1910. (International Grenfell Association photograph collection, The Rooms Provinical Archives Division, VA 118-97.4)

Another difference between Labrador's Inuit-Métis and descendants of the western Canadian Métis Nation is rooted in Newfoundland and Labrador's late entry into Canada and in the Newfoundland government subcontracting the administration of Inuit to the Moravian church (Rompkey 2003:37–48). Our position is that south/central Labrador Inuit-Métis and northern Labrador Settlers were essentially one people who would be divided administratively. Those in the north, once accepted by the Moravian church in the 1850s, would be invited in the 1970s to join Inuttitut-speaking Inuit in the LIA and are now legally Inuit, whereas those further south, the people this book concerns, would be excluded. Thus, the state-sanctioned Moravian tutelage of Labrador Inuit, and later Settlers, had monumental consequences for the social history of Labrador and may be unique to the region (Rollmann, chapter 9).

A final "difference" surrounds the old and likely irresolvable question of who is or is not legitimately Métis. Put differently, can all biracial Aboriginal–European communities be considered Métis or should the term be confined to the "pure" Red River or Northwest Métis? As explained above, the 1982 Constitution Act did not resolve this question, but the fact that the *Powley* case concerned Great Lakes Métis suggests a broader geographic application of the term. Unquestionably, the complex economic, cultural, and political history of the Northwest Métis is distinct from the history reported in this book. Saskatchewan-born Métis scholar Chris Andersen (2008) blames the Canadian state and recent court decisions for a system allowing biracial peoples to self-identify as Métis, albeit that their grandparents might not have used the word. Yet the Latin and later French-based word "métis" or its capitalized "Métis" has not always been used to refer to the mixed-ancestry peoples from the Great Lakes westward. Furthermore, French–Indian *métissage* in eastern Canada during the seventeenth century predates such unions further west. Even in the Labrador case, the Aboriginal roots of some Inuit-Métis families are as deep as those of their western counterparts (Stopp, chapter 8; Way, chapter 7). While the debate over the exclusivity of "Métis" continues, the authors of section 35 of the Constitution Act, 1982 understood both sides and may have agreed *in their indecision* to use "Métis" to refer to all Canadian communities of mixed Aboriginal–European heritage.

On the other hand, Labrador's Inuit-Métis share with other Canadian Métis a historically stigmatized identity that once motivated many Métis to "pass" as whites. Just as in Labrador, some Manitoba Métis were taught to be ashamed of their heritage and consequently denied being Métis (Harrison, quoted in Bell 2013:7–8). As hybrid peoples, both Labrador and other Métis—past and present—struggle with identity. Depending on time and local context, Métis like the nineteenth-century American George Bent may navigate between the worlds of Aboriginal and European origin, in Bent's case both fighting alongside Indians and translating for whites (Halaas and Masich 2004). Other Métis, like Nicholas Chatelain, were important intermediaries and translators between First Nations (in his case the Anishinabeg), the HBC, and government (Lytwyn 2012). Still others, like the iconic Maria Campbell (1973), overcame the poverty and shame associated with a degraded identity to introduce Canadians to the racism and violence faced by Métis, particularly women. Deeply personal struggles with identity occur in rural and urban contexts, the latter examined in Bonita Lawrence's eloquent and moving account of her own identity as a mixed-blood Montreal Native (Lawrence 2004). While many Métis, including those in Labrador, struggle with identity, a 2013 report from Canada's Senate concludes that the federal government must take concrete steps to understand who Canadian Métis are and allow Métis communities to determine their membership and identity (Canada 2013).

The Book

The chapters that follow break new ground on a number of archaeological and ethnohistorical issues. Most of the chapters using archaeological methods investigate the nature and extent of Inuit occupancy of southeastern Labrador. Those using ethnohistorical methods explore questions relevant to Inuit-Métis history and their renascence as a people;

our focus is more empirical then theoretical. Here I offer the broader context of many chapters.

Archaeologists call the last Inuit people who populated the Canadian Arctic and Labrador the "Thule Inuit" after the place in northwest Greenland where their remains were first discovered in 1916. Following Hawkes, archaeologists have emphasized the pre-contact whale-hunting economy of Thule Inuit, considering them a Labrador variant of the ancient north Alaskan whaling culture (Hawkes 1916:139–140; Larsen and Rainey 1948; Schledermann 1971; Taylor 1985). Until recently, archaeologists believed that beginning around AD 1000–1200, Thule Inuit left northern Alaska and hunted their way eastward, reaching Greenland around AD 1200, and possibly Labrador as early as AD 1250 (Fitzhugh 2009; Kaplan 1997:181).

While not dismissing the importance of whaling, archaeologists are increasingly recognizing another dimension of Thule life: their attraction to European technologies and materials, particularly iron. We have long known that Thule Inuit used iron in the central Arctic (e.g., McCartney and Mack 1973), yet this dimension of Thule culture until recently has played second fiddle to the interpretative emphasis on their prehistoric whaling economy. Now, however, the interpretative tide appears to be changing. Scholars such as Robert McGhee (1984, 2009) have for some years emphasized the Inuit fondness for and use of iron.[14] Similarly, research by Patricia Sutherland (2009) on Baffin Island has unearthed evidence that Greenlandic Norse traded with the "Tunit," or Dorset Inuit, immediate predecessors of the Thule, who may have later acquired iron, even if indirectly (Stopp 2011).

New radiocarbon dates of bone have advanced the date of the Thule exodus from northern Alaska to the thirteenth century (Friesen and Arnold 2008). Archaeologists now believe that the Thule migration eastward may have only taken a few years and that they may have been searching for iron (Friesen and Arnold 2008; Stopp 2011). Stopp (2011) summarizes contacts between the Thule Inuit and Greenlandic Norse that began in the thirteenth century. Rankin (2009:19; Ramsden and

Rankin 2013) concludes that the Thule Inuit entered Labrador in the late fifteenth century, just before the arrival of Europeans, and seeking European materials.

Archaeologists agree that the Thule Inuit were genetically and culturally Inuit, the immediate ancestors of the Inuit described by the French, Dutch, and other European visitors. Thule Inuit harnessed dogs to wooden sleds and practised a way of life that focused on hunting sea mammals through the ice or in open water (Park 1998:115). It now seems plausible that Thule Inuit may have entered Labrador during the fifteenth century aware of iron and, perhaps, of Europeans. Assuming archaeological research continues to unearth evidence of trade, we may begin to consider the interregional trade described by Kaplan (1983) and discussed below as the persistence of an ancient Thule way of life, rather than something that began in Labrador (Fay, chapter 4).

Archaeologically, much of our research examines the extent, nature, duration, and fate of Labrador Inuit occupation of southeastern Labrador and the Quebec North Shore (Martijn and Clermont 1980). Among other questions, papers in the Martijn and Clermont collection debated whether, prior to 1763, Inuit occupied southeastern Labrador year-round or only visited seasonally to trade with Europeans or pilfer their posts (Rankin, chapter 2; Crompton, chapter 5; Fitzhugh 2009). In the years preceding publication of the Martijn and Clermont collection, some areas along this long coastline had been studied, others not. One relatively well-studied area at the time was the Strait of Belle Isle, where archaeologists Jim Tuck and Bob McGhee had worked for several years, enabling Tuck to propose in 1975 a dated sequence of cultural traditions spanning nine millennia (Tuck 1976). Around the same time but in Lake Melville, William Fitzhugh's (1972) encyclopedic dissertation proposed a similar sequence. Meanwhile, the long stretch of coast and interior between where Tuck and Fitzhugh were working—the location studied in most of the papers to follow—was, as Kaplan concluded, "poorly known archaeologically" (Kaplan 1983:342). Archaeologist William Fitzhugh wrote what others may have thought. Based on his 1981 survey of southeastern Labrador made while sailing south, Fitzhugh (1982:53) concluded that "the coast between Groswater Bay and Battle Harbour appears less heavily settled in prehistoric times than was the coast north of Makkovik."

The emergence of identity politics in the 1970s appeared to confirm that Aboriginal peoples only inhabited portions of Labrador well north of the southeastern coast, a notion reinforced by new Inuit and Innu claims. The confluence of these two factors—southeastern Labrador as an archaeological *terra nullius* and as a region well south of lands claimed by Aboriginal groups—led many to conclude that the region lacked an Aboriginal past. This conclusion was not challenged in several fine studies (Anderson 1984; Southard 1982; Schneider 1984; Szala-Meneok 1992) based on long-term fieldwork in several parts of the region that made little or no reference to Aboriginal peoples.

Between 1979 and 1983, curiosity led me to new research in Labrador, where I lived in three southeastern Labrador communities. There I discovered what is explained in Chapter 11, namely, that the stigma of everything "Native" or "Skimo" led locals with Aboriginal ancestry to deny having it. Marianne Stopp's research also challenged old and persistent stereotypes about southeastern Labrador. Over three summers between 1986 and 1992, Stopp and her colleagues conducted the first comprehensive archaeological survey of the coast between Blanc-Sablon and Trunmore Bay, discovering numerous prehistoric and historic sites (Stopp 1997).

Now and finally, the research reported in this volume is part of the first consolidated archaeological attempt to learn what actually lies beneath the sods. The excavations of Rankin and Murphy (chapter 3), and of Stopp (2012) at the mouth of St. Michael's Bay establish beyond any doubt that Inuit occupied the southeastern Labrador region year-round between the late sixteenth to mid-eighteenth centuries. Our work replaces the conjectures of the 1980 collection with fact (Rankin and Crompton 2013) and challenges earlier assumptions that southern Labrador was only peripheral to the core Inuit settlement areas further north (Rankin, chapter 2).

Lisa Rankin in Chapter 2, "Inuit Settlement on the Southern Frontier," summarizes archaeological investigations from Sandwich Bay that show it was on the "southern frontier" of Inuit occupation, and an essential part of the Inuit trade network through which Labrador Inuit maintained a cohesive identity. Since Rankin began work in Sandwich Bay, in 2001, a total of 32 probable Inuit sites have been found, of which 18 are confirmed to be Inuit. Rankin applies Jordon and Kaplan's (1980) three-phase, culture-history model to her materials, finding that it works as well in Sandwich Bay as further north. House 1, one of four Inuit houses excavated on Huntingdon Island, dates from the early seventeenth century and is especially interesting. European artifacts (e.g., iron, roofing tiles, and the like) were clustered in different parts of the house and appear associated with the different families tending separate lamps. House 1 does not appear to be a true communal house but may have housed several trading families travelling and living together. Given its early date, and that it is one of only two houses in Labrador illustrating this pattern, House 1 may represent a transitional form leading to true communal houses. Moreover, and as predicted in the model, more recent house strata contain increased amounts of European items, including trade beads, suggesting greater trade with Europeans, likely the French. Rankin concludes by comparing Sandwich Bay area Inuit houses with Inuit houses further north. They are similar in form and number, but southern houses are smaller and richer in European artifacts.

In Chapter 3, "Exploring the Communal House Phase in Sandwich Bay," Phoebe Murphy and Lisa Rankin report on their 2010 excavation of House 3, an early eighteenth-century communal house on Huntingdon Island, Sandwich Bay. Ever since Bird (1945; cited in Woollett 1999:371) coined the term "communal" houses, archaeologists such as Schledermann (1971) have attempted to explain the sudden shift during the eighteenth century from oblong single-family sod houses to larger communal houses, where multiple lampstands indicate several families lived.[15] Schledermann (1971), Kaplan (1983), Woollett (1999), and others date the beginning of this transition to the late seventeenth century (Rankin,

chapter 2).[16] Murphy and Rankin first describe the architecture and associated artifact assemblage of House 3 in order to situate it within the
context of the broader communal house phase. House 3 resembles communal houses in northern Labrador except in its length of occupation.

Until Murphy and Rankin's excavation, and with the possible exception of the Seal Island house near Henley Harbour, excavated by
Reginald Auger (1991) in 1986, archaeologists set the southern boundary of the communal house phase at Lake Melville (Jordon 1977). As
with Rankin's findings, the communal house excavated by Murphy and
Rankin means that the boundary of Inuit occupation must now be
moved south to Sandwich Bay. Stopp (2002:85, 1997) predicted that this
would be the case, having recorded more than 210 sod houses during
her archaeological surveys.

In Chapter 4, "Big Men, Big Women, or Both? Examining the Coastal Trading System of the Eighteenth-Century Labrador Inuit," Amelia
Fay uses documentary and archaeological evidence to discuss a famous
early Labrador Inuit woman, Mikak, one of the nine Inuit captured following the autumn 1767 Inuit raid on an English post at Cape Charles.
Fay's contribution is twofold. First, Fay excavated a sod house at Khernertok (near Nain), where the Moravians recorded that in 1776 Mikak
lived, and second, following Cabak (1991) and supported by available
historical documentation, Fay argues that some Inuit women participated
in the middleman trade alongside Inuit "big men." Female entrepreneurs acquired the prestigious trade goods that elevated their social
position and laid the groundwork for subsequent changes to the traditional gendered division of labour.

Amanda Crompton in Chapter 5, "The Many Habitations of Pierre
Constantin: Exploring the History of French Residence in Southern Labrador in the Early to Mid-Eighteenth Century," uses archival records to
examine the activities of the early eighteenth-century French concessionaire, Pierre Lavallée Constantin. Crompton distinguishes between
the earlier, Laurentian seigneurial system and the concessions granted
by the French Crown in Labrador. These were non-agricultural tracts

permitting grant holders exclusive rights to harvest resources and trade with Aboriginal peoples. Constantin began his career at several posts near Port au Choix, Newfoundland, where conflicts between the French and Inuit were common. Constantin would later be employed by fellow, and ultimately competing, concessionaire Courtemanche, and obtained a concession in Labrador in 1713. In 1716, Constantin was granted a concession at St. Modet. His tenure at this post is particularly well documented because two prominent Quebec bureaucrats litigated its boundaries. Crompton concludes with a description of a failed attempt by Inuit to trade at Red Bay, leading to deception and, finally, to a deadly skirmish between Inuit and the French, in 1719. Given that French goods are commonly unearthed in sites such as those described by Rankin and Murphy (chapter 3) and by Rankin (chapter 2), it is not inconceivable that Inuit living at these sites may have traded with Constantin's men.

In Chapter 6, "The Inuit-Métis Archaeology in Sandwich Bay, Labrador," Laura Kelvin and Lisa Rankin use local interviews, relevant historical documentation, and archaeology to identify possible differences between the vernacular housing of Newfoundland fishers, Inuit-Métis, and Inuit in Sandwich Bay. Kelvin and Rankin's research follows Auger (2001) and Beaudoin (2008) in attempting to discover the archaeological footprint of Inuit-Métis. Their chapter, as well as their overall project, pursues one goal of this book, that is, to discern archaeologically diacritical differences between houses and settlement strategies in socially diverse regions such as Sandwich Bay. Kelvin and Rankin conclude that Inuit-Métis sites can be differentiated from Inuit or European sites by their unique house construction and settlement pattern.

Whiteley (1977:21), Kennedy (1995:80–88), and Rollmann (2008) list the names of many European, mainly Anglo (Stopp, chapter 8), men who came to Labrador after 1763 to work as fishers and trappers. During the late eighteenth and early nineteenth centuries, many of these men married Inuit or part-Inuit women, then the most available choice of spouses along the coast. Borlase (1994), Fitzhugh (1999), and the NCC land claim study (2010:123–126, 227–232) describe the Inuit-Métis offspring of these initial mixed unions. Chapters here by Way, Stopp, and Rollmann use historical, genealogical, and ethnographic data to introduce some of these European husbands and their Inuit or part-Inuit wives.

In Chapter 7, "The Story of William Phippard," Labrador genealogist Patricia Way presents the case of William Phippard (also, Fippard or Pippard), whose union with the Inuit woman Sarah represents one of the two earliest-known first-generation European–Inuit unions. Way's method involves piecing together the existing shreds of evidence from oral history, cemetery headstones, HBC journals, Anglican Church records, and other sources. Phippard, originally from the Isle of Wight, came to Labrador around 1780 to work for British merchant Jeremiah Coghlan. Phippard trapped and fished at Coghlan's Sand Hill River and Black Bear Bay posts. Following service with Coghlan, Phippard moved north to the Rigolet–Double Mer area where he met and married Sarah. Way's detailed Phippard genealogy, spanning four generations, reveals two more general points about Inuit-Métis history. First, second-generation Inuit-Métis usually married others of their own kind, a pattern Kleivan (1966:100) discovered in northern Labrador. Second, although the surname Phippard is no longer found in Labrador, Sarah's Inuit pedigree, and those of subsequent marriages, continues in Inuit-Métis descendants with extant surnames, such as Reeves and Blake.

Labrador archaeologist/historian Marianne Stopp, in Chapter 8, "'I, old Lydia Campbell': A Labrador Woman of National Historic Significance," presents the story of Lydia Campbell, one of Labrador's best-known and cherished historical figures. Lydia Campbell's (1818–1905) life was typical of the lives of nineteenth-century Inuit-Métis women, except that she wrote a diary describing the Hamilton Inlet of her time, which would motivate subsequent Labrador diarists. A self-identified "half-breed," Campbell clearly distinguishes between her people and nearby "Esquimaux and Indians," suggesting that an earlier ethnogenesis of people of mixed ancestry had occurred, a point revisited in my chapter on identity politics. Campbell's perceptions of her own identity reveal the subtle prejudice or stigma of the era. Stopp describes changing attitudes of the HBC towards their employees of mixed descent and briefly places Lydia Campbell within the broader discussion of Canadian Métis women.

Religious historian and Moravian scholar Hans Rollmann, in Chapter 9, "Settler Families on Labrador's North Coast: The Family of Leah (Lea) and Robert Mitchell at Adlatôk Bay," relies on Moravian diaries, church books, and correspondence from Hopedale from the middle of the nineteenth century that describe Anglos who moved north at that time. Rollmann's detailed and nuanced account of Devonshire native Robert Mitchell reveals as never before the social and emotional dynamics of first-generation mixed unions. While the Moravians initially considered strangers like Mitchell threats to "their" Inuit charges, later in life the Inuit wives of many of these men would long for the familiar and meaningful church of their youth. This would eventually lead the mission to accept Settler converts, a decision with consequences that continue (Kennedy, chapter 11). Moreover, and following Kleivan (1966), Rollmann's account of Mitchell illustrates an important theme of mid-nineteenth-century Labrador: that many Anglo or Inuit-Métis males began their careers in south/central Labrador before moving north into Moravian Labrador. The photo of Leah Mitchell that Rollmann found in the Moravian Archives at Bethlehem, Pennsylvania, may be the only extant photograph of a first-generation Inuit spouse.

In Chapter 10, "'We Don't Have Any Klick or Spam in the House— How About a Piece of Boiled Salmon for Lunch?': Country Food in NunatuKavut," Greg Mitchell brings our story to the present, describing how contemporary Inuit-Métis harvest and consume land and sea resources. Extensive random survey and map biography data reveal that the vast majority of people continue to hunt, fish, and trap the country foods that figure prominently in daily diets. Mitchell reports that species such as caribou are now in decline and he also explains how the Labrador Road affects traditional "wooding" (woodcutting), trapping, and hunting practices. Notwithstanding the 1992 moratorium on cod fishing, the continued harvest of country foods by Inuit-Métis remains a source of sustenance and meaning.

John C. Kennedy's Chapter 11, "Identity Politics," reports on social anthropological data collected during fieldwork in 2013 in 10 of the 11 permanent communities between Lodge Bay and Cartwright. Identity politics, the political mobilization of a group based on a common history and culture, is changing the way Labrador people view their identity, their past, and their future. The historic stigma once tarnishing "Skimo" or Aboriginal identities continues to wane and people are increasingly willing to talk about their Inuit ancestry. The chapter proposes an increasing south-to-north continuum of "Inuitness" that becomes greater as one moves north along the Labrador coast. Near the northern end of the region, for example, at Spotted Islands, people have a small vocabulary of Inuttitut words and concepts. They also have a word that historically referred to visiting Newfoundland fishers, which is discussed in relationship to ethnogenesis. Further south, "Whitemen" live alongside long-time Inuit-Métis neighbours, and identity politics has changed social relations as well as inequities following creation of the Nunatsiavut government.

How does stigma relate to the notion of "renewal" in our title? In the 1970s, stigma prevented people of mixed European–Inuit heritage who lived south of the area claimed by the new Labrador Inuit Association from acknowledging their history and seeking membership in this new organization. Both individually and collectively, pride and a new confidence would not begin to replace stigma until the formation of the Labrador Metis Association. The Labrador Metis Association (now the NunatuKavut Community Council) organized Inuit-Métis and began to reverse what otherwise would have been their inevitable assimilation. In sum, the work reported here is discovering a lost history and witnessing the renascence of a nearly forgotten people.

Notes

1.   In alphabetical order our research team included Mario Blaser, John C. Kennedy, Greg Mitchell (until 2012), Evelyn Plaice, Lisa Rankin (the team's Principal Investigator), Hans Rollmann, Marianne Stopp, and Patricia Way.

2. Until the 1970s, Labrador Aboriginal peoples who had long called themselves Inuit (singular Inuk) were referred to as Eskimos, a word of contested etymology.

3. Several years prior to her death in 2004, bilingual educator Beatrice [Ford] Watts, originally from Nain, and a respected educator and colleague, proposed the Inuttitut term "Nunatsiavut," meaning "our beautiful land," as the name of the self-governed region in northern Labrador. Inuit-Métis adopted the Inuit word "NunatuKavut," meaning "our ancient land," in 2010.

4. An important distinction is that the dialect of the language historically spoken in or around Rigolet is referred to as either Inuktut or Inuktitut (Douglas Wharram, personal communication 2014).

5. In 2005, at the invitation of the federal Department of Justice, Dr. Yves Labrèche and I completed two reports for the Minaskuat Limited Partnership as part of a Justice initiative to assess the national applicability of the *Powley* "test." Ours was one of eight areal studies across Canada and our sense is that the Department of Justice found that the *Powley* test might apply more generally than it had hoped, leading the department only to accept those studies where Métis assimilated into neighbouring Indian bands or ceased to exist, neither being the case in Labrador. This said, the NCC and other Métis organizations received federal funding through the Powley Initiative for research related to resource harvesting rights.

6. Unless noted, details of my account are found in Brantenberg (1977); Anger (1983); Tanner (1993, 1998); and Kennedy (1975, 1982, 1987, 1988, 1997). Until recently, Maritime and Newfoundland Mi'kmaq were popularly known as Micmac. Newfoundland Mi'kmaq living at Conne River successfully lobbied to become status Indians under the Indian Act in 1987. Mi'kmaq living elsewhere in Newfoundland, organized as the Federation of Newfoundland Indians, negotiated with and litigated the federal government and became the Qalipu Mi'kmaq First Nation in 2011. Applications to the Qalipu band rose from 26,000 in 2009 to over 100,000 in 2012, but the process was closed in 2014.

7. Just before and during the Trudeau era several programs funded various rural development initiatives, including the short-lived Local Employment Assistance Program (LEAP), the Agriculture Rehabilitation and Development Act (ARDA), the Central Mortgage and Housing Corporation (CMHC), and the Department of Regional Economic Expansion (DREE).

8. During my interview with the President of LIA in 1993, as part of research that I conducted with both LIA and LMA for the Royal Commission on Aboriginal Peoples, the LIA President recalled the LIA's decision to include Settlers and wondered aloud, "hindsight may show that the LIA made a terrible mistake, allowing in the Kablunângajuit. The real Inuit will have dug their own grave." There is much that could be said about this, perhaps most positively, that in 1974 "the real Inuit" did not want to divide communities, as might have happened if more

culturally/linguistically exclusive, less geographically based criteria had been adopted. Moreover, it is a fundamental Aboriginal right that organizations such as the [former] LIA define and determine their own membership criteria, as they did.

9. The Indian Act does not legally define "Inuit," but the Labrador Inuit Association (2003:9, 33–34) does so in its land claim agreement with the federal government, defining Kablunângajuit (literally, "almost White" or Native Settlers) with or without Inuit ancestry (LIA 2003:34) as "Inuit." Statistics Canada reports that "Inuit represent 89.1 percent of the total population of Nunatsiavut" (Statistics Canada, 2011). Of this population of 2,325, 555 or 23.8 per cent speak Inuttitut (Statistics Canada 2011b).

10. While I first learned of the Native Labradorian Association of Labrador in the fall of 1981, more recently Greg Mitchell kindly provided me with a copy of the notes of their founding meeting, which are housed at the NCC library. The approximately 20 people attending came from coastal communities between West St. Modeste and Nain; most are now either Nunatsiavut beneficiaries or NCC members. Finally, the generic term "Labradorian" was popularly used by English-speaking Aboriginal and non-Aboriginal residents who had lived in Labrador for varying periods of time. Rarely do Innu-eimun-speaking Innu or Inuttitut-speaking Inuit use the term. The term is useful for distinguishing between people living in Labrador and those residing on the island of Newfoundland. For further explanation on the term, see Kennedy (1995).

11. LIA elders sought to avoid dividing communities and thus privileged geographically based eligibility criteria. The LIA's definition of Kablunângajuit and "Whites" connected to the Labrador Inuit land claims area as "Inuit" (see note 9, above; LIA 2003:33–38) may explain why the NCC calls Inuit-Métis "southern Inuit." For a legal analysis of the membership rules in Aboriginal organizations, see Grammond (2009).

12. Rupert's Land was named after Prince Rupert of the Rhine (1619–1682), and consists of lands draining to Hudson Bay, and part of the territory granted to the Hudson's Bay Company by England in 1670.

13. I am using the older, original meaning of *métissage* rather than that used by literary theorists as a metaphor for writers who bridge "distinct" autobiographical, mainstream, and alternative genres (Amanda Crompton, Personal Communication, 20 November 2013).

14. Indeed, a recent and controversial documentary by anthropologist Niobe Thompson (2009) on Canadian television claims that belligerent Thule Inuit initially ventured east from north Alaska searching for iron no longer available through trade after Ghengis Khan blocked East Asian trade routes in the thirteenth century.

15. Communal houses from this period are distinct, one assumes, from the massive snow or stone *kashim* or ceremonial houses reported by Taylor (1990).

16. A similar and coeval change to communal houses also occurred in Greenland and further comparisons, now including communal houses from southeastern Labrador, might reveal similar causes.

References Cited

Anderson, David
  1984 The Development of Settlement in Southern Coastal Labrador with Particular Reference to Sandwich Bay. *Bulletin of Canadian Studies* 8(1):23–49.

Andersen, Chris
  2008 From Nation to Population: The Racialization of "Métis" in the Canadian Census. *Nations and Nationalism* (14)2:347–368.

Anger, Dorothy
  1983 Pulling It Back Together: Micmac Political Identity in Newfoundland. Unpublished Master's thesis, Department of Anthropology, Memorial University of Newfoundland, St. John's.

Auger, Reginald
  1991 *Labrador Inuit and Europeans in the Strait of Belle Isle: From the Written Sources to the Archaeological Evidence.* Collection Nordicana, No. 55. Université Laval, Québec.

Bakker, Peter
  2012 The Genesis of Michif and Other Mixed Languages. In *Contours of a People: Family, Mobility, and History*, edited by Brenda Macdougall, Nicole St.-Onge, and Carolyn Podruchny, pp. 169–193. University of Oklahoma Press, Norman.

Beaudoin, Matthew
  2008 Sweeping the Floor: An Archaeological Examination of a Multi-Ethnic Sod House in Labrador (FkBg-24). Unpublished Master's thesis, Department of Anthropology, Memorial University of Newfoundland, St. John's.

Bell, Gloria Jane
  2013 Oscillating Identities: Re-presentations of Métis in the Great Lakes Area in the Nineteenth Century. In *Métis in Canada: History, Identity, Law & Politics*, edited by C. Adams, G. Dahl, and I. Peach, pp. 3–58. University of Alberta Press, Edmonton.

Ben-Dor, Shmuel
  1966 *Makkovik: Eskimos and Settlers in a Labrador Community.* Newfoundland Social and Economic Studies No. 4. Institute of Social and Economic Research (ISER), Memorial University of Newfoundland, St. John's.

Borlase, Tim
  1994 *The Labrador Settlers, Metis, and Kablunangajuit.* Labrador East Integrated School Board, Happy Valley-Goose Bay.

Boisvert, David, and Keith Turnbull
1985 Who Are the Metis? *Studies in Political Economy* 18:107–147.

Brantenberg, Terje
1977 Ethnic Commitments and Local Government in Nain, 1969–76. In *The White Arctic*, edited by R. Paine, pp. 376–410. Newfoundland Social and Economic Papers No. 7. ISER, Memorial University of Newfoundland, St. John's.

Brown, Jennifer
1985 Métis. In *The Canadian Encyclopedia*, pp. 1124–1127. Hurtig, Edmonton, Alberta.

Budgel, Richard
1984 Canada, Newfoundland, and the Labrador Indians: Government Involvement with the Montagnais-Naskapi 1949–69. *Native Issues* IV(1):38–49.

Burley, David, Gayle Horsfall, and John Brandon
1988 Stability and Change in Western Canadian Métis Lifeways: An Archaeological and Architectural Study. Manuscript on file, Archaeological Resource Management Section, Saskatchewan Department of Culture and Recreation, Regina.

Cabak, Melanie Ann
1991 Inuit Women as Catalysts of Change: An Archaeological Study of 19th Century Northern Labrador. Unpublished Master's thesis, University of South Carolina, Columbia.

Campbell, Maria
1973 *Halfbreed*. McClelland and Stewart, Toronto.

Canada
2013 *"The People Who Own Themselves": Recognition of Métis Identity in Canada*. Report of the Standing Committee on Aboriginal Peoples, Ottawa.

Clark, Sandra, Harold Paddock, and Marguerite MacKenzie
1999 Labrador Inuktitut (Inuttut). Newfoundland and Labrador Heritage Website. Electronic document, http://www.heritage.nf.ca/society/language.html, accessed December 9, 2013.

Cumming, P. A., and N. H. Mickenberg
1972 *Native Rights in Canada*. General Publishing, Toronto.

Dahl, Gregg
2013 A Half-Breed's Perspective on Being Métis. In *Métis in Canada: History, Identity, Law and Politics*, edited by C. Adams, G. Dahl, and I. Peach, pp. 93–139. University of Alberta Press, Edmonton.

Duncan, Norman
1902 The Labrador Liveyere. *Harper's Monthly Magazine* 108(648):514–523.

Elliot, D. W.
1985 Aboriginal Title. In *Aboriginal Peoples and the Law: Indian, Metis and Inuit Rights in Canada*, edited by B. W. Morse, pp. 48–121. University of Carleton Press, Ottawa.

Ens, Gerhard J.

2012 The Battle of Seven Oaks and the Articulation of a Metis National Tradition, 1811–1849. In *Contours of a People: Family, Mobility, and History*, edited by B. Macdougall, N. St.-Onge, and C. Podruchny, pp. 93–119. University of Oklahoma Press, Norman.

Fitzhugh, Lynn

1999 *The Labradorians*. Breakwater Books, St. John's.

Fitzhugh, William

1972 *Environmental Archaeology and Cultural Systems in Hamilton Inlet*. Smithsonian Contributions to Anthropology No. 16. Smithsonian Institution Press, Washington, D.C.

1982 Smithsonian Surveys in Central and Southern Labrador in 1981. *Archaeology in Newfoundland and Labrador, 1981*, edited by J.S. Thomson and C. Thomson, pp. 32-55. Government of Newfoundland and Labrador, Historic Resources Division, Annual Report No. 2, Department of Culture, Recreation and Youth, St. John's.

2009 Exploring Cultural Boundaries: The Less "Invisible" of Southern Labrador and Quebec. In *On the Track of the Thule Culture from Bering Strait to East Greenland*, edited by B. Gronnow, pp. 129–148. Studies in Archaeology & History, Volume 15. Publications from the National Museum, Copenhagen.

Foster, John E.

2001 Wintering, the Outsider Adult Male and the Ethnogenesis of the Western Plains Métis. In *The Western Métis: Profile of a People*, edited by P. C. Douard, pp. 91–103. University of Regina Press, Regina, Saskatchewan.

Friesen, T. Max, and Charles D. Arnold

2008 The Timing of the Thule Migration: New Dates from the Western Canadian Arctic. *American Antiquity* 73(3):527–538.

Grammond, Sébastien

2009 *Identity Captured by Law: Membership in Canada's Indigenous Peoples and Linguistic Minorities*. McGill-Queen's University Press, Montreal and Kingston.

Halaas, D. F., and A. E. Masich.

2004 *Halfbreed: The Remarkable True Story of George Bent*. Da Capo Press, Cambridge, Massachusetts.

Handcock, Gordon

2008 A Review of the 1773 Curtis Map. In Toponymic and Cartographic Research Conducted for the Labrador Métis Nation, edited by Lisa Rankin, pp. 23–31. September 2008.

Hawkes, E. W.

1916 *The Labrador Eskimo*. Government Printing Bureau, Ottawa.

Hiller, James K.

1977 Moravian Land Holdings on the Labrador Coast: A Brief History. In *Our Footprints Are Everywhere*, edited by C. Brice-Bennett, pp. 83–94. LIA, Nain, Labrador.

2009 Eighteenth-Century Labrador: The European Perspective. In *Moravian Beginnings in Labrador*, edited by Hans Rollmann, pp. 37–52. Occasional Publication of Newfoundland and Labrador Studies, No. 2. Faculty of Arts Publications, Memorial University, St. John's.

Jordan, Richard, and Susan Kaplan

1980 An Archaeological View of the Inuit/European Contact Period in Central Labrador. *Études/Inuit/Studies* 4(1–2):35–45.

Kaplan, Susan

1983 Economic and Social Change in Labrador Neo-Eskimo Culture. Unpublished PhD dissertation, Bryn Mawr College, Bryn Mawr, Pennsylvania.

1997 Developments in Labrador Inuit Archaeology Research. In *Fifty Years of Arctic Research: Anthropological Studies from Greenland to Siberia*, edited by R. Gilberg and H. C. Gullov, pp. 181–186. Ethnographical Series Volume 18. Department of Ethnography, National Museum, Copenhagen.

Kelvin, Laura

2011 The Inuit-Métis of Sandwich Bay: Oral Histories and Archaeology. Unpublished Master's thesis, Memorial University of Newfoundland, St. John's.

Kennedy, John C.

1975 New Ethnic Minority Organizations in Northern Labrador: Some Preliminary Observations. Paper presented at the 34th Annual Meeting of the Society for Applied Anthropology.

1982 *Holding the Line: Ethnic Boundaries in a Northern Labrador Community*. Newfoundland Social and Economic Studies No. 27. ISER Books, St. John's.

1987 Aboriginal Organizations and Their Claims: The Case of Newfoundland and Labrador. *Canadian Ethnic Studies* 19(2):13–25.

1988 The Changing Significance of Labrador Settler Ethnicity. *Canadian Ethnic Studies* 20(3):94–111.

1995 *Peoples of the Bays and Headlands: Anthropological History and the Fate of Communities in the Unknown Labrador*. University of Toronto Press, Toronto.

1997 Labrador Metis Ethnogenesis. *Ethnos* 62(3–4):5–23.

2015 *Encounters: An Anthropological History of Southeastern Labrador*. McGill-Queen's University Press, Montreal and Kingston.

Kleivan, Helge

1966 *The Eskimos of Northeast Labrador: A History of Eskimo–White Relations, 1771–1955*. Norsk Polarinstitutt, Oslo.

Labrador Inuit Association

2003 Labrador Inuit Land Claims. Initialed at St. John's, Newfoundland and Labrador, this 29th Day of August, 2003.

Labrèche, Yves, and John C. Kennedy
2007 Héritage culturel des Métis du Labrador central. *Recherches amérindiennes au Québec* XXXVII(2–3):61–75.

Larsen, H., and F. G. Rainey
1948 *Ipiutak and the Arctic Whale Hunting Culture*. Anthropological Papers of the American Museum of National History, Vol. 42. American Museum of Natural History, New York.

Lawrence, Bonita
2004 *"Real" Indians and Others: Mixed-Blood Urban Native Peoples and Indigenous Nationhood*. University of British Columbia Press, Vancouver.

Lytwyn, Victor P.
2012 In the Shadows of the Honourable Company: Nicholas Chatelain and the Métis of Fort Frances. In *Contours of a People: Family, Mobility, and History*, edited by Brenda Macdougall, Nicole St.-Onge, and Carolyn Podruchny, pp. 194–229. University of Oklahoma Press, Norman.

Macdougall, Brenda, Carolyn Podruchny, and Nicole St. Onge
2012 Introduction: Cultural Mobility and the Contours of Difference. In *Contours of a People: Family, Mobility, and History*, edited by Brenda Macdougall, Nicole St. Onge, and Carol Podruchny, pp. 3–21. University of Oklahoma Press, Norman.

Mailhot, José
1997 *The People of Sheshatshit*. Social and Economic Studies No. 58. ISER Books, St. John's.

Martijn, Charles, and Norman Clemont (editors)
1980 Les Inuit du Québec–Labrador méridional/The Inuit of Southern Québec–Labrador. *Études/Inuit/Studies* 4(1–2):77–104.

McCarthy, A. P., and D. J. Mack
1973 Iron Utilization by Thule Eskimos of Central Canada. *American Antiquity* 38:328–339.

McGhee, Robert
1984 Contact between Native North Americans and the Mediaeval Norse: A Review of the Evidence. *American Antiquity* 49(1):4–26.
2009 When and Why Did the Inuit Move to the Eastern Arctic. In *The Northern World, AD 900–1400*, edited by H. Maschner, O. K. Mason, and R. McGhee, pp. 155–163. University of Utah Press, Salt Lake City.

Moss, Wendy
1988 *Constitutional Responsibility for the Aboriginal Peoples of Newfoundland*. A Report Prepared for Jack Harris, M.P., by the Research Branch of the Library of Parliament, Ottawa.

Native Association of Newfoundland and Labrador (NANL)
1973a Organizational meeting, February 2–4, 1973. Sponsored by the Secretary of

State and Reported by the Extension Service of Memorial University of New-foundland.

1973b Native Housing Conference, Goose Bay, Labrador. September 21–23, 1973. Sponsored by NANL in Co-operation with CMHC. Reported by the Extension Service of Memorial University of Newfoundland.

Neary, Peter

2012a The First Nations and the Entry of Newfoundland into Confederation, 1945–54, Part I. *Newfoundland Quarterly* 105(2):36–42.

2012b The First Nations and the Entry of Newfoundland into Confederation, 1945–54, Part II. *Newfoundland Quarterly* 105(3):41–49.

Newfoundland

1974 *Report of the Royal Commission on Labrador.* 6 vols. Government of Newfoundland and Labrador, St. John's.

NunatuKavut Community Council

2010 Unveiling NunatuKavut: Document in Pursuit of Reclaiming a Homeland. Unpublished manuscript on file with NunatuKavut, Happy Valley-Goose Bay, Labrador.

Pace, Jessica E.

2008 This Is Where I Live, But It's Not My Home: Archaeology and Identity in Sandwich Bay, Labrador. Unpublished Master's thesis, Department of Anthropology and Archaeology, Memorial University of Newfoundland, St. John's.

Powley

2003 *R. v. Powley* 2003 SCC 43, 2 S.C.R. 2007.

Ramsden, Peter, and Lisa Rankin

2013 Thule Radiocarbon Chronology and Its Implications for Early Inuit–European Interaction in Labrador. In *Exploring Atlantic Transitions: Archaeologies of Transience and Permanence in New Found Lands,* edited by Peter E. Pope with Shannon Lewis-Simpson, pp. 299–309. Society for Post-Medieval Archaeology Monograph 8. Boydell Press, Woodbridge, United Kingdom.

Rankin, Lisa

2009 An Archaeological View of the Thule/Inuit Occupation of Labrador. Unpublished document submitted to the Labrador Métis Nation. Electronic document, http://www.mun.ca/labmetis/pdf/thule_inuit%20final%20report.pdf, accessed December 9, 2013.

Rankin, Lisa, and Amanda Crompton

2013 The Labrador Metis and the Politics of Identity: Understanding the Archaeological Past to Negotiate a Sustainable Future. *International Journal of Heritage and Sustainable Development* 3(2):71–79.

Richling, Barnett

1978 Hard Times, Them Times: An Interpretative Ethnohistory of Inuit and Settlers in the Hopedale District of Northern Labrador, 1752–1977. Unpublished Ph.D. dissertation, McGill University, Montreal.

Rollmann, Hans

2008 Anglican Beginnings and Aboriginality in 19th Century Southern and Central Labrador: Evidence from the Episcopal Visitations to Labrador, Records of the Society for the Propagation of the Gospel, and Hitherto Unexamined Church Records of 1848 and 1849. Contract Research for the Labrador Métis Nation, on file with NunatuKavut, Happy Valley-Goose Bay, Labrador.

Rompkey, Bill

2003 *The Story of Labrador.* McGill-Queen's University Press, Montreal and Kingston.

Sawchuck, Joe

1978 *The Metis of Manitoba: Reformulation of an Ethnic Identity.* Peter Martin Associates, Toronto.

1998 *The Dynamics of Native Politics: The Alberta Métis Experience.* Purich, Saskatoon, Saskatchewan.

2001 Negotiating an Identity: Métis Political Organizations, the Canadian Government, and Competing Concepts of Aboriginality. *American Indian Quarterly* 25(1):73–85

Schledermann, Peter

1971 The Thule Tradition in Northern Labrador. Unpublished Master's thesis, Department of Anthropology, Memorial University of Newfoundland, St. John's.

Schneider, Robert H.

1984 The Formation of Attitudes toward Development in Southern Labrador. Unpublished Ph.D. dissertation, McGill University, Montreal.

Southard, Frank E.

1982 Salt Cod and God: An Ethnography of Socio-Economic Conditions Affecting Status in a Southern Labrador Community. Unpublished Master's thesis, Memorial University of Newfoundland, St. John's.

Statistics Canada

2011a Aboriginal Peoples of Canada. First Nations Peoples, Métis and Inuit. Statistics Canada, Ottawa. Electronic document, http://www12Statcan.gc.ca/nhs-enm 2011/as-sa, accessed March 28, 2014.

2011b Aboriginal Peoples and Language. Statistics Canada, Ottawa. Electronic document, http://www12.Statcan.gc.ca/nhs-enm 2011/as-sa, accessed March 28, 2014.

Stopp, Marianne

1997 Long-term Coastal Occupancy between Cape Charles and Trunmore Bay, Labrador. *Arctic* 50(2):119–37.

2002 Reconsidering Inuit Presence in Southern Labrador. *Études/Inuit/Studies* 26(2):71–106.

2011 *Thule Inuit and Greenlandic Norse in the Eastern Canadian Arctic: A Discussion.* Historic Sites and Monuments Board of Canada, Report Number 2011–27.

Government of Canada, Ottawa.

2012 The 2011 Field Season at North Island-1 (FeAx-3). *Provincial Archaeology Office 2011 Archaeology Review* 10:166–168.

Sutherland, Patricia D.

2009 The Question of Contact between Dorset Paleo-Eskimos and Early Europeans in the Eastern Arctic. In *The Northern World, AD 900–1400*, edited by H. Maschner, O. Mason, and R. McGhee, pp. 279–299. University of Utah Press, Salt Lake City.

Szala-Meneok, Karen

1992 Time and Contingency: Temporal Organization in Southern Labrador. Unpublished Ph.D. dissertation, McMaster University, Hamilton, Ontario.

Tanner, Adrian

1993 History and Culture in the Generation of Ethnic Nationalism. In *Ethnicity and Aboriginality: Case Studies in Ethnonationalism*, edited by Michael D. Levin, pp. 75–96. University of Toronto Press, Toronto.

1998 The Aboriginal Peoples of Newfoundland and Confederation. *Newfoundland and Labrador Studies* 14(2):238–52.

Taylor, J. Garth

1985 The Arctic Whale Cult in Labrador. *Études/Inuit/Studies* 9(2):121–132.

1990 The Labrador Inuit Kashim (Ceremonial House) Complex. *Arctic Anthropology* 27(2):51–67.

Tompkins, Edward

1988 *Pencilled Out: Newfoundland and Labrador's Native People and Canadian Confederation, 1947–1954*. A report prepared for Jack Harris, M.P., on the impact of the exclusion of Newfoundland and Labrador's native people from the Terms of Union in 1949. House of Commons, Ottawa.

Thompson, Niobe

2009 *Inuit Odessey*. Documentary Film written and produced by Niobe Thompson and Tom Redford. CBC The Nature of Things (aired February 8, 2009).

Tremblay, Hughette

1977 *Journal des voyages de Charles Arnaud 1872–1873. Recherche et transcription*. Les Presses de l'Université du Québec, Montreal.

Tuck, James A.

1976 *Newfoundland and Labrador Prehistory*. Van Nostrand Reinhold, Toronto.

Whiteley, W. H.

1977 Newfoundland, Quebec, and the Labrador Merchants, 1783–1809. *Newfoundland Quarterly* 73(4):18–26.

Woollett. James M.

1999 Living in the Narrows: Subsistence Economy and Culture Change in Labrador Inuit Society during the Contact Period. *World Archaeology* 30(3):370–387.

Inuit Settlement on the Southern Frontier

Lisa Rankin

Over the past decade a number of early contact period Inuit archaeological sites have been located and excavated in and around Sandwich Bay, an area once considered peripheral to the "core" Inuit settlement zones of central and northern Labrador. These sites, which span the period between the late sixteenth and the mid-eighteenth centuries, not only challenge the assumption of a "core" settlement area, but have the potential to shed light on Inuit colonization and the related processes of Inuit trade and interaction with Europeans in southern Labrador. In short, the addition of new information concerning the Inuit presence in southern Labrador allows for a much more comprehensive interpretation of their history, and presents an opportunity to revise older models concerning Inuit settlement and trade patterns during this volatile period of their history.

Background

Researchers have always understood that the southern coast of Labrador played an important role in Inuit mobility and culture patterns (Kaplan 1985; Martijn and Clermont 1980a; Taylor 1977, 1984). This region was a hub of early modern European fishing and whaling activity and therefore an important region for Inuit access to the European material culture. Historical documentation has been used to suggest that Inuit travelled south specifically to trade with Europeans or raid their camps and settlements for desirable materials, perhaps since the sixteenth century. However, the spotty nature of the historical record has resulted in an ongoing debate concerning the nature of the Inuit occupation of the southern coast. One side of the debate, spearheaded by Taylor (1977, 1980, 1984), purports that the Inuit presence in southern Labrador was largely limited to seasonal and brief forays for the purposes of acquiring European goods. In contrast, Martijn (1980, 2009) and Stopp (2002) have suggested that both maps and written documents indicate a regular and year-round presence of the Inuit in southern Labrador and along the Quebec North Shore by the mid- to late seventeenth century. In other words, the south became a place of Inuit occupation before the permanent European settlement of the region.

Unfortunately, Martijn and his supporters have had only minimal material evidence (in contrast to the substantial Inuit historical and archaeological record from central and northern regions) to support their convictions of a southern Labrador Inuit settlement system. Archaeological sites reported by Auger (1991) at Seal Islands, Dumais and Poirier (1994) at Baie des Belles Amours, Fitzhugh (1989) at Snack Cove, Martijn and Clermont (1980b) at Kettle Head, and Stopp (2002) at various low-elevation locations on the south coast offer tantalizing but often confusing, limited, or insecure data—none sufficient to prove year-round Inuit settlement. In the absence of a significant archaeological record, even some archaeologists have seemed unwilling to believe that the Inuit ventured south outside of the summer months (Jordan 1977:43; 1978:176). By failing to unequivocally substantiate the presence of an Inuit settlement zone in southern Labrador, these historical tidbits have unwittingly marginalized the significance of the Inuit's southern frontier. Instead of perceiving the south as a nexus of Inuit cultural activity, they have enhanced a view of the south as peripheral to the northern homeland of Labrador Inuit. Thus, the south has remained largely absent from scholarly interpretations of Labrador Inuit social, cultural, and economic history.

As it stands, the most inclusive Inuit culture-history sequence remains that espoused by Jordan and Kaplan (1980). This broad, diachronic model identifies three phases of Inuit socio-economic development in the historic period and suggests that the Inuit followed a similar pattern of adaptation from the north coast through their settlement terminus in Groswater Bay, central Labrador. During the early Colonization Period (AD 1600–1700) the Inuit occupied small, single-family semi-subterranean winter homes with long entrance passages; acquired European goods from infrequent raiding and trading in southern Labrador; and maintained a relatively traditional Inuit culture pattern (Jordan and Kaplan 1980:40–41). Throughout the Intermittent Trading Period (AD 1700–1800) Inuit occupied large communal houses; formalized trade with Europeans, thereby increasing the number and types of European goods available to them; and developed a highly structured social hierarchy based around powerful shaman/traders who controlled access to European commodities (Jordan and Kaplan 1980:42). These middlemen-traders became responsible for moving European goods to more northerly Inuit settlements while bringing Inuit-produced commodities such as baleen, furs, and sea mammal oils south to European consumers (Jordan and Kaplan 1980). At some point during this period, Inuit shifted their settlements away from outer-coast locations, which most resembled the landscapes of their Arctic homeland, to the more protected inner island and mainland locations (Kaplan 1983, 2012:21). This provided access to a wider resource base, which was capable of supporting larger communities and perhaps reflected an evolving Inuit understanding of the Labrador landscape. Finally, during the nineteenth century Trading Post Period (AD 1800–1870), the social hierarchy supporting communal houses and long-distance trade routes collapsed; trapping and cash economies were adopted; and single-family homes re-emerge as European goods became available directly to nuclear families engaged in the trading post economy (Jordan and Kaplan 1980:43).

Similar schemes, such as those proffered by Schledermann (1971) and Woollett (1999), have noted that there may have been environmental reasons for the adoption of communal houses. Schledermann (1971) suggested that climatic cooling during the seventeenth century may have limited the number of whales available for Inuit consumption and forced the Inuit to merge together into houses where seal resources could be better shared. Later research by Woollett (1999) determined that Labrador experienced rather mild temperatures during this period, leading him to suggest that declining sea ice may have increased the possibilities for open-water sealing—a task best completed by an organized group—which may have been best organized and controlled by the head of a communal household.

These models explained the majority of historical, environmental, and archaeological evidence available, and it is a tribute to the scholarly work of the authors that their ideas continue to act as the dominant explanatory frameworks of the contact period Inuit settlement and economy. According to Fitzhugh (2009), the persistence of such schemes also reflects the difficulty that archaeologists have faced finding Inuit sites in southern Labrador. In southern Labrador archaeologists face numerous difficulties, both in finding and in interpreting Inuit sites, that do not exist in central and northern settings. The more temperate and vegetated landscape means that Inuit sites may not be located; the ephemeral nature of summer settlements means that they might not be readily recognized; and European settlement of southern Labrador after AD 1700 means that distinguishing Inuit and European sod houses is difficult (Fitzhugh 2009:134–135). Nevertheless, archaeologists have persevered and throughout the last decade have brought significant new data to the fore.

There is now a growing body of archaeological data from Inuit sites in southern Labrador and the Quebec North Shore (Brewster 2006; Fitzhugh 2009; Fitzhugh et al. 2011; Murphy 2011; Ramsden and Rankin 2013; Rankin 2006, 2010a, 2010b, 2012, 2013; Rankin et al. 2012; Stopp 2002, 2012; Stopp and Jalbert 2010; Stopp and Wolfe 2011). For the first time, archaeologists have proof that southern Labrador was a permanent home to the Inuit and a genuine part of the Inuit landscape. It is now time to evaluate our recent contributions and incorporate these new data into our understanding of Labrador Inuit socio-economic history. As with central and northern Labrador, we can now begin to see the south as a place where the daily lives of Inuit families played out, where economic and cultural interaction with Europeans and other Inuit occurred, and where Inuit practised a meaningful way of life. My contribution to this research concerns Inuit sites discovered in and around Sandwich Bay.

Sandwich Bay Context

The area studied includes portions of Sandwich Bay proper as well as mainland areas to the southeast as far as Cape North, and north to the tip of Cape Porcupine, along with many adjacent islands (see Figure 1). It is a region of diverse ecosystems, from the rocky, windswept headlands and outer islands to a heavily forested mainland, as well as a 60-km stretch of sand dune beach, known as the Porcupine Strand, running from the north side of Sandwich Bay to the southern edge of Hamilton Inlet. Sandwich Bay is the second largest bay on the Labrador coast. Two major salmon rivers drain into its base, but other food resources include several species of seal and whale, caribou, black bear, polar bear, small fur bearers, over 250 species of sea birds, and diverse freshwater and marine fishes; as well, edible berries and lichen are seasonally abundant (King 1983; Peterson 1966; Speiss 1993; Todd 1963).

The first archaeological investigation of potential Inuit sites was carried out in this region in 1986 by William Fitzhugh of the Smithsonian Institution. He recorded four probable Inuit sites on Huntingdon Island and Newfoundland Island (1989:168–171). Stopp visited the region in 1992 (1997, 2002) and recorded another series of "historic period sites" in the southern periphery of the region that, by 2002, she had begun to suspect were of Inuit origin. My own research, and that of my students, began in the area in 2001 as part of the "Porcupine Strand Archaeology Project," a multi-year archaeological survey of the region, and this work has continued more recently under the Social Sciences and Humanities Research Council of Canada-sponsored project, "Understanding the Past to Build the Future." Among that project's many goals is to locate and excavate Inuit habitation sites in the Sandwich Bay region.

Sandwich Bay Finds

Thirty-two probable Inuit sites have thus far been recorded in the Sandwich Bay region. While the classification of some sites remains tenuous, 18 have now been confirmed as Inuit and further investigation of the remaining sites may yet confirm them as Inuit (Table 1). Nine of these sites contain sod-walled houses, six contain tent rings and associated features, one is an isolated burial, and the remaining two contain stone fox traps with associated caches and features. To date, excavations have been undertaken at four habitation sites: Snack Cove 1 and 3, Huntingdon Island 5, and Pigeon Cove 1 (Figure 1). This is not only the order in which they were excavated, but also follows a rough chronology of when they were occupied.

Table 1. Confirmed Inuit Sites in Sandwich Bay.

Site	Site Type
GbBi-19	Boulder tent rings, stone caches, hunting blinds, rock crevice burials
FlBf-02	Boulder houses, boulder caches
FlBf-06	Sod house (semi-subterranean with entrance passage)
FkBg-03	Sod houses (semi-subterranean with entrance passages), tent rings, fox trap, boulder burial)
FkBg-34	Tent rings, possible sod houses
FkBf-01	Tent rings, cache
FkBf-02	Tent ring, caches, fox trap
FkBe-01	Tent rings with intact hearths
FkBe-03	Sod houses (semi-subterranean with entrance passages), cache, burial, kayak stands
FkBe-06	Tent rings with intact hearths
FkBe-08	Cache, fox trap, box hearth
FkBe-16	Burial
FkBd-10	Stone fox trap
FlBg-07	Sod house (semi-subterranean with entrance passage)
FkBd-20	Sod houses (semi-subterranean filled by an old growth of trees)
Cape Porcupine	Sod house, earthenware pottery sherd
Dumpling Island	Sod house, Inuit bone pendant
Pack's Harbour	Sod house (semi-subterranean)

Snack Cove 1 (FkBe-01) and 3 (FkBe-03) are related—with Snack Cove 3 containing a minimum of four sod-walled winter dwellings while the adjacent Snack Cove 1 contains three contemporaneous summer tent rings (Rankin et al. 2012). Numerous other features such as kayak supports and boulder burials span the area between the two site locales. The sod dwellings had slab stone floors and were framed with timber, which is common in this part of Labrador. The excavated dwellings were small, averaging 6 m in width and 3 m long. Each contained a single room with rear sandy platform, and a long entrance passage with cold trap (Figure 2). They were likely occupied by a single family. On other parts of the Labrador coast Inuit winter houses of similar style have been associated with the early period of Inuit settlement circa AD 1450–1700 (Jordan and Kaplan 1980; Kaplan 2012; Schledermann 1971). Radiocarbon dates taken from all three excavated winter houses as well as one of the tent rings indicate that both summer and winter dwellings at Snack Cove may have been occupied by the late sixteenth century,

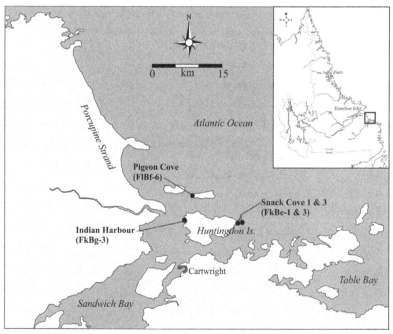

Figure 1. Study area.

but the highest probability for occupation is the early to mid-seventeenth century (Brewster 2006:27; Ramsden and Rankin 2013). The houses contain limited material culture, with fewer than 100 artifacts recovered from each dwelling and thin middens. This is indicative of a limited-term occupation, but the presence of both summer and winter house forms demonstrates that the settlement was used for at least two seasons (Brewster 2006; Rankin et al. 2012). Material culture such as harpoon paraphernalia and ulus indicates that both men and women were present at these sites, and the substantial faunal assemblage suggests that they were following a traditional seal-based subsistence pattern (Brewster 2006; Rankin 2010b). The occupants of Snack Cove were aware of Europeans and were using European material culture, predominantly iron and ceramics. No formal trade items such as beads were present and there is little to indicate that the Inuit occupants of Snack Cove had any direct contact with Europeans. Many of the European items present were modified into traditional Inuit tools such as iron ulus, but a cache of iron nails with heads removed suggests that this group was also preparing European iron for trade with other Inuit groups (Brewster 2006:25; Rankin et al. 2012).

Figure 2. Excavated Snack Cove house.

Like other early colonization period Inuit settlements in central and northern Labrador, the Snack Cove sites are located in a sheltered cove, but an outer island environment, at the extreme eastern end of Huntingdon Island. This may suggest that the seventeenth-century Inuit were relatively new to the region and therefore inhabiting the kinds of landscapes and ecosystems with which they were most familiar. However, the Snack Cove sites were well placed to take advantage of a nearby portage to Table Bay (Figure 1), which would have provided faster and safer access to points further south than by rounding Cape North in kayaks. Therefore, the location of the site may well have been strategically placed to take advantage of the access to European goods further south.

Huntingdon Island 5 (FkBg-3) is located on Indian Island—a small promontory of land connected to the western edge of Huntingdon Island at low tide (Figure 1). The site is located in a sheltered environment from which the mainland is visible. A swift current a few hundred metres to the west of the site ensures access to open water and seal hunting even in the depths of winter. The site contains five sod-walled houses and six summer tent rings. To date we have excavated four of the houses and undertaken extensive testing on one tent ring.

House 1, dating to the early to mid-seventeenth century (ca. AD 1620–1680), was occupied first (Ramsden and Rankin 2013). Although contemporary with the houses at Snack Cove, House 1 on Indian Island is quite different from them (Figure 3). This larger (8 m x 7 m), rectangular house had a slab stone floor, side and rear platforms, and four lamp stands, as well as a long entrance passage with cold trap and lintel entryway. Its layout resembles communal houses from central and northern Labrador, yet its early to mid-seventeenth-century occupancy makes it an early example of communal houses. Faunal remains indicate that the inhabitants relied on both seal and caribou. Like the houses at Snack Cove, the number of artifacts (approximately 350) was small, and these were of both Inuit and European origin. Most of the European items were modified into traditional Inuit forms and were clearly being fashioned to meet Inuit needs. Most interesting, however, is the distribution

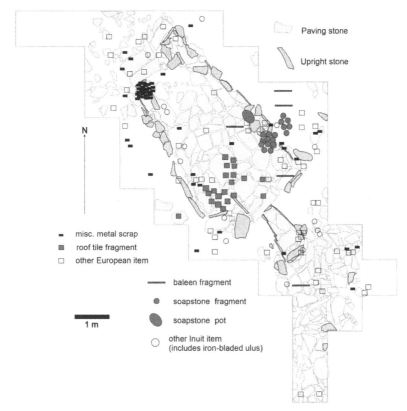

Figure 3. Huntingdon Island 5, House 1 distribution map.

of material culture throughout the house. There is a bilateral distribution of goods, with most European items found along the left side of the house and Inuit items along the right side (Figure 3). Given that many of the Inuit items were associated with women's kitchen duties, this may reflect a gendered division of space. Yet another distribution pattern seems to indicate that different types of material culture, including European-manufactured roofing tiles and iron, as well as baleen, were kept by different segments of the household, suggesting an unequal control of commodities within the house (Figure 3). These patterns may suggest that even within a small household, decisions about the significance of material culture were being negotiated differently. House 1 marks the transition from the single-family homes at Snack Cove to a multi-family household, yet the types and numbers of European artifacts present were ultimately similar, suggesting that Inuit socio-economic structures were changing even before there was increased access to European trade goods. Only one similar house has been recorded in Labrador, located at the site of Eskimo Island 3 in Hamilton Inlet, which also dates to the same time period (Kaplan 1983:420). This suggests that this type of household might have been a southerly phenomenon.

House 2, which also dates from the early to mid-seventeenth century, shares the entrance passage with House 1, but appears to have been occupied slightly later (Figure 4). This square structure (measuring 7 m x 6 m) included three lamps stands and an artifact assemblage twice the size of that recovered from House 1 (approximately 600 artifacts). The faunal assemblage is made up almost exclusively of harp and ringed seal. The quantity and type of European artifacts, including items such as beads, suggest that formal trade with the French had begun. As with the other houses, items of material culture associated with women were more prevalent than men's objects, reflecting the domestic nature of household space. However, the distribution of artifacts and artifact types is much more random than in House 1, suggesting perhaps that this multi-family house functioned as a unit and goods were shared among occupants. The presence of new materials, such as a lead sheet cold-hammered into bowl shapes and used as oil lamps and decorative beads, indicates that women were benefiting from the new trade. Moreover, a single miniature soapstone pot, likely a child's toy, is our first indication both that children were present and that they were learning the tasks necessary for survival.

Houses 3 and 4 date from the early to mid-eighteenth century and are true communal houses, similar in size and form to those found in central and northern Labrador (approximately 7 m x 7 m) (Figure 5, and see Murphy and Rankin, this volume). Larger artifact assemblages of 1,000–1,500 items were unearthed in each. Most artifacts were manufactured from European-derived materials, but many traditional objects and forms, including children's toys, were still present. There were

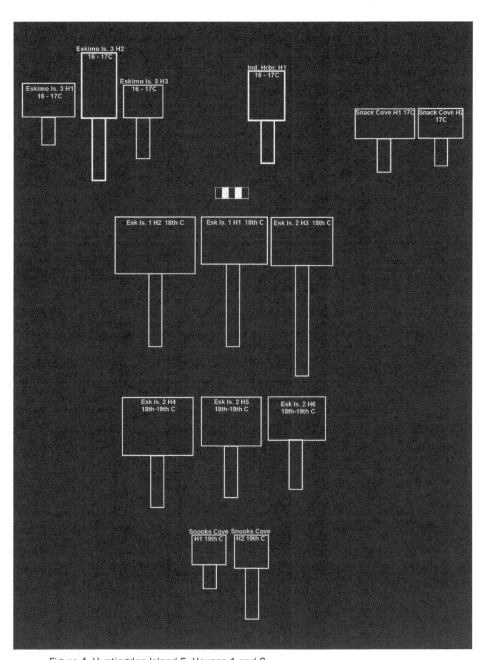

Figure 4. Huntingdon Island 5, Houses 1 and 2.

many items of personal adornment including beads, pendants made from coins, and in one instance, a French sword hilt (see Murphy and Rankin, this volume). Communal houses are thought to be representative of the increasing status and power of individual men who were able to co-ordinate the labour and support of others and use this influence to enhance their success in trade. However, many of the European-derived artifacts from these houses are indicative of women's activities and demonstrate that they too used new commodities, made significant contributions to the household, and, given the number of beads and pendants, were actively enhancing their own social status. The faunal assemblages, comprised of several thousand remains, indicated that sealing was the predominant activity.

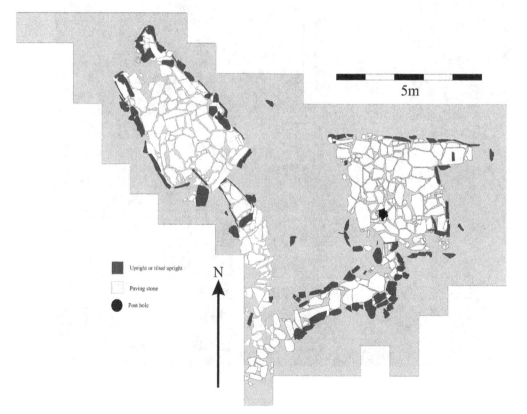

Figure 5. Huntingdon Island 5, House 4.

The house remains at Huntingdon Island 5 indicate that there was both a formalization of trade (most likely with the French), and a realignment of household structure over time. For example, the two earliest houses have the largest range of European material culture. It is as if the Inuit collected every exotic item they encountered. Within 100 years this had changed. Houses 3 and 4 have much more European material culture but the selection of items is more limited, suggesting that the Inuit had decided which European goods had the most cultural or economic value to them. As these communal households became more acquainted with European material culture the distribution of these goods within the houses also changed. In House 1 specific European goods were associated with distinct segments of the house as if they were

Figure 6. Pigeon Cove, House 1.

controlled by different household members, but in Houses 3 and 4 this distribution is more random, indicating that internal household relationships, and the relationships of individual household members with these goods, changed over time with most household members having access to most things. That said, unique items such as the sword hilt pendant were rare and highly valued.

In the summer of 2012, we began excavations at Pigeon Cove (FIBf-06), a sheltered cove on an island just north of Huntingdon Island 5. This site was chosen because it contained only a single winter house, and was therefore unlike both Snack Cove and Huntingdon Island 5. We are currently completing the analysis of this site, but some data are available. Pigeon Cove contains a large communal house and the material culture recovered suggests that the occupation dates to the mid-eighteenth century (Figure 6). As with the other houses, terrestrial mammal bone recovered from the house will be sent for carbon dating. Both traditional Inuit material culture and European materials, predominantly French in origin, are present at the site. The artifact collection is the largest we have recovered to date. Cataloguing is ongoing but we have now surpassed 4,200 items—almost three times the size of the largest collection from Huntingdon Island 5. Items recovered include artifacts associated with men, women, and children. Thousands of faunal remains were also excavated and have recently been sent to Université Laval for analysis.

The house is large, approximately 10 m x 12 m in size, and contains multiple platforms, storage niches, lamp stands, and a rather odd entrance passage. The house appears to have been occupied longer than any of the other houses we have excavated in Sandwich Bay. The size of both the artifact and faunal assemblage hint at this, but alterations to the southern wall and entrance passage suggest that the occupants had to reconstruct their home at least once. Excavations at Pigeon Cove are not yet complete, and further research at this site will no doubt demonstrate that there is an even greater diversity to the Sandwich Bay settlement system than we had previously thought.

The sites that we have investigated, combined with the other Inuit sites recorded in Sandwich Bay, demonstrate that there was considerable Inuit settlement here predating the arrival of Europeans on this part of the coast. Furthermore, the settlements we have observed do not appear to represent the camps of traders, making rapid trips south. Rather, these settlements were the homes of families, large and small, living at specific locations for extended periods, spanning multiple seasons. There can be little doubt now that the Inuit inhabited the coast south of Groswater Bay by the mid-seventeenth century, supporting Martijn's (1980) and Stopp's (2002) interpretation of the historic record.

Comparisons to Other Labrador Inuit Regions

The Inuit sites in Sandwich Bay are remarkably similar in form and number to Inuit settlements elsewhere on the Labrador coast. For example, the Newfoundland and Labrador provincial site records indicate that Nain Bay has 11 confirmed Inuit sod-house settlements dating to the mid-eighteenth century or earlier; Okak has four, Makkovik has two, Hopedale has six, and there are five near Rigolet in Hamilton Inlet (Table 2). If we add in tent rings and sites with associated cache and burial features, the number of Inuit sites is between 20 and 30 for each of these more northerly regions. With nine sod-house sites and 18–32 potential Inuit sites, the Sandwich Bay area has about the number of Inuit sites as further north. The Inuit occupation of Sandwich Bay also follows another trend seen elsewhere in Labrador: from early, small sod-house settlements in outer-coastal settings to later, larger communal houses located on the inner islands (Kaplan 2012)—although communal houses may occur earlier than they do further north. Like elsewhere, the Inuit living in Sandwich Bay learned how to live in specific areas, and they learned what local resources were best to exploit. They had increasing access to European goods and selected European commodities with more care over time. These transitions occurred all along the Labrador coast, and as Kaplan (2012:21) points out, it is likely that certain families preferred and became associated with certain regions of the coast. Historic documentation makes it seem that particular Inuit families settled in Sandwich Bay. By 1773, Curtis records the Inuit name for the Sandwich Bay region as "the place where there are many jar [ringed] seals" (Handcock 2008:23–31; Wharram 2008:97). Later on, there are Moravian references to Inuit who were born or died in this region (Hans Rollmann, personal communication, 2011). By the mid-nineteenth century, Hudson Bay records refer regularly to "Cartwright" Inuit (Patty Way, personal communication, 2012). Ultimately, some Inuit who resided in Sandwich Bay referred to themselves as "the people of the place of the ringed seals" (Hawkes 1916), suggesting a lengthy period of Inuit occupation of Sandwich Bay.

Table 2. Regional Distribution of Eighteenth-Century Inuit Sod-House Sites in Labrador.

Region	Sod-House Sites
Nain	Eleven sites: HcCh-10; HkCk-01; HdCh-32; HeCi-15; HeCg-08; HdCg-15; HdCg-23; HcCk-05; HcCi-01; HcCi-02; HcCj-01
Okak	Four sites: HkCl-23; HhCk-05; HjCl-05; HjCl-09
Makkovik	Two sites: GgBu-01; GgBq-01
Hopedale	Six sites: GlCb-06; GiCa-02; GiCb-01; GjCb-03; GjCb-06; GkCc-01
Rigolet	Five sites: GaBp-01; GaBp-02; GaBp-03; GbBm-02; GbBo-02

Note: Data from Newfoundland and Labrador Site Record forms Database, December 2011.

However, there do appear to be some real differences between the Inuit settlements in Sandwich Bay and those elsewhere. These include the small size of settlements, with no more than five winter houses at any site identified to date; the relatively short period of house occupation, as demonstrated by the lack of reoccupation and thin middens at most sites; and seemingly limited amounts of European material when compared to large Inuit settlements such as Eskimo Island in Groswater Bay (Jordan and Kaplan 1980). To better understand these differences my students and I have begun a series of targeted comparisons examining household architecture and length of occupation (Murphy 2011; Murphy and Rankin, this volume); the presence, absence, and distributions of exotic and prestige items (Fay 2012); gender-associated tools (Davies 2012); and European ceramic use (Collins 2012).

While Murphy (2011; Murphy and Rankin, this volume) sees little difference in the architectural form of Inuit houses along the coast of Labrador, she acknowledges that the duration of occupation in the southern settlements appears brief. Murphy (2011) has suggested that Inuit occupation may be somewhat different in the south because Inuit population numbers were probably minimal and because they had access to abundant resources for house construction. Therefore, the Inuit could move around the region in response to local events rather than remain in one settlement locale each year. This process would result in smaller sites with smaller amounts of refuse at each settlement. Alternatively, Kennedy (2009) suggests that the short duration of occupation may reflect the mobility southern Inuit needed to intercept and trade with those aboard visiting European ships. However, as more house comparisons are made, it is beginning to appear that, especially with small settlements, limited duration of occupancy was more widespread than previously thought (Fay 2012). Furthermore, archaeological data collection strategies have emphasized the larger, more recognizable settlements rather than smaller, seasonally occupied settlements. If this is the case, then the settlement system we see in Sandwich Bay may not be that different from the majority of Inuit settlements elsewhere.

As we have begun to compare the archaeological collections from each of the Inuit houses from Sandwich Bay with individual houses located on the central and northern coast, we are finding that the amount and type of discard is not dissimilar. In fact, many of the Sandwich Bay houses contain greater numbers of European goods than individual houses further north (Collins 2012; Davies 2012). This may be explained by the relative proximity of access to European commodities afforded to the Inuit who lived on the southern Labrador frontier, but given the thin depth of middens at the Inuit houses in Sandwich Bay, it is somewhat unexpected. What we can state now is that discard is greater at those

Inuit sites in central and northern Labrador, which have lengthy histories of reoccupation and direct connections to the trade in European commodities (such as the sites on Eskimo Island thought to be associated with significant middlemen/traders). In order to add more substance to our comparisons, more emphasis on the excavation of complete houses (rather than strategic trenching) is needed in the future, and more control will be required over the chronological provenience of artifacts recovered from reoccupied houses. Only then will we ascertain whether discard at some of the larger settlements was similar over the short term, and what the real differences are.

Conclusion

Interpreting Sandwich Bay as a southern Inuit settlement area resolves some questions about the range of Labrador Inuit settlement. It is no longer possible to accept Groswater Bay as the southern terminus of Inuit settlement because year-round settlement was occurring in Sandwich Bay. Furthermore, settlement strategies in the south follow similar patterns over time to those seen elsewhere in Labrador, while allowing for an expected amount of regional variation in response to local circumstances.

However, other questions have yet to be answered. The historic record makes it clear that northern Inuit were travelling south to access European commodities and that prestigious Inuit middlemen helped to move Inuit and European goods back and forth between the two groups—in this manner many central and northern Inuit contributed to the success of the trade network. It also appears that this burgeoning coastal trade network was strongly correlated to changes in Inuit settlement patterns over time (Jordan and Kaplan 1980). Yet the collections recovered from the Sandwich Bay sites suggest that while the southern trade was important to Inuit households it was not necessarily the primary focus of this population, who, for all intents and purposes, were at the front of the line in this network. Certainly they accumulated large amounts of European commodities, but much less than those Inuit inhabiting Eskimo Island, for example (Jordan and Kaplan 1980). It is possible that trading the exotic goods they had access to and holding onto the information about where to acquire them were of greater value to the southern Inuit than amassing prestige through accumulation (Townsend 1976). Trade would help to keep lines of communication open with Inuit living far from the frontier, allowing information to flow between groups and for culture patterns to be maintained over the length of the coast. Living on the southern frontier was essential to the maintenance of the coastal trade network, a network that no doubt helped the Inuit to maintain a cohesive identity throughout the early historic period.

References Cited

Auger, Reginald
> 1991 *Labrador Inuit and Europeans in the Strait of Belle Isle: From Written Sources to the Archaeological Evidence.* Collection Nordicana No. 55. Centre d'études Nordiques, Université Laval, Québec.

Brewster, Natalie
> 2006 *The Inuit in Southern Labrador: The View from Snack Cove.* Occasional Papers in Northeastern Archaeology No. 15. Copetown Press, St. John's.

Collins, David Andrew
> 2012 Putting the Pieces Together: Labrador Inuit Acquisition, Use, Reuse and Distribution of European Ceramics during the Labrador Communal Sod House Phase. Paper delivered at the 18th Inuit Studies Conference, Washington, D.C.

Davies, Michelle
> 2012 Activities and Agency of Inuit Women in the Communal House Phase of 18th Century Labrador. Paper delivered at the 18th Inuit Studies Conference, Washington, D.C.

Dumais, P., and J. Poirier
> 1994 Témoinage d'un site Archéologiques Inuit, Baie des Belle Amours, Basse-Côte-Nord. *Études/Inuit/Studies* 22(1):5–35.

Fay, Amelia
> 2012 The One Percent: Exploring the Haves and Have Nots of the Inuit Coastal Trade Network during the 18th Century in Labrador. Paper delivered at the 18th Inuit Studies Conference, Washington, D.C.

Fitzhugh, William W.
> 1989 Hamilton Inlet and Cartwright Reconnaissance. In *Archaeology in Newfound-*

land and Labrador 1986: Annual Report #7, edited by J. Callum Thomson and Jane Sproull Thomson, pp. 164–181. Historic Resources Division, Newfoundland Museum. Department of Municipal and Provincial Affairs, St. John's.

2009 Exploring Cultural Boundaries: The Less "Invisible" Inuit of Southern Labrador and Quebec. In *On the Track of the Thule Culture from Bering Strait to East Greenland. Papers in Honour of Hans Christian Gulløv*, edited by Bjarne Grønnow, pp. 129–148. Publications from the National Museum Studies in Archaeology and History Volume 15. National Museum, Copenhagen.

Fitzhugh, William W., Anja Herzog, Sophia Perdikaris, and Brenna McLeod
2011 Ship to Shore: Inuit, Early Europeans and Maritime Landscapes in the Northern Gulf of St. Lawrence. In *The Archaeology of Maritime Landscapes: When the Land Meets the Sea*, edited by Ben Ford, pp. 99–108. Springer, New York.

Hancock, Gordon
2008 A Review of the 1771 Curtis Map. In Toponymic and Cartographic Research Conducted for the Labrador Metis Nation, edited by Lisa K. Rankin, pp. 21–32. Report on file with the NunatuKavut Community Council, Goose Bay, Labrador.

Hawkes, E. W.
1916 *The Labrador Eskimo*. Geological Survey of Canada, Memoir 91. Government Printing Bureau, Ottawa.

Jordan, Richard
1977 Inuit Occupation of the Central Labrador Coast since AD 1600. In *Our Footprints are Everywhere: Inuit Land-use and Occupancy in Labrador*, edited by Carol Brice-Bennett, pp. 3–48. Labrador Inuit Association, Nain.

1978 Archaeological Investigations of the Hamilton Inlet Labrador Eskimo: Social and Economic Responses to European Contact. *Arctic Anthropology* 15(2):175–185.

Jordan, Richard, and Susan Kaplan
1980 An Archaeological View of the Inuit/European Contact Period in Central Labrador. *Études/Inuit/Studies* 4(1–2):35–45.

Kaplan, Susan
1983 Economic and Social Change in Labrador Neo-eskimo culture. Unpublished Ph.D. dissertation, Bryn Mawr College, Bryn Mawr, Pennsylvania.

1985 European Goods and Socio-economic Change in Early Labrador Inuit Society. In *Cultures in Contact*, edited by William Fitzhugh, pp. 45–69. Smithsonian Institution Press, Washington, D.C.

2012 Labrador Inuit Ingenuity and Resourcefulness: Adapting to a Complex Environmental, Social and Spiritual Environment. In *The Nunatsiavummiut Experience: Settlement, Subsistence and Change among the Labrador Inuit*, edited by David C. Natcher, Lawrence Felt, and Andrea Proctor, pp. 15–42. University of Manitoba Press, Winnipeg.

Kennedy, John C.

2009 Two Worlds of Eighteenth Century Labrador Inuit. In *Moravian Beginnings in Labrador: Papers from a Symposium held in Makkovik and Hopedale*, edited by Hans Rollmann, pp. 23–36. Occasional Publication of Newfoundland and Labrador Studies No. 2. Faculty of Arts Publication, Memorial University of Newfoundland, St. John's.

King, Judith E.

1983 *Seals of the World*. 2nd ed. British Museum of Natural History, Oxford University Press, Oxford.

Martijn, Charles A.

1980 The "Eskimaux" in the 17th and 18th Century Cartography of the Gulf of St. Lawrence: A Preliminary Discussion. *Études/Inuit/Studies* 4(1–2):77–104.

2009 Historic Inuit Presence in Northern Newfoundland Circa 1550–1800 CE. In *Painting the Past with a Broad Brush: Papers in Honour of James Valliere Wright*, edited by David L. Keenlyside and Jean-Luc Pilon, pp. 65–101. Canadian Museum of Civilization Mercury Series, Gatineau, Quebec.

Martijn, Charles A., and N. Clermont

1980a The Lande God Alloted to Caine. *Études/Inuit/Studies* 4(1–2):5–16.

1980b Les Structures de Pierres et la Mandible du site EiBk-3. Basse Côte-Nord, Quebec. *Études/Inuit/Studies* 4(1–2):127–134.

Murphy, Phoebe

2011 *Identifying the Inuit Communal House Phase in Southern Labrador*. Occasional Papers in Northeastern Archaeology No. 19. Copetown Press, St. John's.

Peterson, Randolph L.

1966 *The Mammals of Eastern Canada*. Oxford University Press, Oxford.

Ramsden, Peter, and Lisa K. Rankin

2013 Thule Radiocarbon Chronology and Its Implications for Early Inuit–European Interaction in Labrador. In *Exploring Atlantic Transitions: Archaeologies of Permanence and Transience in New Found Lands*, edited by Peter E. Pope with Shannon Lewis-Simpson, pp. 299–309. Society for Post-Medieval Archaeology Monograph No. 7. Boydell and Brewer, Woodbridge, Suffolk.

Rankin, Lisa K.

2006 The Porcupine Strand Archaeological Project: Interim Report on the 2005 Field Season. On File, Provincial Archaeology Office, Department of Tourism, Culture and Recreation, St. John's.

2010a Indian Harbour, Labrador. *Provincial Archaeology Office 2009 Archaeology Review* 8:119–121.

2010b A People for All Seasons: Expressions of Inuit Identity over the Past 500 Years in Southern Labrador. In *Identity Crisis: Archaeological Perspectives on Social Identity*, edited by Lindsay Amundsen-Meyer, Nicole Engel, and Sean Pickering, pp. 332–340. University of Calgary, Calgary.

2012 Indian Harbour, Labrador. *Provincial Archaeology Office 2011 Archaeology Review* 10:126–129.

2013 The Role of the Inuit in the European Settlement Process in Sandwich Bay, Labrador. In *Exploring Atlantic Transitions: Archaeologies of Permanence and Transience in New Found Lands*, edited by Peter E. Pope with Shannon Lewis-Simpson, pp. 310–319. Society for Post-Medieval Archaeology Monograph No. 7, Boydell and Brewer, Woodbridge, Suffolk.

Rankin, Lisa K., Matthew Beaudoin, and Natalie Brewster

2012 Southern Exposure: The Inuit of Sandwich Bay, Labrador. In *The Nunatsiavummiut Experience: Settlement, Subsistence and Change among the Labrador Inuit*, edited by David C. Natcher, Lawrence Felt, and Andrea Proctor, pp. 61–84. University of Manitoba Press, Winnipeg.

Schledermann, Peter

1971 The Thule Tradition in Northern Labrador. Unpublished Master's thesis, Memorial University of Newfoundland.

Speiss, Arthur

1993 Caribou, Walrus and Seals: Maritime Archaic Subsistence in Labrador and Newfoundland. In *Archaeology of Eastern North America: Papers in Honour of Stephen Williams*, edited by James B. Stoltman, pp. 73–100. Archaeological Report No. 25. Department of Archives and History, Jackson, Mississippi.

Stopp, Marianne P.

1997 Long-Term Coastal Occupancy between Cape Charles and Trunmore Bay, Labrador. *Arctic* 50(2):119–137.

2002 Reconsidering Inuit Presence in Southern Labrador. *Études/Inuit/Studies* 26(2):71–106.

2012 The 2011 Field Season at North Island-1 (FeAx-3). *Provincial Archaeology Office 2011 Archaeology Review* 10:166–168.

Stopp, Marianne P., and Catherine Jalbert

2010 Searching for the Inuit in the Unknown Labrador — A Community University Research Alliance (CURA) Project. *Provincial Archaeology Office 2009 Archaeology Review* 8:156–160.

Stopp, Marianne P., and Kara Wolfe

2011 Report of 2010 Excavations at North Island-1. *Provincial Archaeology Office 2010 Archaeology Review* 9:172–174.

Taylor, J. Garth

1977 Traditional Land Use and Occupancy by the Inuit. In *Our Footprints Are Everywhere: Inuit Land-use and Occupancy in Labrador*, edited by Carol Brice-Bennett, pp. 49–58. Labrador Inuit Association, Nain.

1980 The Inuit of Southern Quebec–Labrador: Reviewing the Evidence. *Études/Inuit/Studies* 4(1–2):185–193.

1984 Historical Ethnography of the Labrador Coast. In *Handbook of North American Indians: Volume 5, Arctic,* edited by David Damas, pp. 508–521. Smithsonian Institution Press, Washington, D.C.

Todd, W.E. Clyde
1963 *Birds of the Labrador Peninsula and Adjacent Areas.* University of Toronto Press, Toronto.

Townsend, Joan
1976 European Trade Goods: Questionable Indicators of Contact Intensity. Paper presented at the Annual Meeting of the Canadian Archaeological Association, Winnipeg.

Wharram, Douglas
2008 Translations of Some Inuit "Tribal" Names and Toponyms. In Toponymic and Cartographic Research Conducted for the Labrador Metis Nation, edited by Lisa K. Rankin, pp. 95–100. Report on file with NunatuKavut Community Council, Goose Bay.

Woollett, J. M.
1999 Living in the Narrows: Subsistence Economy and Culture Change in Labrador Inuit Society during the Contact Period. *World Archaeology* 30(3):370–387.

CHAPTER 3

Exploring the Communal House
Phase in Sandwich Bay

Phoebe Murphy and Lisa Rankin

During the eighteenth century the French began overwintering on the Labrador coast and interactions between the Inuit and Europeans intensified. This process appears to be associated with a dramatic change in Inuit housing, from small single-family dwellings to larger dwellings accommodating several families, which is referred to as Labrador's "Communal House phase." The sudden adoption of communal houses by Inuit was short-lived, continuing for only a century or so. The building of large communal houses is likely linked to increased trade relations between the two groups and the rise of influential Inuit traders, including men such as Tuglavina (see Fay, chapter 4). Inuit–European interaction during this period was more direct and sustained than during previous centuries (Jordan 1978; Jordan and Kaplan 1980; Kaplan 1983; Taylor 1976).

Labrador Inuit communal houses were large, rectangular semi-subterranean structures that generally housed three or more families, averaging 20 or more people (Taylor 1974:15). Communal houses ranged in size from 6 m by 7 m to 6 m by 16 m (Kaplan 1983:238), compared to earlier winter houses that typically measured 3 m by 6 m, and housed only six to eight people (Kaplan 1983:220; Kaplan and Woollett 2000:352). Archaeologists believe the Communal House phase in northern and central Labrador began in the early eighteenth century and continued until the turn of the nineteenth century (Jordan 1978; Kaplan and Jordan 1980; Schledermann 1971). Until recently, archaeologists believed central Labrador was the southernmost boundary of the Communal House phase and, indeed, of Inuit occupancy. Recently, however, new archaeological and archival findings challenge that boundary (Beaudoin 2008; Brewster 2006; Rankin 2009; Rankin et al. 2011; Rankin, chapter 2; Stopp 2002), and include southern Labrador within the customary Inuit land use area. The communal house at Sandwich Bay discussed in this chapter further suggests that Inuit lived in southern Labrador in much the same manner as they did further north.

In the summer of 2010, a research team from Memorial University investigated an Inuit winter house, House 3, located at the Huntingdon Island 5 site (FkBg-3) in Sandwich Bay (Figure 1). Excavation and analysis revealed that House 3 was a large communal Inuit winter dwelling occupied during the early decades of the eighteenth century (AD 1720–1740). In the 1980s, Auger (1989) unearthed a similar dwelling in the Strait of Belle Isle that he initially identified as Inuit. However, the Inuit cultural affinity of this structure has recently been questioned (Gaudreau 2011). Assuming Gaudreau is correct, House 3 at the Huntingdon Island 5 site is the first Inuit communal house fully excavated in southern Labrador. This chapter presents the results of the House 3 excavation and then discusses the purpose of Inuit communal houses in southern Labrador.

Communal House Context

Europeans began to frequent the Labrador coast in the sixteenth century. European fishermen and whalers used the coast seasonally, to harvest cod and whale stocks, and returned to Europe with their catches at the end of the summer. This seasonal presence continued (though experiencing fluctuations in intensity) in the ensuing centuries (Trudel 1980). By the early eighteenth century, some French began overwintering in Labrador (see Crompton, chapter 5). These seasonal and resident Europeans provided the Inuit with a source of new materials, particularly metals. The Inuit obtained these new objects by trade, by raiding, or by scavenging the seasonally abandoned European fishing and whaling stations.

The increased presence of Europeans in Labrador, and the expanded opportunities for obtaining European materials, led to increased socioeconomic differentiation within Inuit society. As European fishing and

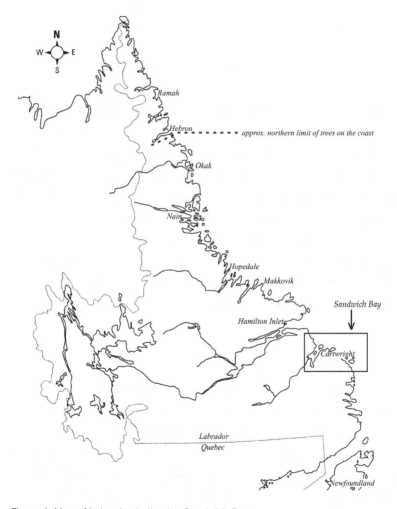

Figure 1. Map of Labrador, indicating Sandwich Bay.

whaling occurred primarily off southern Labrador, this provided the opportunity for ambitious Inuit individuals to become middlemen traders, ferrying goods to Inuit in far northern Labrador (Jordan 1978; Jordan and Kaplan 1980; Kaplan 1983; Taylor 1976). These traders occupied large communal houses, often had multiple wives, owned sleds pulled by many dogs, and acted as intermediaries between the Europeans and other Inuit groups (Richling 1993; Taylor 1974:80–81; also see Fay, chapter 4).

Middlemen traders travelled south with the purpose of acquiring European goods that were scarce in the north (Jordan and Kaplan 1980). The traders then travelled north with European items to trade with northern Inuit populations who had little, if any, access to these items. In exchange, these traders collected and transported baleen, oil, and other seal and whale products that the Europeans in the south desired (Taylor 1976). It follows that Inuit middlemen only distributed European goods at the household level and through this process easily attracted more members to their household unit (Taylor 1976). Thus, the large houses that define the Communal House phase were home to wealthy Inuit traders and their extended families.

House 3, Huntingdon Island 5 (FkBg-3)

Huntingdon Island, in Sandwich Bay, contains a number of Inuit sites representing both summer and winter habitations (Brewster 2006; Murphy 2011; Rankin 2009, 2010a, 2010b; Rankin et al. 2011) (Figure 2). The Huntingdon Island 5 site contains at least five semi-subterranean Inuit winter houses and as many summer tent rings (Figure 3). All of the winter houses are clustered within metres of each other on the western side of the island. Excavation revealed that House 3 was a large, communal-style dwelling oriented to the northwest with a sunken cold-trap entrance passage extending to the southeast (Figure 4). The internal dimensions of House 3, excluding the entrance passage, were 7 m by 8.5 m, constituting a 60 m^2 living area.

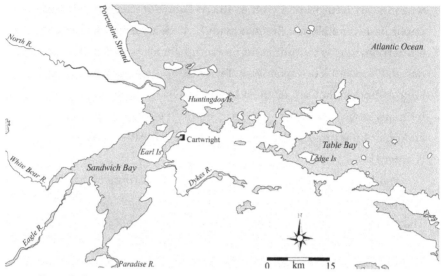

Figure 2. Sandwich Bay.

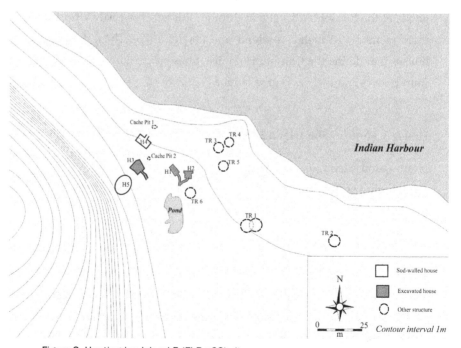

Figure 3. Huntingdon Island 5 (FkBg-03) site map.

The Inuit constructed House 3 with sand, turf, and large rocks with timber structural elements. The floor and sunken cold-trap entrance passage consisted of tightly placed and levelled flagged floor stones. A large portion of exposed bedrock near the eastern wall of the house composed part of the central floor space. The entrance passage also consisted of levelled floor stones and measured 4.5 m in length. Raised sleeping platforms of sand and fine gravel lined the three interior walls around the periphery of the floor area. Organic remains demonstrate that the platforms were likely covered with bark, plant matting, and skins for insulation and comfort. Vertical rocks positioned in an angular arrangement around the junction between the platform edge and the central floor space created discrete

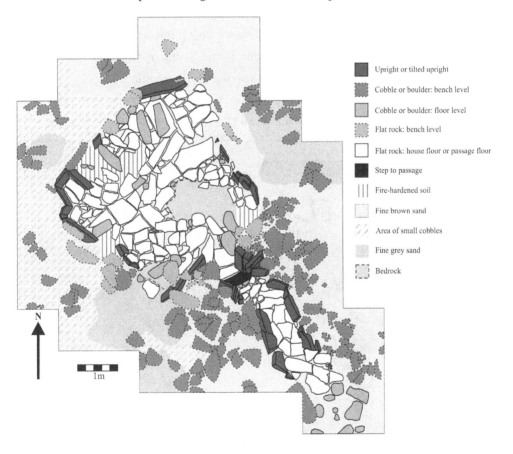

Figure 4. House 3 at Huntingdon Island 5 (FkBg-03).

alcove or niche areas. Associated with each of these alcove areas were horizontal tabular rocks, interpreted as bench or seating areas.

A large midden or refuse area was not located; however, two small external faunal deposit areas were positioned on either side of the entrance passage. Nonetheless, neither deposit was large or deep enough to suggest sustained accumulation over multiple seasons. Distinct and separate midden deposits associated with Inuit winter houses were generally the result of a fall season interior cleaning of the house prior to the reoccupation of the structure (McGhee 1984:78). The absence of a large midden suggests that House 3 was only occupied for one or two winters. The absence of visible and complex stratigraphic layers and the absence of any rebuilding episodes support the idea that this site was only occupied for a short period of time. This contrasts with other communal houses constructed in central and northern Labrador, which were occupied during multiple seasons and over multiple years.

The number of discrete alcove and bench areas in House 3 suggests that five families, or between 20 and 25 people, resided there (Kaplan

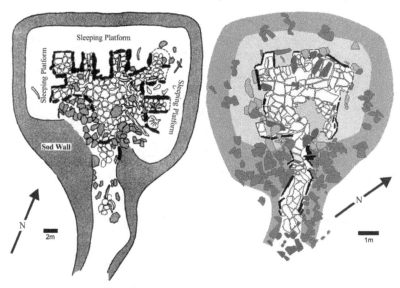

Figure 5. House plans from Huntingdon Island 5, House 3 (right) and Ikkusik House 8 (left). Ikkusik House 8 is redrawn from Schledermann (1976:Figure 4).

1983:312–313). According to ethnographic documents, the families were probably agnatically related, such as fathers and their married sons (Taylor 1974). Each family had a separate alcove and bench area and the central floor area was a common living space. Each of the alcove areas may have functioned as lampstands for preparing meals, as lighted work areas, and as storage locations for each individual family. In its size (60 m^2) and layout (multiple sleeping platforms and multiple lamp stands), House 3 is consistent with the typical Labrador Inuit communal house form (Kaplan 1983:220, 238). For instance, House 3 resembles Ikkusik House 8, an Inuit communal house located in Saglek Bay near the northern tip of Labrador. The similarities in these two structures reveal clear parallels in the organization and use of space in Labrador communal houses (Figure 5). These two houses were over 800 km apart; however, the correlation in design suggests a standardization of communal houses throughout the entire region.

Material Culture

The House 3 excavation recovered 753 artifacts, including objects of European origin, traditional Inuit items, and hybrid European–Inuit objects (Table 1). Traditional Inuit artifacts include whalebone sled parts and tools, soapstone pots and lamps, baleen, pyrite strike-a-lights, and pieces of animal hide. Yet the majority of House 3 material culture is of European manufacture. These objects include nails, fish hooks, ceramics, glass bottles, glass beads, lead projectiles, roof tiles, utensils, pipes, gunflints, coins, sword parts, an axe, a padlock, a finger ring, and many more miscellaneous fragments of iron and other metals (Murphy 2011). A number of European artifacts had been cut, drilled, hammered, or bent to transform them into different objects. Excavation recovered approximately 50 items of this type, including five iron ulus, one traditional-style iron men's knife, hammered nails, and punctured coins.

Table 1. Origin of Artifacts Recovered in House 3.

Origin	Number	Per cent
Inuit	52	7
European	554	73
European-modified	52	7
Unknown	95	13

The artifacts also demonstrate the daily activities of the household. For instance, whalebone and iron sled parts indicate winter travel, while iron fish hooks and a bone wound pin suggest fishing and seal-hunting activities. The presence of lead projectiles and gunflints suggests that the inhabitants possessed firearms. Iron-bladed ulus and a man's stemmed end-blade knife demonstrate the Inuit adapted European objects to traditional tool types. The overall importance of iron tools at the site is further demonstrated by the large number of metal items and tools in the assemblage, and by the presence of whetstones and roof tile abraders that were used to sharpen these tools.

At House 3, the Inuit used soapstone pots and lamps fueled by sea mammal oil for cooking, heating, and lighting, indicating continuation of customary Inuit food preparation practices. Traditional Inuit communal meals were liquid-based stews and broths, prepared in soapstone, baleen, or wooden pots (Jurakic 2007:81). All of the ceramics recovered, with the exception of one Ligurian-style platter, were hollowware vessels. This too suggests a continuation of traditional Inuit foodways. Inuit did not rely on soapstone lamps and pots alone; Normandy stoneware vessel bases also served as substitutes for these objects. The stoneware vessel bases have scorch marks and were found around the sleeping platform and alcove areas, where soapstone pots are typically found. Hollowware ceramics were also likely used in the consumption of traditional communal meals, replacing wooden or soapstone pots (Jurakic 2007).

The House 3 assemblage contains objects of adornment, which would have either been attached to clothing or suspended for display within houses. For example, the small, tri-lobed lead drop pendants would have been attached to the fringes of clothing in much the same manner that perforated animal teeth and amulets were traditionally used (Karklins 1992:198–199; Woollett 2003:348). The glass beads in the assemblage would also have been used in the same manner. In addition, three pierced copper coins (one of which has been identified as a George II halfpenny, dating 1729–1754) were used as pendants. Ethnographic accounts document the Labrador Inuit using "coins of various countries attached to the arms and dress" (Turner 2001 [1894]:212). Other pendants were made from a pair of French grenadier copper cast sword hilts (dating 1725–1750). Both hilts were missing the knuckle guard; one of the hilts was hammered flat and had leather tied around the quillon, presumably to facilitate the wearing or hanging of this item. The Inuit at House 3 may have decorated their clothing and bodies with European items in an overt display of wealth and power intended to impress other Inuit and Europeans alike.

Conclusion

As explained in the preceding chapter, until recently, archaeologists considered southern Labrador to be south of the limits of permanent Inuit settlement. This study adds further support to the growing body of evidence suggesting a sustained and long-standing Inuit occupation of the south. The artifacts uncovered from House 3 demonstrate the continuation of traditional Inuit activities such as seal hunting, fishing, winter travel by sled, and preparation of communal meals over soapstone oil lamps. Datable artifacts from House 3 were manufactured in France or England, generally between ca. AD 1720–1740. House 3 was occupied during the period that France held rights to Labrador (up to AD 1763), and this material culture was obtained either through direct trade with the French or by scavenging abandoned French sites. Inuit were attracted to these items as substitutes for traditional Inuit items and objects of adornment.

As a result of their geographic position, the southern Inuit populations began to explore and develop barter-based economies that relied on trading both with the Europeans in the south and with Inuit in the north. The southern Inuit became front-line traders, middlemen, and information gatherers who had direct access to Europeans (Kaplan 1983; Kennedy 2009; Taylor 1976). The short length of occupation of House 3 may in fact be correlated with the lifestyle of the southern front-line traders who required a more mobile settlement system in order to move to and from various parties involved in the complex trade networks of the eighteenth century (Kennedy 2009).

The examination of House 3 from the Huntingdon Island 5 site revealed that, except for the duration of occupancy, this structure was a typical Labrador Inuit communal house. House 3 demonstrates that communal houses were indeed built and used by the Inuit in southern Labrador. It is apparent that the construction of communal houses coincides with increased access to foreign manufactured goods, enhanced trade networks, and the rise of a class of middlemen traders. Our research demonstrates that the Inuit cultural tradition, including the Communal House phase, clearly persisted south of Groswater Bay.

References Cited

Auger, Reginald
>   1989 Labrador Inuit and Europeans in the Strait of Belle Isle: From the Written Sources to the Archaeological Evidence. Unpublished Ph.D. dissertation, Department of Archaeology, University of Calgary, Calgary.

Beaudoin, Matthew
>   2008 Sweeping the Floor: An Archaeological Examination of a Multi-Ethnic Sod House in Labrador (FkBg-24). Unpublished Master's thesis, Department of Archaeology, Memorial University of Newfoundland, St. John's.

Brewster, Natalie
>   2005 The Inuit in Southern Labrador: A View from Snack Cove. Unpublished Master's thesis, Department of Archaeology, Memorial University of Newfoundland, St. John's.
>   2006 *The Inuit in Southern Labrador: The View from Snack Cove.* Occasional Papers in Northeastern Archaeology, No. 15. Copetown Press, St. John's.

Gaudreau, Nathalie
>   2011 Stratégies de Subsistance et Identité Culturelle des Occupants Seal Islands (FaAw-5) au Labrador Méridional Entre 1760–1820. Unpublished Master's thesis, Department of History, Université Laval, Québec City.

Jordan, Richard H.

1978 Archaeological Investigations of the Hamilton Inlet Labrador Eskimo: Social and Economic Responses to European Contact. *Arctic Anthropology* 15(2):175–185.

Jordan, R. H., and S. A. Kaplan

1980 An Archaeological View of the Inuit/European Contact Period in Central Labrador. *Études/Inuit/Studies* 4(1–2):35–45.

Jurakic, Irena

2007 Up North: European Ceramics and Tobacco Pipes at the Nineteenth-Century Contact Period Inuit Winter Village Site of Kongu (IgCv-7), Nachvak Fiord, Northern Labrador. Unpublished Master's thesis, Department of Archaeology, Memorial University of Newfoundland, St. John's.

Kaplan, Susan A.

1983 Economic and Social Change in Labrador NeoEskimo Culture. Unpublished Ph.D. dissertation, Department of Anthropology, Bryn Mawr College, Bryn Mawr, Pennsylvania.

Kaplan, Susan A., and Jim M. Woollett

2000 Challenges and Choices: Exploring the Interplay of Climate, History, and Culture on Canada's Labrador Coast. *Arctic, Antarctic, and Alpine Research* 32(3):351–359.

Karklins, Karlis

1992 *Trade Ornament Usage Among the Native Peoples of Canada: A Source Book.* National Historic Sites Parks Service, Ottawa.

Kennedy, John C.

2009 Two Worlds of Eighteenth-Century Labrador Inuit. In *Moravian Beginnings in Labrador*, edited by Hans Rollman, pp. 23–36. Occasional Publications No. 2. Newfoundland and Labrador Studies, St. John's.

McGhee, Robert

1984 *The Thule Village at Brooman Point, High Arctic Canada.* Archaeological Survey of Canada Paper No. 125, Mercury Series. National Museums of Canada, Ottawa.

Murphy, Phoebe

2011 The Southern Component of the Labrador Inuit Communal House Phase: The Analysis of an 18th-Century Inuit House at Huntingdon Island 5 (FkBg-3). Unpublished Master's thesis, Department of Archaeology, Memorial University of Newfoundland, St. John's.

Rankin, Lisa K.

2009 *An Archaeological View of the Thule/Inuit Occupation of Labrador.* Report on File with the Labrador Métis Nation, Goose Bay.

2010a A People for All Seasons: Expressions of Inuit Identity over the past 500 Years in Southern Labrador. In *Identity Crisis: Archaeological Perspectives on*

Social Identity, edited by L. Amundsen-Pickering, N. Engel, and S. Pickering, pp. 320–328. Proceedings from the 42nd Annual Chacmool Conference. University of Calgary, Calgary.

2010b *Huntingdon Island 5 (FkBg3) Huntingdon Island, Labrador*. A Report on Activities Conducted under Permit 09.22 in 2009. On File at the Provincial Archaeology Office, Government of Newfoundland and Labrador, St. John's.

Rankin, Lisa K., Matthew Beaudoin, and Natalie Brewster
2011 Southern Exposure: The Inuit of Sandwich Bay, Labrador. In *Settlement, Subsistence and Change among the Inuit of Nunatsiavut, Labrador*, edited by David Natcher, Larry Felt, and Andrea Proctor. Northern Studies 61 Series. University of Manitoba, Winnipeg.

Richling, Barnett
1993 Labrador's "Communal House Phase" Reconsidered. *Arctic Anthropology* 30(1):67–78.

Schledermann, Peter
1971 The Thule Tradition in Northern Labrador. Master's thesis, Department of Archaeology, Memorial University of Newfoundland, St. John's.

Stopp, Marianne
2002 Reconsidering Inuit Presence in Southern Labrador. *Études/Inuit/Studies* 26(2):71–106.

Taylor, J. G.
1974 *Labrador Eskimo Settlements of the Early Contact Period*. Publications in Ethnology No. 9. National Museum of Canada, Ottawa.

1976 The Inuit Middleman in the Labrador Baleen Trade. Paper presented at the 75th Annual Meeting of the American Anthropological Association, Kansas City.

Trudel, François
1980 Les relations entre les Français et les Inuit au Labrador méridional, 1660–1760. *Études/Inuit/Studies* 4(1–2):135–146.

Turner, Lucien M.
2001 [1894] Ethnology of the Ungava District, Hudson Bay Territory. *11th Annual Report of the Bureau of American Ethnology for the Years 1889–90*, 11:159–350. Originally published 1894, Smithsonian Institution, Washington, D.C.

Woollett, James M.
2003 An Historical Ecology of Labrador Inuit Culture Change. Ph.D. dissertation, Department of Anthropology, City University of New York, New York.

CHAPTER 4

Big Men, Big Women, or Both? Examining the Coastal Trading System of the Eighteenth-Century Labrador Inuit

Amelia Fay

By the eighteenth century, an extensive coastal trade network had developed in Labrador where European goods from the south were being traded for baleen, oil, and furs from the north. This trade network is conventionally thought to have been co-ordinated by Inuit "big man" traders who travelled up and down the coast; indeed, the majority of European documents from this time mention specific Inuit men responsible for coastal trade. While women presumably played an important role in the changing economy, they are seldom mentioned in historical documentation. An exception to this is the well-documented life of the Inuit woman, Mikak (ca. 1740–1795).

The movement of goods was thoroughly entwined with the movement of people, and increased involvement in trade meant that Inuit expeditions travelled the entire coast of Labrador. In this chapter, I examine the development and importance of the coastal trade network and explore the role of major players like Mikak and her husband for a time, Tuglavina (ca. 1738–1798), who was a successful trader. At the same time, I highlight some preliminary results from the archaeological record of eighteenth-century Inuit sod houses in the Nain area, including one that Mikak was believed to have lived in, and reflect on how the incorporation of archaeological data may enhance our understanding of gender roles and the trade network itself.

Brief Labrador Contact History

The first instances of European contact with the Labrador Inuit were sporadic and fleeting. Basque whalers were among the first Europeans to exploit Labrador's rich resources, having set up seasonal whaling stations in such harbours as Red Bay and Chateau Bay during the sixteenth and early seventeenth centuries. Contact between the Inuit and Basques consisted of opportunistic trade or, more likely, the scavenging of vacant Basque work sites during the winter months. There is little evidence of any formal exchange system between the two groups (Kaplan 1985:56). Early European contact was even less substantial along the northern coast (Nain and northward), although it is likely that the northern Inuit occasionally traded with Dutch whalers during the seventeenth century (Kaplan 1980). Direct and sustained contact did not occur in either the northern or southern coastal regions until the eighteenth century.

European expansion in Labrador during the eighteenth century was largely dependent on political and social developments beyond Labrador. The Treaty of Utrecht in 1713 facilitated the French occupation of coastal Labrador, and, as Crompton (chapter 5) explains, French concessionaires were granted land from which they were permitted to participate in the seal and cod fisheries, as well as trade with Aboriginal peoples (Kaplan 1985; Stopp 2008). In 1763, the Treaty of Paris saw control switch from the French to the British. This created a more restricted economic regime that banned Newfoundland and New England residents from fishing in Labrador waters and forbade landownership and year-round fishing and trading rights (Stopp 2008:14). In 1765 Governor Hugh Palliser visited Chateau Bay to establish and sign a treaty in the hopes of promoting peaceful relations between the British and the Inuit (see NunatuKavut Community Council, 2010; Kennedy, chapter 1).

Hostilities decreased, so that by 1770 Captain George Cartwright, and later British merchants, began to pursue the cod and seal fisheries on the southern coast. Some of the male servants employed by these merchants decided to remain in Labrador and would marry the only available choice of spouses: Inuit women. Thus began the history of Labrador's Inuit-Métis.

After 1763, British policy sought to contain Inuit in the north to prevent them from interfering with the planned fishery in the south. Coincidentally, Moravian missionaries wanted to establish a mission among the Labrador Inuit. To do so, they agreed to work with the British government towards limiting Inuit activities in the south, in exchange for land to set up their mission stations (Hiller 1971; Kaplan 1985). The Moravians established their first mission station at Nain in 1771 and over the next two centuries would open and operate at least nine more. As Europeans in a new world, the missionaries relied on the help of Inuit, and fortunately, we know something about two of their earliest helpers, Mikak and Tuglavina.

Mikak

J. Garth Taylor and Marianne Stopp have pieced together the details of Mikak's life story from written sources, such as ships' journals and the station diaries of Moravian missionaries, and through an examination of portraiture and oral histories (Taylor 1983, 1984, 2000; Stopp 2009). According to Taylor's and Stopp's research, Mikak first enters the historical record in 1765 when she, along with a large group of Inuit, hosted Jens Haven and the Moravian Brethren, who were temporarily storm-bound during their reconnaissance to Labrador. At this time she was in her early twenties, had a partner whose identity is unknown, and also had a young son named Tutauk (Stopp 2009). In 1767 Mikak, her son, and seven others were captured as part of a revenge attack on a group of Inuit who had stolen wooden boats and killed three Englishmen at a whaling station north of Chateau Bay (Taylor 1983). The commander of the vessel, Francis Lucas, who also was in his twenties, took an immediate interest in Mikak, and they began to teach each other words in their respective languages (Taylor 1983:5). That summer, Lucas took his prisoners to St. John's where they met Governor Hugh Palliser, who Mikak may have remembered from the visit he paid to Chateau Bay in 1765 to establish the peace treaty. Palliser was greatly impressed with Mikak's intelligence and knowledge of Inuit numbers and settlements. He realized he could use her and the other prisoners to establish good communications and trade with other Inuit along the coast (Stopp 2009:48; Taylor 1983:6). Palliser decided to take Mikak, her son Tutauk, and an orphan named Karpik to winter in London, where Mikak was reintroduced to the missionary Jens Haven and learned of his goal to secure a land grant for a mission post in Labrador (Taylor 2000). For unknown reasons, Mikak championed the cause of the Moravians while she was in London and offered her assistance to encourage her fellow Inuit to be amenable to their message. Some have suggested that her enthusiasm may have helped the Moravian cause, for they received their land grant in 1769 (Taylor 1983). During her stay in London, Mikak was visited by a number of well-connected members of London society, had her portrait painted by John Russell, and was given many gifts. She returned to Labrador during the summer of 1769 and encouraged Inuit to welcome the Moravians (Stopp 2009; Taylor 2000).

In 1770, the missionaries found Mikak and her family, just north of Hamilton Inlet. By this time she had married Tuglavina, a shaman and influential trader along the coast. It should be noted that during this time period marriage was recognized when a couple started living together, and was not the result of any sort of formal ceremony (Stern 2010:12). Together Mikak and Tuglavina helped guide the missionaries north to establish the first mission post in Nain (Hood 2008; Taylor 1983, 2000). Many Inuit disagreed with locating the mission at Nain, arguing that they could not make a living there for more than two months in a year, yet the Moravians persisted in their choice in location, perhaps in an attempt to follow the conditions of their land grant from the British by keeping the Inuit in the north (Stopp 2009:51). On their journey with the missionaries,

Mikak and Tuglavina seemed responsive to the Christian message, yet once the Nain mission was established in 1771, they declined the invitation to winter there and only visited to trade (Taylor 1984).

Traditional Inuit settlement patterns began to change during this time. Typically in the winter months, Inuit would move into semi-subterranean sod houses, hunting seals at the *sîna* (ice edge) or *polynyas* (ice-free corridors). From spring to autumn they became increasingly mobile, as they travelled to acquire different marine and terrestrial resources. With the arrival of the Moravians, the Inuit developed a desire to remain close to the mission for supplies, at the same time attempting to maintain their traditional seasonal resource harvesting patterns (Stopp 2009). The Moravians wanted to keep the Inuit close, to prevent them from engaging in cultural practices they frowned upon, such as polygamy, spousal exchange, and shamanic rituals, but they also wanted the Inuit to remain economically independent, so as not deplete the mission's foods and supplies. This presented the missionaries with a serious dilemma: they did not want to alter the traditional subsistence economy, but that economy required Inuit families to be mobile and thus beyond the watchful eye of the mission. Many Inuit families, including Mikak and Tuglavina's, continued to follow a traditional way of life, often staying away from the mission station for long periods.

According to Taylor's (1984) summary of the Moravian records, Mikak's family quarrelled with other families in the region over their wealth, as Mikak and Tuglavina enjoyed substantial wealth and prestige. Turner (1894:189) noted that when a family was prosperous, the husband would often take a second wife, and that wife exchange occurred frequently. Shortly after marrying Mikak, Tuglavina claimed a second wife, arguing that Mikak's stay in London made her barren. This second wife happened to be Mikak's sister and Mikak was supposedly unhappy with the new arrangement, but if she complained Tuglavina beat her (Taylor 1984:20). In 1773, Tuglavina exchanged wives with Pualo, whose wife was also Mikak's sister. Pualo was not heavily involved in coastal trade and his name only enters the Moravian documents during

this transaction with Tuglavina. Mikak's association with Pualo low-
ered her standing among fellow Inuit, as Pualo was a less prestigious
partner than Tuglavina. Immediately after the exchange, Tuglavina left
on a month-long trip with his new spouse. Upon his return, the missionaries urged him to stay with Mikak and, though he promised that he
would, he broke that promise the following year (Taylor 1984).

By 1775, Tuglavina and Mikak were heavily involved in the baleen
trade and his success enabled him to take a third wife, Pualo's daughter.
Mikak's final wife exchange from Tuglavina to Pualo occurred in 1776.
Although the Moravians report that Pualo had treated Mikak better, she
had to adjust to a lower standard of living since Pualo did not even own
a boat, then emblematic of success (Taylor 1984:21). In 1780, both Pualo
and Mikak's son Tutauk were baptized but Mikak was left off the list,
most likely due to the Moravian lot system, which made many decisions
by lottery (Taylor 1984). Two years later, against Moravian wishes, Mikak
and Pualo decided to go south, at the urging of Tuglavina. By this time,
Tuglavina had four wives, a measure of his affluence and influence.
More wives not only provided more labour but also required considerable wealth (Taylor 2000). Mikak and Pualo's trip was successful, as
they returned north with a new boat and musket, which encouraged
them to continue with trips to the south for trade (Taylor 1984). Mikak
lived out the remainder of her life trading in the south with occasional
trips north. Pualo died in 1783 but Mikak was not widowed for long; a
few years later, she remarried a younger man. Little is known about her
life during this time, for after her baptismal rejection she remained very
mobile and continued to trade between the north and south. She returned to Nain in 1795, where she died at age 55, after finally being
baptized (Stopp 2009; Taylor 1984).

Tuglavina

Tuglavina's life has been described by Bryan Hood (2008) based on information from the Moravian Periodical Accounts and by Taylor (1969,
1974, 1984, 2000). Tuglavina first enters the documentary record in 1770

when the Moravians returned to Labrador to explore for a mission location and to find Mikak. Hood (2008:216) speculates about whether Tuglavina's marriage to Mikak was a deliberate strategy on his part to facilitate access to European goods and enhance his status, as she had close ties with the English and Moravians. Mikak's return to Labrador may have attracted the interest of other Inuit males, as her time in England and her European goods would have been quite desirable. Tuglavina was an *angekok* (shaman), a good hunter, and an influential man among his fellow Inuit (Hood 2008; Taylor 2000). During the early years of the mission, the Moravians vacillated between considering Tuglavina a nuisance or, at other times, an influential Inuk who could assist them (Hood 2008:217). In 1775 he took three missionaries in his boat to search for the site of a new mission station later called Hopedale and in 1780 he allowed one of the missionaries to accompany him on a caribou hunting trip in the interior (Taylor 1969, 2000).

Mikak's marriage to Tuglavina was tumultuous, although it was likely similar to what other Inuit women endured during that time. Polygyny and wife-swapping were common, and in this sense Mikak and Tuglavina's marriage was not unique. In contrast, Tuglavina's success at securing wives (he had four by 1782) was exceptional, and an indication of his power and prestige. During and after his marriage to Mikak, Tuglavina sailed his two-masted sloop north to acquire baleen, which he would then exchange for European goods at Chateau Bay. Tuglavina acquired firearms, which he transported north, since initially the Moravians were unwilling to supply guns, and he often convinced others to join him on these trips south to acquire European goods (Rollmann 2011). However, his career as a trader ended in 1790 when his two-masted sloop became unseaworthy and, as Taylor (2000) writes, he had only one dog to pull his sled. His once meteoric career in tatters, Tuglavina and his one remaining wife joined the mission settlement in Nain (Hood 2008; Taylor 2000). Although baptized at Chateau Bay in 1783, when he was seriously ill, he failed to meet Moravian expectations and did not join the congregation until 1793, in Nain. He died in 1798 at the age of 60 (Taylor 2000).

Big Women?

Mikak's southern trade forays with her husband Pualo invite the question as to whether she rather than he might have conducted the actual trade, yet most of the literature confines the occupation of traders to men, or as Richling (1993) called them, "big men." But were all traders men? What evidence is there to support the idea that women, like Mikak, were also "big women" in the coastal trading network?

Among northern foraging societies, a relatively consistent, pan-Arctic gendered division of labour is common (Bodenhorn 1990; Frink 2007, 2009; Jarvenpa and Brumbach 2006; LeMoine 2003). This gendered division is actually a complex symbiotic relationship where the success of one depends on the other. While tasks occasionally overlapped—for example, men will sometimes sew but only women will make skin clothing—men and women tended to avoid encroaching on each other's productive spheres (Frink 2007:353). Stern (2010:9) describes how this relationship is deeply rooted in Inuit cosmology where women are associated with *the* essential role in attracting the animals needed for food, clothing, and fuel. Despite recognition of women's important role within the subsistence economy, in practice women had very little power or control over their lives (Stern 2010:13). Evidence for this is most pronounced in the aforementioned practices of spousal exchange and polygyny. As Stern (2010:16) further elaborates, "this lack of women's power in sexual relations contrasts markedly with the important role that women played in subsistence work and cosmology, and the two situations are not easily reconciled."

The introduction of new technologies would have changed household activities and altered subsistence strategies. By the end of the eighteenth century fish hooks, needles, knives, nets, traps, and guns were all available at both the Moravian and Hudson's Bay Company trading posts (Kleivan 1966). It was no longer necessary to fashion stone or bone tools when steel tools were readily available, nor was it necessary to sew seal skins together to make *umiaks* (large skin-covered boats) when wooden boats could be obtained. This meant that male hunters and trappers could spend more time away from home acquiring the goods for trade, and that the women could also participate in the market economy through their increased involvement in the cod fishery. In this sense, the introduction of European technology gradually changed Labrador Inuit social and economic strategies. Increased trade participation altered relationships among individuals by producing some changes in the division of labour, gender roles, and the status system (Cleland 1993). Yet there is an indication of continuity, at least in terms of the gendered division of labour. Although the tasks performed by men and women changed, and the locations of these tasks were altered, the symbiotic economic-based relationship continued. The technological changes introduced by Europeans do not appear to have disrupted this feature of Inuit society.

The Moravians kept detailed records and accounts of their travels and trades along the coast. That said, gender roles are not often described. Typically, the lives of women are not mentioned; an exception, of course, is the life of Mikak, who appears fairly frequently in Labrador's documentary history. Men's and women's roles are mentioned occasionally, such as, for example, by Lieutenant Roger Curtis in 1774. Curtis writes:

> The Esquimaux men are extremely indolent and the women are the greatest drudges upon the face of the earth. They do every thing except procure food, and even in that they are frequently assistants; so that they are at continual labour [Curtis 1774:385].

From this description Curtis acknowledges the fact that women often helped with food procurement, highlighting this symbiotic gendered division of labour.

Lucien Turner (1894) provides a detailed account of men's and women's roles in the Ungava region. He states that while the men go off to hunt larger game, the women bring the wood and water, make skin clothes and boots, as well as hunt small game (Turner 1894:205–206). Again, the work of men and women is framed symbiotically, and although women's work seems never-ending, Turner (1894:206) emphasizes how the two roles work perfectly well together: "The entire family accompany the [hunting] expeditions; and as the females are often the more numerous portion of the population, they row the umiak at their leisure." Women participated in hunting and trading expeditions, yet they are seldom referred to, most especially by name. For example, when missionary William Turner travelled with a group of Inuit inland to hunt caribou in 1780 he mentions women so infrequently that one wonders if they were there at all. Only occasionally does he mention their presence: "Tuglavina ordered everyone to be ready, that we might go in the night. His wives were obliged to make a great fire between the tents and the boat, in order to have light in loading our boat" (Taylor 1969:156).

Missionaries Kohlmeister and Kmoch (1814) seldom mention women in their detailed account of their 1811 voyage from Okak to Ungava Bay. Aside from a brief introduction of who was aboard the vessel, in which we learn there were five Inuit women, the remainder of their journal contains one reference to a woman, who suffered a severe head wound after the ship hit a rock (Kohlmeister and Kmoch 1814:38). Presumably these women had specific roles on board the vessel but the missionaries' primary focus was to record the account of their trip and how they preached their Christian message at every stop along the way. With the exception of their captain, Jonathan, they say very little about any of the other passengers, male or female, and refer to everyone by the blanket term "the Esquimaux" (Kohlmeister and Kmoch 1814). This lack of reference to women in these documentary records may be explained both by the historical period when they were written and by the fact that male missionaries and other travellers would have had little contact with Inuit women.

From these few excerpts we can get a sense of male and female roles, and it seems that women were constantly at work either within the home or assisting men with hunting or travelling. As the Inuit economy

shifted throughout the eighteenth century, women might have participated increasingly within the trade network. Cabak (1991:158) states
that during the nineteenth century, Inuit women were "shrewd shop-
pers, often sharper than men, and displayed influence in household
purchasing decisions, often making the final choices." This behaviour
may have developed during the eighteenth century as Inuit women
gained access to prestigious European goods. These ethnographic and
historical sources provide us with some information, albeit written from
a male perspective. While we may never know whether women like
Mikak actually participated in trade, we know that the social status of
the wives of influential male traders increased through the things they
came to possess, and when trade was peaceful, the women themselves
may have participated.

Khernertok

In the 1776 census by Moravian missionary J. L. Beck, Mikak is recorded
with her husband Pualo and his family as the inhabitants of a sod house
on Khernertok, a small island in the Nain archipelago, approximately 30
km northeast of Nain. This site was first located by J. Garth Taylor
during his survey from Nain to Okak in the 1960s. The Inuit toponym
"Khernertok" appears associated with the colour black, and this may
explain its subsequent English name, Black Island (Wheeler 1953). There
are only two sod dwellings (HeCi-15) on the island (see Figure 1).
During the summer of 2010, I visited Khernertok to conduct a test excavation and determine house configurations. Test excavations and details
from Taylor's 1966 report indicate that House 1 appears to be more
modern in construction. Though both dwellings are mentioned in the
1776 census, it appears that House 1 was occupied much longer and
underwent great structural changes. The two dwellings may have been
joined at one point during their occupation, and following House 2's
abandonment the occupants of House 1 might have borrowed structural
materials in the reconstruction (Fay 2011; Taylor 1966). Based on the

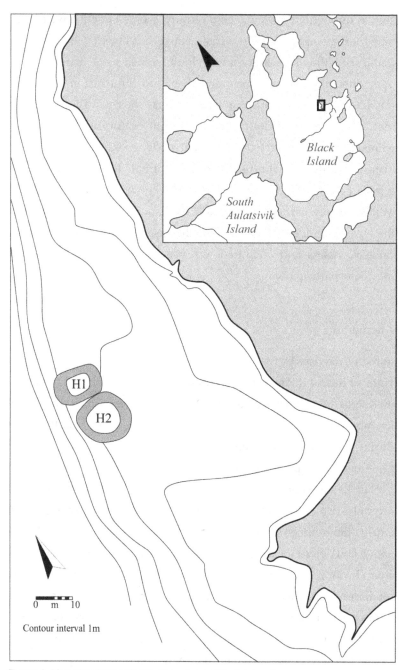

Figure 1. Map showing HeCi-15, Khernertok (Black Island).

layout of the dwelling and the eighteenth-century artifacts unearthed in 2010, House 2 became the focus for my 2011 excavations.

When looking at the artifacts recovered from House 2 during the 2010 and 2011 seasons we see an assemblage representing occupants who wholly embraced European trade objects. Preliminary counts put pipe fragments as the largest artifact category, followed by glass beads, iron nails, ceramic sherds, and glass fragments. Soapstone fragments, which include part of a lamp and a pot fragment with charred fat, are under-represented, as are worked whalebone artifacts (see Table 1). Further analysis will provide a clearer picture of the artifact assemblage and distribution within the house, but these preliminary numbers say a lot, especially when compared to other eighteenth-century Inuit dwellings in the Nain area.

Table 1. House 2, Khernertok (Black Island).

Artifact Category	Number
Pipe fragments	312 (minimum pipe count = 74)
Glass beads	194
Iron nails	185
Ceramic sherds	137 (minimum vessel count = 38)
Glass fragments	128
Soapstone fragments	8
Worked whalebone	65

Comparative Sites

Thus far only two eighteenth-century Inuit sod houses have been fully excavated in the Nain area, House 2 from Khernertok and House 2 from Oakes Bay 1, on nearby Dog Island. Other eighteenth-century sites within the Nain area have been tested, especially the house middens (garbage dumps), but in terms of full household excavations we have limited comparative data to draw upon. That being said, the data collected support tentative comparisons to Khernertok, as midden deposits often depict a fair representation of the household. Two sites within the Nain area that I have identified as useful comparisons are Oakes Bay 1 and Koliktalik 6.

The Oakes Bay 1 site (HeCg-08) consists of six dwellings, three of which are large communal houses, that records indicate were abandoned in 1771–1772, the year the Moravians established a mission in Nain (Woollett 2010). Research at this site is ongoing, but a preliminary look at the assemblages from the tested dwellings (Houses 1, 3, and 4) and the completely excavated dwelling (House 2) reflect a much different lifestyle than that of Khernertok. Soapstone and whalebone artifacts far outnumber other artifact categories, and iron and copper represent the bulk of the European materials (Swinarton personal communication 2012; see Table 2). Although the site was abandoned just as the Moravians arrived in Nain, we know that the long-distance trade network was in full force and that the Inuit in this area (and further north) had access to a diverse range of European materials. Unlike Khernertok, it appears that the Inuit at Oakes Bay had little interest in dealing with Europeans or acquiring trade goods. Indeed, one wonders if this explains their decision to abandon their settlement at the time the Moravians were settling in the area.

Table 2. House 2, Oakes Bay 1 (Dog Island).

Artifact Category	Number
Pipe fragments	0
Glass beads	0
Iron nails	140
Ceramic sherds	6
Glass fragments	3 (all bottle)
Soapstone fragments	55
Worked whalebone	47

Table 3. Ikkeghasarsuk Settlement, Koliktalik Island.

Artifact Category	Number
Pipe fragments	33
Glass beads	12
Iron nails	285
Ceramic sherds	25 (minimum vessel count = 5)
Glass fragments	29
Soapstone fragments	21
Worked whalebone	83

The Ikkeghasarsuk settlement on Koliktalik Island (Koliktalik 6, HdCg-23) was occupied during the same winters as Khernertok (1776–1777 and 1778–1779) and also consists of two sod dwellings. Unfortunately, neither of the dwellings was completely excavated, but the middens from both houses were excavated as was an interior house trench. Though this site was only partially excavated, the data from Koliktalik can still be used to make inferences about what the dwellings might have contained. European-made items are numerous, with a variety of ceramic sherds, pipe fragments, glass beads, window and bottle glass sherds, and iron nails. Worked bone artifacts are also fairly abundant, as are soapstone pot/lamp fragments (see Table 3). This assemblage more closely reflects that of Khernertok, with a fairly large and diverse range of European-made materials and items, yet it still contains significant amounts of traditional Inuit items. The ceramic assemblage consists of a variety of refined stonewares and earthenwares, and a Normandy stoneware jug, representing a minimum vessel count of five; this small number of vessels might explain the increased use of soapstone at this site.

In contrast, Khernertok has a minimum vessel count of 38, which ranges widely from the ubiquitous eighteenth-century creamware to fine Chinese export porcelain. The bead assemblage is also more extensive than at Koliktalik, with a wider range of sizes and colours. If sheer numbers alone do not set Khernertok apart, then surely the diversity and perhaps even the quality of items do. Although based on a small sample, the data from the Nain area currently suggest that Khernertok had better access to and perhaps first choice in European trade goods. The quality and quantity of trade goods at Khernertok further suggest that they might be the prized items that Mikak acquired. As exciting as this suggestion is, more comparative data is needed to strengthen this potential conclusion.

Inuit Entrepreneurs

The documentary and archaeological evidence suggests that both Inuit men and women participated in the burgeoning trade network in some capacity, and that certain individuals possessed entrepreneurial skills that set them apart and created a hierarchy within Inuit society. An uncritical examination of the documentary records and bias within our own interpretations have led to the construction of the Inuit "big man" trader as a key component of the coastal trade network. This assumption does a disservice to the many women who may have played an active role in the trade economy as well. The term "Inuit entrepreneurs" is suggested here, to reflect more accurately the individuals who participated in this trade economy and to remove any gender bias from our understanding of the coastal trade network. It also removes the tendency to place males and females in binary opposition and instead considers their complementary economic roles in Inuit society.

The archaeological record exhibits some interesting patterns, but more research needs to be conducted on eighteenth-century sites in the Nain area and along the coast of Labrador in general. Without access to comparative data it is hard to definitively state whether the quantity and quality of trade goods at the Khernertok site relate to Mikak's presence, but it is an interesting hypothesis. What we do know is that Inuit entrepreneurs gained access to higher-quality materials and were able to increase their status and prestige by doing so. We need to incorporate more data from the entire Labrador coast to further our understanding of the coastal trade network and the families that participated in it.

References Cited

Bodenhorn, Barbara
> 1990 "I'm Not the Great Hunter, My Wife Is": Inupiat and Anthropological Models of Gender. *Études/Inuit/Studies* 14(1–2):55–74.

Cabak, Melanie
> 1991 Inuit Women as Catalysts of Change: An Archaeological Study of 19th Century Northern Labrador. Unpublished Master's thesis, Department of Anthropology, University of South Carolina, Columbia.

Curtis, Roger

1774 Particulars of the Country of Labradore, Extracted from the Papers of the Lieutenant Roger Curtis, of His Majesty's Sloop the Otter, with a Plane-Chart of the Coast. *Philosophical Transactions of the Royal Society* 64:372–388.

Delle, James A.

2000 Gender, Power and Space: Negotiating Social Relations under Slavery on Coffee Plantations in Jamaica, 1790–1834. In *Lines That Divide: Archaeologies of Race, Class and Gender,* edited by James Delle, Stephen Mrozowski, and Robert Paynter, pp. 168–204. University of Tennessee Press, Knoxville.

Fay, Amelia

2011 Excavations on Black Island, Labrador. *Provincial Archaeology Office 2010 Archaeology Review* 9:34–36.

Frink, L.

2007 Storage and Status in Precolonial and Colonial Coastal Western Alaska. *Current Anthropology* 48(3):349–374.

2009 The Social Role of Technology in Coastal Alaska. *International Journal of Historical Archaeology* 13:282–302.

Hiller, James

1971 Early Patrons of the Labrador Eskimos: The Moravian Mission in Labrador, 1764–1805. In *Patrons and Brokers in the East Arctic,* Newfoundland Social and Economic Papers No. 2, edited by R. Paine, pp. 74–97. ISER Books, St. John's.

Hood, Bryan C.

2008 *Towards an Archaeology of the Nain Region, Labrador.* Contributions to Circumpolar Anthropology #7, edited by W. Fitzhugh, Arctic Studies Centre, Smithsonian, Washington, D.C.

Jarvenpa, Robert, and Hetty Jo Brumback

2006 Revisiting the Sexual Division of Labor: Thoughts on Ethnoarchaeology and Gender. *Archaeological Papers of the American Anthropological Association* 16:97–107.

Kaplan, Susan

1980 Neo-Eskimo Occupations of the Northern Labrador Coast. *Arctic* 33(3): 646–666.

1985 European Goods and Socio-Economic Change in Early Labrador Inuit Society. In *Cultures in Contact: The European Impact on Native Cultural Institutions in Eastern North America, A.D. 1000–1800,* edited by W. Fitzhugh, pp. 45–69. Smithsonian Institution Press, Washington, D.C.

Kleivan, Helge

1966 *The Eskimos of Northeast Labrador: A History of Eskimo–White Relations 1771–1955.* Norsk Polarinstitutt Skrifter No. 139. Norsk Polarinstitutt, Oslo.

Kohlmeister, Benjamin, and George Kmoch

1814 *Journal of a Voyage from Okak on the Coast of Labrador to Ungava Bay, Westward to Cape Chudleigh.* W. M. McDowall, London.

LeMoine, Genevieve

2003 Woman of the House: Gender, Architecture and Ideology in Dorset Prehistory. *Arctic Anthropology* 40(1):121–138.

NunatuKavut Community Council

2010 Unveiling NunatuKavut. Document in Pursuit of Reclaiming a Homeland. Describing the Lands and People of South/Central Labrador. Document on file with the NunatuKavut Community Council, Goose Bay, Labrador.

Richling, Barnett

1993 Labrador's "Communal House Phase" Reconsidered. *Arctic Anthropology* 30(1):67–78.

Rollmann, Hans

2011 "So fond of the pleasure to shoot": The Sale of Firearms to Inuit on Labrador's North Coast in the Late Eighteenth Century. *Newfoundland and Labrador Studies* 26(1):6–24.

Stern, Pamela R.

2010 *Daily Life of the Inuit.* Greenwood Press, Westport, Connecticut.

Stopp, Marianne

2008 *The New Labrador Papers of Captain George Cartwright,* introduced and edited by Marianne Stopp. McGill-Queen's University Press, Montreal and Kingston.

2009 Eighteenth Century Labrador Inuit in England. *Arctic* 62(1):45–64.

Taylor, J. Garth

1966 Field Notes: Site Survey in the Nain–Okak Area, Northern Labrador. Report on Activities Carried Out during the Summer of 1966, Submitted to the National Museum of Canada. Manuscript on file at the Canadian Museum of Civilization, Ottawa.

1969 William Turner's Journeys to the Caribou Country with the Labrador Eskimos in 1780. *Ethnohistory* 16(2):141–164.

1974 *Labrador Eskimo Settlements of the Early Contact Period.* National Museum of Man, Publications in Ethnology No. 9. National Museums of Canada, Ottawa.

1983 The Two Worlds of Mikak, Part I. *The Beaver* 31(3):4–13.

1984 The Two Worlds of Mikak, Part II. *The Beaver* 31(4):18–25.

2000 Tuglavina. *Dictionary of Canadian Biography Online,* Vol. IV, *1771–1800.* University of Toronto Press, Toronto. Electronic document, http://www.biographi.ca/en/bio/tuglavina_4E.html, accessed September 10, 2013.

Turner, Lucien M.

1979 [1894] *Indians and Eskimos in the Quebec–Labrador Peninsula* [originally entitled Ethnology of the Ungava District, Hudson Bay Territory]. Coméditex, Quebec.

Wheeler, E. P.

1953 *List of Labrador Inuit Place Names.* Bulletin No. 131. National Museum of Canada, Ottawa.

Woollett, James

2010 Oakes Bay 1: A Preliminary Reconstruction of a Labrador Inuit Seal Hunting Economy in the Context of Climate Change. *Geografisk Tidsskrift–Danish Journal of Geography* 110(2):245–259.

CHAPTER 5

The Many Habitations of Pierre Constantin: The French Presence in Southern Labrador in the Early Eighteenth Century

Amanda Crompton

The eighteenth century was a time of great change in southern Labrador. Inuit, Innu, French, and Basque peoples came together in an increasingly dense set of connections along the Strait of Belle Isle during the early part of the century. Innu and Inuit lived in southern Labrador year-round, and French and Basque seasonal cod fishermen visited the coast every summer. French permanent settlement expanded along the south coast of Labrador beginning in the very early eighteenth century. This chapter explores how, where, when, and why this development occurred, and focuses on the French colonization of Labrador through the experiences of one landowner, Pierre Constantin. In so doing, the wide-ranging and varied nature of the French presence in Labrador will be illustrated, as will the extent of the expanding and increasingly complex relationships between the Inuit and the French. Ultimately, these relationships would contribute to the elaboration of new, hybrid cultural identities in southern Labrador in the centuries that followed.

Background

The Inuit moved southward into Labrador in the sixteenth century, and archaeological evidence accumulated in recent years suggests that the southern Labrador Inuit presence was sustained, widespread, and enduring. The Inuit migration to the south was at least in part a deliberate move to access European materials, which they found in abundance on seasonally abandoned whaling and fishing sites, left behind by French fishermen and Basque whalers (Martijn 1980b; Rankin et al. 2012; Stopp 2002). A detailed understanding of how the French organized themselves in Labrador—where they chose to live, at what times of the year, how they conceived of and organized their landscapes—provides a more complete understanding of the colonial period and the nature of Inuit–French relationships.

This topic has not gone unexplored. Research that specifically focuses on the French in Labrador can be found in the work of Langlois (2000), Morandière (1962), Niellon (1995), and Trudel (1978, 1980). Focused studies of individuals involved in the colonization of French Labrador have also been completed, including those by Pritchard (1974), Robitaille (1955), and Roy (1928). Some archaeological survey and excavation of French sites dating to the French colonial period in Labrador has also been completed. Niellon (2010), Fitzhugh et al. (2011), and others (as summarized in Dubreuil 2007) have worked at sites along Quebec's Lower North Shore. Tuck (1987, 1988, 1989, 1990) conducted exploratory excavations at a French site in Red Bay, thought to be the location of one of Constantin's habitations. Hull and Mercer (2006) have also conducted brief survey work at a suspected French site in West St. Modeste.

However, much remains to be learned about the French in Labrador. The French documentary record has been mined for data on the Inuit presence in southern Labrador, particularly by Clermont (1980), Dorais (1980), Mailhot et al. (1980), Martijn (1980a, 1980b), Stopp (2002), and Trudel (1978, 1980). Since the publication of the special edition of *Études/Inuit/Studies* in 1980, much progress has been made to better understand the timing, nature, and extent of the Inuit presence in southern Labrador, helped in large part by the researchers of the SSHRC-CURA funded project "Understanding the Past to Build the Future." Archaeological investigations, conducted by Rankin (2010; chapter 2) and her students (e.g., Rankin et al. 2012; Kelvin and Rankin, chapter 6; Murphy and Rankin, chapter 3), as well as by Stopp (2002, 2012, 2013), have added a great deal of data to the Inuit story in southern Labrador. At the time of writing, it is fair to say that the French presence in this same region is not nearly as well understood as the Inuit presence.

Achieving a better balance in our knowledge of both the French and the Inuit presence is important. French, Basques, and Inuit had been in contact since the sixteenth century, and their interactions had intensified dramatically by the eighteenth century (Brière 1990:34; Stopp 2002:80; Trudel 1980; Turgeon 1998:537). Though the shifting affairs of European political conflicts resulted in the general ouster of the French from the Labrador coast in 1763, some French presence continued in the region (Whiteley 1969, 1976). After the fall of the French regime, the British were keen to encourage continued trading relationships with the Inuit, albeit with the use of different approaches than the French (Rollmann 2011). Ultimately, sustained relations between Inuit and Europeans in southern Labrador would give rise to *métissage* (or cultural hybridity) between the two, and eventually result in the ethnogenesis of the Labrador Métis (Kennedy 1995:86–88, 1997).

Investigating encounters, contact, and exchange are important parts of understanding the overall process of *métissage*. The intercultural dialogues and accumulated practices that developed between the French and the Inuit—whether these were elaborated in peace, violence, or relative indifference—are all critical elements of *métissage* (e.g., Moussette 2003, Zemon Davis 2001). Others have noted that such cultural practices develop over the long term, and indeed, "histories of interaction are a continuum of contexts and recursive social processes" (Ferris 2009:27). Thus, the early eighteenth-century interactions between French and Inuit constitute one part of a larger process of *métissage*, which would be elaborated in the later eighteenth and nineteenth centuries with the formation of a distinct hybrid cultural identity.

As such, the documentary record for eighteenth-century Labrador certainly deserves to be revisited. Fortunately, this is becoming increasingly easy, as both Library and Archives Canada and the Archives nationales du Québec are making more of their records available on the Internet. This is necessarily an initial study. It is based only on those French records that are Internet-accessible or have been made available as printed primary sources (see Notes, below). This chapter takes a decidedly narrative turn, and focuses on the Labrador experiences of one *canadien* landholder in the early to mid-eighteenth century: Pierre Constantin.

Taking a narrative, biographical focus emphasizes the dynamic and heterogeneous colonial experience in Labrador. Most French colonies shared some very broad characteristics, but French North America was not a uniformly administered political entity, and colonial institutions were transferred unevenly to colonial settlements (Greer 1997:3, 2010:701; Johnston 2001:xix–xx, 303; Marzagalli 1999:71). The diverse settlements and outposts in New France were thus an "unsorted collection of peoples and possibilities and they received 'assembled bits of attention' from the state" (Banks 2002:7). Indeed, French colonial efforts can best be regarded as fundamentally experimental entities (Dawdy 2008:18). Each colony or settlement was a unique product: a result of different agendas of the colonists, different geographical constraints or opportunities, and different historical contingencies. Furthermore, there was not a single European experience in Labrador, for the histories of individual colonists are complex and situationally variable. By restricting this discussion to the experiences of one Labrador landholder, we can observe the process by which Constantin and his employees learned to live in Labrador and construct their settlements there, and begin to understand the variation in their experiences.

The French documentary record for Labrador imposes its own set of limitations. While Brière (1990) and Turgeon (1997, 1998) have demonstrated that French notarial records contain much detail about the port of origin of transient French fishing ships, and sometimes their destination, the experiences those fishermen had during their time in Labrador are not known in nearly as much detail. Administrative documents and correspondence written by the French in Labrador largely focus on the affairs of permanent colonists rather than the seasonal fishermen. This bias, in which documentary records emphasize the activities of resident Europeans at the expense of others (in this case, both Aboriginal residents and transient French fishermen), is a commonly noted problem (e.g., Ferris 2009:13). Furthermore, the documentary record relating to colonization in Labrador is internally uneven. In the case of Pierre Constantin, the majority of the records take the form of administrative reports or documents relating to his legal disputes with rival landowners or with business partners. This renders the documents a thoroughly detailed record of certain issues, such as land tenure, or contractual obligations, but frustratingly silent on many other non-legal or non-administrative issues.

The French in Labrador

Outside of the brief but storied visits by early explorers like Jacques Cartier, the European presence in Labrador begins with the arrival of French and Basque seasonal cod fishing and/or whaling crews in the sixteenth century. Though these crews did not overwinter (at least deliberately) in Labrador, their seasonal presence in Labrador grew quickly, and Europeans might be found in the same harbours repeatedly. Specific harbours quickly became preferred for both their access to good cod stocks and good anchorages with drying grounds (Brière 1990:31–32; Pope 2009). Though not part of a process of directed colonialism per se, these transient fishermen "allowed the French to 'occupy' the coasts of north-eastern North America, to symbolically consume this space and progressively construct a colonial territory" (Turgeon 2009:34). In the course of fishing and whaling, the French and Basques in Labrador harbours began encountering Inuit in increasingly greater numbers, in both friendly and violent encounters (Barkham 1980; Martijn 1980b). Through this contact, Inuit obtained European materials, especially metals, which are amply documented on Inuit archaeological sites in southern Labrador (e.g., Kaplan and Jordan 1980; Rankin 2010; Rankin et al. 2012; Murphy and Rankin, this volume).

For the French, southern Labrador was a part of the royal *domaine*. This territory could be divided and granted to individuals, based on the recommendations of the colonial government in Quebec (Trudel 1978:486). Some of the early Labrador grants of land were made *en seigneurie*, which superficially resembled the more agrarian-based system of land distribution practised further west, in the St. Lawrence River valley. The Labrador grants given as *seigneuries* were for large tracts of land, were conceded in perpetuity, and required the payment of a token yearly royalty to the Crown (Trudel 1978:486). Here, the similarity with the Laurentian seigneurial system ended, for the grantholders in the royal *domaine* were not expected to engage in agriculture, or establish *censitaires* or tenant farmers (Langlois 2000:31–33; Niellon 1995:155–156). Indeed, the land grants given out in Labrador have been best described by Lavoie (2010:37) as "seigneuries d'exploitation," indicating that they were granted for the purposes of natural resource extraction (particularly sealing, fishing, and furring) and trade with Aboriginal people (Lavoie 2010:63–78). The Labrador grants were not unique developments, but were logical extensions of seigneurial grants focused on extractive industries (particularly fishing) established elsewhere in New France (e.g., Francoeur 2008; Landry 2012–2013; Lavoie 2010; Mimeault 1984; Nadon 2004).

Grants *en seigneurie* were not the typical form of French Labrador land tenure. Rather, most land grants, and all of those issued after 1713, were given as concessions rather than *seigneuries*. These were granted for a limited time, typically 10 to 20 years. Most of the later concessions were also smaller in size than the earlier concessions and generally spanned four or five *lieues* (French leagues) of ocean frontage (one French *lieue* equals one league, or about 5 km). Typically, the grantholders had an exclusive right to the seal fishery in their concessions, as well as rights over hunting and trade with Aboriginal people (Lavoie 2010:73–78). Grantholders could also pursue the cod fishery in their concession, but could not deny seasonal fishermen access to beaches not in use (Trudel 1978:486–489). For the sake of simplicity, the term "concession" is used here to refer to both types of land grants, as concessions were by far the most common form.

Most concessionaires were particularly interested in the profitable seal fishery, and their concessions along the Strait of Belle Isle were particularly well suited to take advantage of the spring and fall harp seal migrations in this area. Seal oil was highly desirable, and the pelts were sold to tanners. The French caught harp seals by stretching nets across narrow stretches of water between the mainland and nearshore islands (Belvin 2006). These locations were highly prized and their ownership often caused disputes (Langlois 2000:76–78; Trudel 1978:486–487).

The preparation for the seal fishery, along with other economic activities that occupied the concessionaires and their crews, meant that concessions were generally occupied year-round (Trudel 1980:137). Some concessionaires may have occupied their posts for the year, but many were only seasonally resident, leaving their posts under the management of post-masters. This occupation may not have required full crews all year, and typically overwintering crews were smaller than summertime crews. Crews were hired by contract and received a share of the post's product as compensation. Concessionaires, post-masters, and crews were generally from Quebec, though sometimes, Aboriginal individuals were employed as well (Trudel 1978:486–489). The infrastructure required for these establishments was considerable, and was tailored to render seal fat, assemble barrels, store gear, and house the post-master and his crew (Niellon 2010:13–16).

Pierre Constantin: A History

Much of Constantin's family life can be reconstructed using the Programme de recherche en démographie historique (hereafter, PRDH) genealogical database. The PRDH provided the birth, marriage, and death details discussed in this section, unless otherwise noted. Pierre Constantin (sometimes known as Pierre Constantin Levallée) was born on April 21, 1666, in the parish of Sillery, New France, to Guillaume Constantin and Jeanne Masse. As a child, he is recorded as living in Ste. Foy in several *recensements*. In 1691, at the age of 25, Constantin was engaged by the Sieur de la Tourette for a voyage to the *pays d'en haut*, and indeed Constantin is described shortly after his marriage in 1696 as a *voyageur* (Niellon 1995:32; Pritchard 1974). In 1696, at the age of 28, he married Marie Marguerite Suzanne Guyon Durouvray (who was 18 years old), in the parish of St. Augustin, in the *seigneurie* of Maure, New France.

Constantin's marriage brought him into a family of well-known traders (Roy 1928:257). In the years immediately following his marriage, Constantin became involved with individuals who had an interest in Labrador ventures. In April of 1700, he was employed by Augustin Le Gardeur de Courtemanche to explore southern Labrador (Niellon 1995:32). Constantin had returned to St. Augustin by September, where he was present at the baptism of his third child. Interestingly, a witness at this baptism was one Martel, described as a *marchand* and *bourgeois*. This is almost certainly Raymond Martel, a notable Quebec merchant who was a close business associate of Augustin Le Gardeur de Courtemanche (Bryden 1969). Constantin continued his association with both men; beginning in 1701 he was engaged several years to seasonally explore Labrador on behalf of Courtemanche, to trade with Aboriginal people, and to help with the establishment of Courtemanche's settlements (initially located at Rivière St. Paul, and shortly thereafter moved to Baie Phélypeaux) (Niellon 1995; Robitaille 1955). These early years allowed Constantin to become acquainted with this territory and the Aboriginal people who lived there.

Though Constantin was consistently involved in Labrador ventures after 1700, he did not apparently move his family to Labrador, nor did he become a more or less permanent resident of the region. Over a 30-year period, his wife gave birth to 16 children in St. Augustin, six of whom died as children. Almost all his children were born with reasonably regular birth spacing, between one and three years, suggesting Constantin was regularly present in the family home. Constantin was an active landowner in St. Augustin, and continued to buy and sell property there throughout his adult life (e.g., Pierre Constantin au Robert Fouché, contrat de vente, 8 November 1710, Cote E1,S4,SS1,D237,P5, Archives nationales du Québec [ANQ]). He was frequently present at birth, marriage, and death events for associates and family in Quebec, and his general correspondence indicates that he probably only spent summers in Labrador. He became an officer in the Quebec militia, and by the last years of his life was described as a *commandant de milice* in the *seigneurie* of Desmaures. He still retained an active interest in his Labrador concession as late as 1748 (Niellon 1995:162). He was buried in St. Augustin on April 21, 1751, approximately a year and a half after the death of his wife.

Constantin in Newfoundland

Constantin's first involvement as a concessionaire in his own right stems from this association with Courtemanche and Martel. In 1702, the baptism of Constantin's son Joseph was witnessed by Courtemanche and also by one "Hazur," described as a *marchand* and *bourgeois* (PRDH). This is almost certainly François Hazeur, an important seigneur, merchant, and government official in Quebec (Zoltvany 1969). In 1705, Hazeur was granted a large concession *en seigneurie*, centred around Port au Choix on the island of Newfoundland, which extended 20 leagues along the shore, and 10 leagues inland (Martijn 2009:71). Though Hazeur was the initial concessionaire, he had applied for it at Constantin's urging (undoubtedly relying on Constantin's knowledge of the Strait of Belle Isle region). By 1708, Constantin had been made a formal joint partner in the concession (Martijn and Dorais 2001:321–322).

In early 1708, the partners agreed by contract that Constantin would travel to the Port au Choix concession (referred to in later documents as the Saint Marie à la Point aux Ancres concession). Once arrived, he was responsible for surveying the limits of their concession and assessing the work completed by the four *engagés* who had overwintered there (Roy 1928:258–259). Their main economic pursuits had been the seal fishery and the salmon fishery, though Constantin was also charged with determining where the best cod-fishing locations were. His final task for the season was to determine the best place for a new establishment. Clearly, as Hazeur had overwintering *engagés* from the previous season, some structures must have been erected for shelter. However, Constantin was resolved to find a new location for an establishment, using his best judgement following his survey, though the partners had provisionally suggested Ferolle as a suitable location (Roy 1928:259–260). These plans were thrown into disarray when Hazeur died a month after this document was signed. The concession was in Hazeur's name, but by arrangement with his heirs and creditors, Constantin was appointed as the concession's sole proprietor in 1709. The price of 100 *livres* bought Constantin the small house that had been constructed on the concession, as well as the supplies and gear left there (Niellon 1995:158; Roy 1928:261).

The documentary record is largely silent about Constantin's progress at Port au Choix, though we might safely assume he encountered Aboriginal people. The original land grant issued to Hazeur in 1705 defined the limits of the concession using Innu toponyms, which may well have been obtained from Innu informants by Pierre Constantin in his previous travels around the Strait of Belle Isle region. Furthermore, Inuit ventured across the Strait of Belle Isle regularly (Martijn and Dorais 2001:321–322, Martijn 2009:67). Conflict between Inuit and French frequently occurred in this area. For example, a letter of 1713 refers to three Basque fishing ships leaving Port au Choix due to conflict with the Inuit (Lettre de Courtemanche, 4 October 1713, Col.C^{11}A, Vol. 123, f. 90, Archives nationales d'outre-mer [ANOM], Aix-en-Provence, France). Other early eighteenth-century letters record several episodes in which Inuit attacked (or at least threatened to attack) fishing crews based at Port au Choix (Martijn 2009:78–79).

Constantin's Newfoundland concession was affected by the 1713 Treaty of Utrecht. Under the terms of the treaty, Newfoundland was ceded to the British. The French were to abandon their permanent settlements on the island, and were only allowed to catch and dry cod in the summer season on the geographically restricted French Shore, which stretched from Point Riche to Cape Bonavista (Hiller 1991:31). Constantin lost the right to use his Port au Choix concession. In 1714, he applied for a passport to journey from Quebec to Port au Choix, to retrieve his brothers-in-law who resided there, and to begin anew in Labrador (Passeport accordé par Vaudreuil à Constantin, 9 March 1714, ANOM, $C^{11}A$, v.109, f. 137).

However, the Treaty of Utrecht did not bring an end to French concessions in Newfoundland. In a region that was remote from centres of authority, individual adherence to the terms of the treaty was apparently far from rigorous. In 1732, Constantin had a document notarized in Quebec, by which he rented his concessions in Labrador *and* in Newfoundland to three men, one of whom was his son-in-law (Bail par Pierre Constantin à F. Trefflé, P. Trefflé et P. Hamel, 4 November 1732, ANOM, $C^{11}A$, v.109, f. 241). Confirmation of Constantin's continued presence in Newfoundland for the period between 1714 and 1732 is lacking, though the aforementioned documentation suggests his continued involvement in the area.

Whatever Constantin's presence was, by 1736 it was the subject of competing claims by Joliet Mingan and Antoine Marsal. Permission was granted to Marsal to have the exclusive right of the seal fishery in this area for a period of nine years (Permission à Marsal, 15 December 1736, Col. E, v.303, f.8; Ordonnance de Hocquart, 26 February 1738, ANQ, E1,S1,P2985, f. 56–57). This was a carefully prepared document, which spoke of granting permission only to use the land, rather than granting title to it. The Treaty of Utrecht should have rendered this situation impossible; however, the continued French presence there is testimony to the ability of French concessionaires to creatively subvert the dictates of international treaties, at least in the earlier part of the eighteenth century.

Constantin in Southern Labrador

After the apparent loss of Port au Choix, Constantin was granted another concession in southern Labrador in 1713. The initial grant was a very large concession, measuring 30 *lieux* of coastline frontage and 10 *lieux* inland, and was granted for a period of 10 years (Niellon 1995:159). The exact location of the bounds of the concession was not clearly established; he was instructed to settle at least 20 leagues from Courtemanche, "beyond Bellisle." As was typical, Constantin was granted the right to exclusively hunt, fish, and trade within the boundaries of his concession, and to keep the shore free for all cod fishermen, with the exception of that shoreline he required for his own fishery (Concession à Pierre Constantin, 18 May 1713, ANOM, C¹¹A, v.109, f. 137–137v). Three years later, in 1716, the Governor and Intendant of New France decreased the size of this concession, to measure four leagues inland and four leagues along the coast (including adjacent islands and islets), centred on the spot "presently called the habitation of Sieur Constantin, situated northeast of the Riviere des Francois." This concession was granted to him for his lifetime, and once again Constantin had the exclusive right to trade with Aboriginal people, hunt, seal, and fish cod concurrently with the seasonal fishermen (Brevet du concession pour Constantin, 31 May 1716, ANOM, C¹¹A, v.109, f.313, v.314; Délibération du Conseil de Marine, 31 March 1716, ANOM, C¹¹A, v.123, f. 167–168v).

In the early years especially, Constantin ranged around the landscape, much in the same way he had at Port au Choix. Constantin's locations can be tracked, not only by statements in letters he wrote, but in the statements and testimony of others as well. In 1714, Constantin engaged four men to journey to his post at Red Bay, which consisted of a small *cabanne* made of wood that had been built in the summer by his crews fishing for cod. The crew moved south to the Rivière des François (Pinware River), where they built another *cabanne* for overwintering (Procès-verbal des déclarations des quatre témoins, 7 December 1734, ANOM, C¹¹A, v.109, f. 152v; Placet au ministre par Constantin, [1736],

ANOM, C[11]A,v.109, f. 131v). In 1715, Courtemanche accused Constantin of having made a post somewhere above Forteau, and addresses the letter to Constantin at the Rivière des Francois (Lettre de Courtemanche à Constantin, 22 July 1715, ANOM, C[11]A, v.109, f. 239–240). Courtemanche and Constantin had fallen out in the previous years; Courtemanche now saw his former employee as a rival, and began to agitate unsuccessfully for his removal from the Labrador coast (Niellon 1995).

Other testimony further corroborates Constantin's location in the early years of his concession. In 1716–1717, Constantin was said to have fished at both Red Bay and Petit St. Modet and to have small residences in both harbours. He also, reportedly, had other *cabannes* built at L'Anse au Loup and Forteau. This information is drawn from witness testimony recorded in a 1730s dispute over the boundaries of Constantin's concession, so we must treat these data cautiously, for they may be influenced by the passage of time and the predisposition of the witnesses to be for or against Constantin's case (Procès-verbal, 7 December 1734, ANOM, C[11]A, v.109, f. 152–152v; Robitaille 1955). As of 1719, Constantin's Red Bay establishments consisted of a fort "de pieux," plus several buildings, including a shelter for his fishing gear (Procès-verbal, 7 December 1734, ANOM, C[11]A, v.109, f.150v; Niellon 1995:160; Robitaille 1955). Constantin's servants were overwintering in Red Bay during this time as well (Résumé d'une lettre de Brouague, February 1721, ANOM, C11A, v.109, f. 9–13).

Constantin's establishment in Red Bay was attacked by the Inuit during a raid in September 1719. In 1721, Constantin rebuilt his post in Red Bay (Lettre de Brouague à Conseil de Marine, 17 September 1721, ANOM, C[11]A, v.109, f. 102–106). In 1723, he writes of "mon poste a Baye Rouge" where he and his business partners from St. Malo, France, were to work the seal fishery there together (Procès verbal de Constantin contre Pasquier, 28 July 1723, ANOM, C[11]A, v.109, f. 142–143v). In 1723, he is still described as having a post near the Rivière des François, half a *lieue* to the northeast of the river, where he focused on the seal fishery (Déclaration de Porrau et Rasset, ANOM, C[11]A, v.109, f. 135). In 1729, Constantin requested an extension of his concession by one *lieue* to the west-southwest; he argued that this space has a good elevated location on which a fort could be built to prevent the incursion of the Inuit (Placet de Constantin à Maurepas, 1729, ANOM, C11A, v.51, f. 33). His request was apparently refused the following year (Conseil de la Marine à Beauharnois et Hocquart, 21 March 1730, ANOM, Col. B, v.54, f. 393).

However, this requested extension would have encompassed an elevated hillside in present-day West St. Modeste, in which a site locally known as Constantin's Fort is located. It is certainly possible that Constantin constructed a fort here, even without official permission to do so, and testing of the site by Newfoundland and Labrador's Provincial Archaeology Office uncovered artifacts consistent with an eighteenth-century French occupation (Hull and Mercer 2006). In 1733, after Constantin had leased his concession to his son-in-law and two other associates for seven years (though he seemed to continue to take an active role in its affairs), overwintering employees built two new cabins at the Rivière des François (Procès-verbal, 7 December 1734, ANOM, C¹¹A, v.109, f. 150v). This is also borne out by a map, drawn about 1735, on which Constantin's post is shown above the Rivière des François (Plan de la concession de Constantin dressée par Pellegrin, [1735], ANOM, C¹¹A, v.109, f. 139).

These data also indicate that Constantin experienced some friction with other concessionaires. His presence on the coast of southern Labrador certainly appears to have alienated his former employer, Courtemanche. By 1714, Courtemanche had been appointed as the commandant of the coast of Labrador, with the power to settle disputes in the region, particularly regarding the fisheries (Corley 1969). Interestingly, Constantin never availed himself of the commandant's authority in settling disputes, not even when François Martel de Brouague was appointed as commandant following Courtemanche's death. Rather, when Constantin had to resolve a dispute with a transient merchant from France, he approached the fishing admiral in Forteau. Though the admiral replied that he had no authority to dispense justice in the matter, Constantin registered his complaint with the admiral, and then later registered the complaint with a notary in Quebec (Procès-verbal, 28 July

1723, ANOM, C¹¹A, v.109, f. 142–143v; Lettre à Lieutenant-général de l'Amirauté par Constantin, 13 August 1734, ANOM, E, dossier de Sieur Boucault, v.43, f. 7–13). Thus, it seems that the authority of the commandant in Labrador was not one that Constantin preferred to turn to, possibly because he was also a fellow concessionaire who might not be an unbiased arbiter in mediating disputes.

And certainly, such disputes occurred. In the 1730s, Constantin became embroiled in a challenge to his concession launched by Nicolas-Gaspard Boucault and François Foucault, both important bureaucrats in the colonial government at Quebec. The details of the case are complex and have been well documented elsewhere by Robitaille (1955) and Pritchard (1974). Boucault and Foucault established a seal-fishing concession at Grand St. Modet and attempted to argue through legal challenges that this land did not fall within the boundaries of Constantin's original concession. The two men seized on a sentence from the original land concession, which said that Constantin's concession was centred on the place commonly known as the *habitation de Constantin* and extended two *lieux* above and two *lieux* below this point. Boucault and Foucault argued that Constantin's sole *habitation* was located at Red Bay, not the Rivière des François; as a result, their occupation of Grand St. Modet was perfectly appropriate, as it fell outside the boundaries of the Constantin concession. Initially, the Governor and Intendant of New France supported Boucault and Foucault, but Constantin's appeal to higher colonial authorities in France eventually upheld his original concession and Boucault and Foucault were denied. As Pritchard (1974) notes, "the significance of the outcome is that it favoured a small entrepreneur of peasant background against two important individuals who were supported by the highest officials in the colony."

Constantin faced other challenges in running his concession. In 1722, he had made an agreement to a partnership with a merchant from St. Malo to jointly exploit the seal fishery at Red Bay. In 1723, the merchant's ship arrived in Red Bay, and the merchant's representative wanted to retract from the partnership. The settlement eventually reached between the two parties is not clear, but this episode demonstrates that Constantin's links were not just with merchants in Quebec, but also extended to merchants in France as well (Procès-verbal, 28 July 1723, ANOM, C^{11}A, v.109, f. 142–143v).

By contrast, the documentary record does not reveal many disputes with the transient cod-fishing ships that populated the beaches of southern Labrador in the summer months. Records indicate that Constantin took care of the seasonal fishermen's *chaloupes*[1] and supplies if the fishing crews chose to leave them behind at his establishments at the end of the season. Courtemanche (and later Brouague), living further south in the Baie de Phelypeaux, made the same arrangements. This was intended to keep their fishing gear safe from Inuit raiders, who would seize unguarded boats and gear (Placet au Vaudreuil par les captains de navires, 22 July 1717, ANOM, C^{11}A, v.109, f. 243; Mémoire de Brouague au Conseil, 1717, ANOM, C^{11}A, v.37, f. 405v). In his relations with seasonal fishermen, Constantin appears to have followed the terms of his concession, which required him to allow the fishermen access to unused beaches. Records document the presence of seasonal cod-fishing crews working out of Red Bay and St. Modet as well (Brouague au Conseil de Marine, 27 August 1720, ANOM, C^{11}A, v.109, f. 75–91; Procès-verbal, 7 December 1734, ANOM, C^{11}A, v.109, f. 150v).

These crews may have been present some years in substantial numbers. In 1718, a survey of the fishing crews in St. Modet recorded five ships, with a total of 273 crew aboard; in 1726, three ships with 170 crew; and in 1729, one ship with 25 crew. Indeed, selected harbours in southern Labrador were busy, populous places in the summer months, and were visited by 1,000–2,000 seasonal fishermen annually (Trudel 1978:Tableau III). The sheer number of French fishermen, compared to the small crews (of a dozen or less) employed by concessionaires, may well mean that Inuit had the opportunity to trade with seasonal fishermen more frequently than with concessionaires. Additionally, with this degree of seasonal visitation of the coast of Labrador, it is not surprising that Inuit intent on raiding harbours frequented by the fishing crews often waited until their boats departed for good at the end of the season.

In his early years, Constantin was said to have received "mille ami-tieés" from the Inuit (Mémoire concernant le Labrador, 1715, ANOM, C¹¹A, v.109, f. 23). However, the relationship between Constantin, his employees, and the Inuit deteriorated from wary to violent. In 1719, Constantin returned to Quebec, leaving four men to overwinter. Two were his brothers-in-law (Lettre de Pierre Constantin, 18 October 1722, ANOM, C¹¹A, v.122, f. 145). In September of that same year, a group of Inuit raided Constantin's Red Bay post, as described in a letter written by François Martel de Brouague, the commandant for the Labrador coast (Lettre de Brouague au Conseil de Marine, 27 August 1720, ANOM, C¹¹A, v.109, f. 75–91). During the month of September, the Inuit had frequently been sighted in and around Red Bay. Over one day and into the night, the Inuit were said to have frequently cried out and shouted, making the overwintering crewmen nervous. On the morning of September 16, a group of Inuit expressed their desire to trade at a point near the water. Three of the crewmen gathered firearms and went to meet the Inuit, leaving the fourth man (whose name we do not know) behind in the dwelling to keep watch. Distracted by their negotiations, the three Frenchmen by the waterfront did not notice four Inuit men hidden in nearby woods. The Inuit emerged from the woods with bows drawn. The man in the dwelling shouted an alarm to his compatriots, who immediately stood up and looked to the water to see what the problem was. While their attention was directed towards the sea, the Inuit exited the woods and cut off the Frenchmen's route of escape. None of the Frenchmen had time to raise their firearms before being shot with multiple arrows. The fourth man, who had been waiting in the house, ran, and later claimed that the Inuit fired arrows after him; with bad luck, he claimed, one of the arrows apparently pierced his bag of gunpowder. Perhaps the surviving man was trying to find a reason to explain why he did not return fire. Whatever the reason, the survivor took to the hills behind the residence and hid (Lettre de Brouague au Conseil de Marine, 27 August 1720, ANOM, C¹¹A, v.109, f. 75–91).

By the evening, the Inuit had set sail in six *chaloupes*, and the surviving man returned to see if anyone remained alive. Two were already dead. The wounded third man had arrows in his head and belly, but was still alive. The surviving man helped the wounded man remove the arrows from the belly. This apparently made the wounds worse (the survivor said that the wounded man's intestines spilled out), and the wounded man died in the survivor's arms. Afterwards, the survivor surveyed the settlement and noted that it had been looted. The Inuit had taken the *chaloupes*, which they set sail in, as well as nets, ropes, and supplies. They also smashed the barrels for holding seal oil (Lettre de Pierre Constantin, 18 October 1722, ANOM, C¹¹A, v.122, f. 144–145).

The surviving crewman made his way to Baie Phelypeaux to seek refuge with the commandant of the Labrador coast. Several days later, some of Brouague's men spotted three Inuit men, two boats, and several dogs in Blanc-Sablon, but the French avoided any contact with them. Brouague sent one man to accompany the survivor back to Red Bay to bury the three dead men. All the harbours they encountered in between (St. Modet, l'Anse au Loup, and Forteau) bore similar signs of Inuit destruction. By September 28, the Inuit had "returned to their country" (Lettre de Brouague au Conseil de Marine, 27 August 1720, ANOM, C¹¹A, v.109, f. 75–91). Given the violent nature of this interaction, it is not surprising that witnesses still recalled the encounter in later years. In 1722, Constantin referred to this as a remarkable betrayal by the Inuit, noting the loss of his employees and relatives and estimating the substantial financial cost of this attack. Many years later, the mariner Jean Durouvray (Constantin's brother-in-law) testified that he would never return to the area because two of his brothers had been killed there during the raid (Procès-verbal, 7 December 1734, ANOM, C¹¹A, v.109, f. 150v).

Conclusion

Constantin's story illustrates French involvement on Newfoundland's Great Northern Peninsula and southern Labrador. Constantin's many habitations demonstrate the ways in which he and his employees chose to occupy new landscapes. During the early years of concession-building, Constantin and his employees ranged about the landscape, building temporary structures intended to last a season or two. This initial process of landscape-learning is an important step in the colonization process (Rockman 2003). These initial efforts were refined and rebuilt, as Constantin and his employees expanded their familiarity with the region. Furthermore, this study shows that French concessionaires might not have one residence in their lands; like Constantin, they might have many *habitations*. Constantin and his men fished in some harbours and prosecuted the seal fishery in others, and they built structures and *cabannes* accordingly. Archaeologists working on French sites in southern Labrador may well discover that these sites are scattered, thinly occupied, and ephemeral, particularly those which date to the earliest years of settlement.

Constantin's experiences in Labrador illustrate the advantages of living at a distance from authority. Constantin potentially occupied, and certainly rented out, lands at Port au Choix that he officially no longer had access to under the terms of the Treaty of Utrecht. He may have similarly taken advantage of lands outside of his Labrador concession, though the evidence is less clear in this case. Indeed, even when a *commandant* was established in Labrador as a means of providing access to the authority of the Crown, Constantin adopted a strategy of avoidance. He preferred to take his legal dealings directly to officials in Quebec in the wintertime, rather than to the *commandant*. Sometimes, the absence of authority in Labrador caused trouble for Constantin. His land concession was written in only general geographical terms. The offices of government in which he defended his concession were far removed from Labrador, meaning that savvy individuals like Boucault and Foucault could make seemingly credible claims about his concession that were difficult to disprove.

Constantin's interactions with the Inuit at Red Bay demonstrate the tenuous nature that French–Inuit interactions could take in the eighteenth century. The violence that occurred in 1719 illustrates several important points. First, Constantin's employees expected to trade with visiting Inuit, and they knew the procedures for doing so. They were, however, wary of the situation, as demonstrated by the fact that they both armed themselves and left a lookout behind. The Inuit with whom the French traded had clearly considered the best way to take control of the settlement, and planned their attack carefully. They used their experience with established trading procedures to draw the Frenchmen to the waterside. By launching a surprise attack, and carefully controlling any possible lines of retreat, the Inuit were able to instantly kill two of the three well-armed Frenchmen and fatally wound the other.

Pierre Constantin's colonial ventures in Newfoundland and Labrador allow us to meaningfully situate the contexts of interaction between French residents, seasonal fishermen, and the Inuit in Labrador. The analysis of the contact between these different peoples requires an equally detailed understanding of both French and Inuit histories in this region. French colonization in Labrador was a risky venture, and Constantin's history demonstrates that to survive successfully in this area, concessionaires needed to be flexible and situationally adaptable. And finally, Constantin's history demonstrates that in southern Labrador, the initial steps in the development of *métissage*—encounter, contact, and exchange—could be unpredictable and volatile, even for experienced and seasoned French crews.

Note

1.   A *chaloupe* (or shallop) is a small undecked rowing boat with a small mast, used in the cod fishery (Balcom 1984).

Notes on Archival Sources

A full list of archival references for the documents cited in the text is given below. This will allow readers to locate the archive that holds the original document and the archives that hold microfilmed copies.

ANOM, Col. B: Original documents at Archives nationales d'outre-mer, Aix-en-Provence, France. Fonds ministériels, premier empire colonial Série B (Correspondance au départ). Internet-accessible images of microfilmed copies were consulted as Series MG1-B at the Library and Archives Canada website.

ANOM, Col. C^{11}A: Original documents at Archives nationales d'outre-mer, Aix-en-Provence, France. Fonds ministériels, premier empire colonial Série C^{11}A (Correspondance à l'arrivée, Canada et colonies du nord de l'Amérique, Canada). Internet-accessible images of microfilmed copies were consulted as Series MG1-C^{11}A at the Library and Archives Canada website.

ANOM, Col. E: Original documents at Archives nationales d'outre-mer, Aix-en-Provence, France. Fonds ministériels, premier empire colonial Série E (Personnel colonial ancien). Internet-accessible images of microfilmed copies were consulted as Series MG1-E at the Library and Archives Canada website.

ANQ, Cote E1, S1: Original documents at Archives nationales du Québec, Quebec. Cote E1 (Fonds Intendants), S1 (Ordonnances). These documents are Internet-accessible via the ANQ.

ANQ, Cote E1,S4,SS1: Original documents at Archives nationales du Québec, Quebec. Cote E1 (Fonds Intendants), Série 4 (Papiers terriers de la Compagnie des Indes occidentales et du Domaine du roi, Sous-série 1 (Cahiers d'intendance). These documents are Internet-accessible via the ANQ.

PRDH: The Programme de recherche en démographie historique, a searchable demographic database maintained by the Université de Montréal. These records are Internet-accessible at http://www.genealogie.umontreal.ca/en/ (accessed 15 September 2013).

References Cited

Balcom, B. A.
> 1984 *The Cod Fishery of Isle Royale, 1713–58*. Studies in Archaeology, Architecture and History. Parks Canada, Ottawa.

Banks, Kenneth
> 2002 *Chasing Empire across the Sea: Communications and the State in the French Atlantic, 1713–1763*. McGill-Queen's University Press, Montreal and Kingston.

Barkham, Selma
> 1980 A Note on the Strait of Belle Isle during the Period of Basque Contact with Indians and Inuit. *Études/Inuit/Studies* 4(1–2):51–58.

Belvin, Cleophas
2006 *The Forgotten Labrador: Kegashka to Blanc-Sablon*. McGill-Queen's University Press, Montreal and Kingston.

Brière, Jean-François
1990 *La pêche française en Amérique du Nord au XVIIIe siècle*. Fides, Saint-Laurent, Quebec.

Bryden, John
1969 Martel, Raymond. In *Dictionary of Canadian Biography*, Vol. 2. University of Toronto/Université Laval, Toronto and Quebec. Electronic document, http://www.biographi.ca/en/bio/martel_raymond_2E.html, accessed June 11, 2013.

Clermont, N.
1980 Les Inuit du Labrador méridional avant Cartwright. *Études/Inuit/Studies* 4(1–2):147–166.

Corley, Nora T.
1969 Le Gardeur de Courtemanche, Augustin. In *Dictionary of Canadian Biography*, Vol. 2. University of Toronto/Université Laval, Toronto and Quebec. Electronic document, http://www.biographi.ca/en/bio/le_gardeur_de_courtemanche_augustin_2E.html, accessed June 11, 2013.

Dawdy, Shannon Lee
2008 *Building the Devil's Empire: French Colonial New Orleans*. University of Chicago Press, Chicago.

Dorais, L.-J.
1980 Les Inuit du Labrador méridional: données linguistiques. *Études/Inuit/Studies* 4(1–2):167–174.

Dubreuil, Steve
2007 Étude sur les sites archéologiques préhistoriques et historiques caractéristiques de la region de la Côte-Nord du Québec. Rapport final remis à la Direction du Patrimoine, Ministère de la Culture et Communications du Québec, Quebec.

Ferris, Neal
2009 *The Archaeology of Native-Lived Colonialism: Challenging History in the Great Lakes*. University of Arizona Press, Tucson.

Fitzhugh, William W., Anja Herzog, Sophia Perdikaris, and Brenna McLeod
2011 Ship to Shore: Inuit, Early Europeans, and Maritime Landscapes in the Northern Gulf of the St. Lawrence. In *The Archaeology of Maritime Landscapes*, edited by B. Ford, pp. 99–128. Springer, New York.

Francoeur, Marie-Claude
2008 Le développement socio-économique des seigneuries gaspesiennes sous le régime français: Un modèle régionale unique. Unpublished Master's thesis, Département d'histoire, Université Laval, Quebec.

Greer, Allan

   1997 *The People of New France*. University of Toronto Press, Toronto.

   2010 National, Transnational, and Hypernational Historiographies: New France Meets Early American History. *Canadian Historical Review* 91(4):695–724.

Hiller, James

   1991 Utrecht Revisited: The Origins of Fishing Rights in Newfoundland Waters. *Newfoundland and Labrador Studies* 7(1):23–39.

Hull, Stephen, and Delphina Mercer

   2006 Provincial Archaeology Office: Miscellaneous Field Trips. In *Provincial Archaeology Office Newsletter Archaeology in Newfoundland and Labrador 2005*, Vol. 4, pp. 61–67. Government of Newfoundland and Labrador, St. John's.

Johnston, A. J. B.

   2001 *Control and Order in French Colonial Louisbourg, 1713–1758*. Michigan State University Press, East Lansing, Michigan.

Kaplan, S. A., and R. H. Jordan

   1980 An Archaeological View of the Inuit/European Contact Period in Central Labrador. *Études/Inuit/Studies* 4(1–2):35–46.

Kennedy, John C.

   1995 *People of the Bays and Headlands: Anthropological History and the Fate of Communities in the Unknown Labrador*. University of Toronto Press, Toronto.

   1997 Labrador Metis Ethnogenesis. *Ethnos* 62(3–4):5–23.

Landry, Nicolas

   2012–2013 La Compagnie de la pêche sédentaire en Acadie, 1682–1708. *Port Acadie: revue interdisciplinaire en études acadiennes/Port Acadie: An Interdisciplinary Review in Acadian Studies* 22–23:9–41.

Langlois, Janick

   2000 Les pêcheries de loup-marin en Nouvelle-France. Unpublished Master's thesis, Université du Québec à Chicoutimi. Chicoutimi, Quebec.

Lavoie, Michel

   2010 *Le Domaine du roi 1652–1859: Souveraineté, contrôle, mainmise, propriété, possession, exploitation*. Septentrion, Quebec.

Mailhot, J., J.-P. Simard, and S. Vincent

   1980 On est toujours l'Esquimau de quelqu'un. *Études/Inuit/Studies* 4(1–2):59–76.

Martijn, Charles A.

   1980a The "Esquimaux" in the 17th and 18th Century Cartography of the Gulf of St. Lawrence: A Preliminary Discussion. *Études/Inuit/Studies* 4(1–2):77–104.

   1980b La présence inuit sur la Côte-Nord du Golfe St. Laurent à l'époque historique. *Études/Inuit/Studies* 4(1–2):105–126.

   2009 Historic Inuit Presence in Northern Newfoundland, Circa 1550–1800 CE. In *Painting the Past with a Broad Brush: Papers in Honour of James Valliere Wright,* edited by David L. Keenlyside and Jean-Luc Pilon, pp. 65–101. Mercury Series Archaeology Paper 170. Canadian Museum of Civilization, Gatineau, Quebec.

Martijn, Charles A., and Louis-Jacques Dorais
2001 Eighteenth-Century Innu (Montagnais) and Inuit Toponyms in the Northern Peninsula of Newfoundland. *Newfoundland and Labrador Studies* 17(2):319–330.

Marzagalli, Silvia
1999 The French Atlantic. *Itinerario* 23(2):70–83.

Mimeault, Mario
1984 Les entreprises de pêche à la morue de Joseph Cadet 1751–1758. *Revue d'histoire de l'Amérique française* 37(4):557–572.

Morandière, Charles de la
1962 *Histoire de la pêche française de la morue dans l'Atlantique septentrionale.* 3 vols. G.P. Maisonneuve et Larose, Paris.

Moussette, Marcel
2003 An Encounter in the Baroque Age: French and Amerindians in North America. *Historical Archaeology* 37(4):29–39.

Nadon, Pierre
2004 *La baie du Grand Pabos: une seigneurie gaspésienne en Nouvelle-France au XVIIIe siècle.* Mémoires de recherche 1. Association des archéologues du Québec, Quebec.

Niellon, Françoise
1995 *S'établir sur la terre de Caïn—Brador: Une tentative canadienne au XVIIIe siècle.* Ministère de la Culture et des Communications, Quebec.
2010 *Le patrimoine archéologique des postes de pêche du Québec.* Direction du Patrimoine et de la Muséologie, Ministère de la Culture, des Communications et de la Condition féminine, Quebec.

Pope, Peter E.
2009 Transformation of the Maritime Cultural Landscape of Atlantic Canada by Migratory European Fishers, 1500–1800. In *Beyond the Catch: Fisheries of the North Atlantic, the North Sea and the Baltic, 900–1850*, edited by Louis Sicking and Darlene Abreu-Ferreira, pp. 123–154. Brill, The Hague.

Pritchard, James S.
1974 Constantin, Pierre. In *Dictionary of Canadian Biography*, Vol. 3. University of Toronto/Université Laval, Toronto and Quebec. Electronic document, http://www.biographi.ca/en/bio/constantin_pierre_3E.html, accessed June 10, 2013.

Rankin, Lisa
2010 A People for All Seasons: Expressions of Inuit Identity over the Past 500 Years in Southern Labrador. In *Identity Crisis: Archaeological Perspectives on Social Identity*, edited by Lindsay Amundsen Meyer, Nicole Engel, and Sean Pickering, pp. 332–340. University of Calgary Press, Calgary.

Rankin, Lisa, Matthew Beaudoin, and Natalie Brewster

2012 Southern Exposure: The Inuit of Sandwich Bay, Labrador. In *Settlement, Subsistence and Change among the Labrador Inuit: The Nunatsiavummiut Experience*, edited by David C. Natcher, Lawrence Felt, and Andrea Procter, pp. 61–84. University of Manitoba Press, Winnepeg.

Rockman, Marcy

2003 Knowledge and Learning in the Archaeology of Colonization. In *Colonization of Unfamiliar Landscapes: The Archaeology of Adaptation*, edited by Marcy Rockman and James Steele, pp. 3–24. Routledge, London.

Robitaille, Benoît

1955 L'habitation de Constantin et la possession du Grand Saint-Modet. *Le bulletin des recherches historiques* LXI:163–168.

Rollmann, Hans

2011 "So fond of the pleasure to shoot": The Sale of Firearms to Inuit on Labrador's North Coast in the Late Eighteenth Century. *Newfoundland and Labrador Studies* 26(1):5–24.

Roy, P.-G.

1928 Documents sur Pierre Constantin. *Le Bulletin des recherches historiques*. XXXIV:257–263.

Stopp, Marianne P.

2002 Reconsidering Inuit Presence in Southern Labrador. *Études/Inuit/Studies* 26(2):71–106.

2012 The 2011 Field Season at North Island-1 (FeAx-3). *Provincial Archaeology Office 2011 Archaeology Review* 10:166–168.

2013 Sod House Archeology in the Seal Islands Area, 2012. *Provincial Archaeology Office 2012 Archaeology Review* 11:160–161.

Trudel, François

1978 Les Inuits du Labrador méridional face à l'exploitation canadienne et française des pêcheries (1700–1760). *Revue d'histoire de l'Amérique française* 31(4):481–499.

1980 Les relations entre les Français et les Inuit au Labrador méridional, 1660–1760. *Études/Inuit/Studies* 4(1–2):135–146.

Tuck, James A.

1987 1987 Fieldwork at Red Bay, Labrador. Unpublished report on file with the Provincial Archaeology Office, Department of Tourism, Recreation, and Culture, Government of Newfoundland and Labrador, St. John's.

1988 Archaeology at Red Bay, Labrador 1988. Unpublished report on file with the Provincial Archaeology Office, Department of Tourism, Recreation, and Culture, Government of Newfoundland and Labrador, St. John's.

1989 Excavations at Red Bay, Labrador 1989. Unpublished report on file with the Provincial Archaeology Office, Department of Tourism, Recreation, and Culture, Government of Newfoundland and Labrador, St. John's.

1990 Archaeology at Red Bay, Labrador, 1990. Unpublished report on file with the Provincial Archaeology Office, Department of Tourism, Recreation, and Culture, Government of Newfoundland and Labrador, St. John's.

Turgeon, Laurier

1997 Bordeaux and the Newfoundland Trade during the Sixteenth Century. *International Journal of Maritime History* 9(2):1–28.

1998 French Fishers, Fur Traders, and Amerindians during the Sixteenth Century: History and Archaeology. *William and Mary Quarterly*, Third Series 55(4):585–610.

2009 Codfish, Consumption and Colonization: The Creation of the French Atlantic World during the Sixteenth Century. In *Bridging the Early Modern Atlantic World: People, Products and Practices on the Move*, edited by Caroline A. Williams, pp. 33–56. Ashgate, Burlington, Vermont.

Whiteley, W. H.

1969 Governor Hugh Palliser and the Newfoundland and Labrador Fishery, 1764–1768. *Canadian Historical Review* 50(2):141–163.

1976 Newfoundland, Quebec and the Administration of the Coast of Labrador, 1774–1783. *Acadiensis* 6(1):92–112.

Zemon Davis, Natalie

2001 Polarities, Hybridities: What Strategies for Decentring? In *Decentring the Renaissance: Canada and Europe in Multidisciplinary Perspective 1500–1700*, edited by Carolyn Podruchny and Germaine Warkentin, pp. 19–32. University of Toronto Press, Toronto.

Zoltvany, Yves F.

1696 Hazeur, François. In *Dictionary of Canadian Biography*, Vol. 2. University of Toronto/Université Laval, Toronto and Quebec. Electronic document, http://www.biographi.ca/en/bio/hazeur_francois_2E.html. Accessed June 11, 2013.

CHAPTER 6

The Inuit-Métis of Sandwich Bay: Oral Histories and Archaeology

Laura Kelvin and Lisa Rankin

The southern coast of Labrador offers a unique opportunity to study Inuit-Métis ethnicity in the archaeological record. Drawing their ancestry from their European and Inuit roots, Labrador's Inuit-Métis mobilized their collective identity in 1985 by establishing the Labrador Metis Association, now NunatuKavut Community Council (see Kennedy, chapter 1). Archaeologists, including those in our CURA team, are now attempting to better understand Inuit-Métis history. The question our work asks is whether archaeological research can help identify the footprint of historic Inuit-Métis sod houses, as distinct from those used by historic Inuit and visiting Newfoundland fishers.

Problematic here is that during the nineteenth century, Inuit, migratory fishermen, and Inuit-Métis all constructed and lived in similar sod dwellings. These dwellings appear almost identical, making it difficult for archaeologists to determine the ethnicity of the occupants. To date, a minimal number of well-defined European and Inuit dwellings have been excavated in southern Labrador, and their ethnic signatures have been tentatively established. Only one known Inuit-Métis sod dwelling has been excavated thus far, FkBg-24, a winter dwelling located on North River in Sandwich Bay, Labrador. The excavation of FkBg-24 allowed Beaudoin (2008) to make some preliminary conclusions about the nature of Inuit-Métis archaeological assemblages and architecture. However, these results have yet to be tested elsewhere and further investigation into Inuit-Métis archaeological sites is needed to determine whether FkBg-24 is representative of the Inuit-Métis life in Sandwich Bay. In order for this to occur, more Inuit-Métis sites need to be excavated—a difficult process considering that the sites are so difficult to recognize.

In hopes of locating further Inuit-Métis settlements we undertook both oral history and archaeological survey work in Sandwich Bay in the summer of 2010. This technique allowed us to identify a number of Inuit-Métis settlements in Sandwich Bay, and ultimately to compare these sites to the known occupations of Inuit and migratory fishermen in the region. The results of this process are encouraging and offer a way forward for the archaeological investigation of the Inuit-Métis.

Inuit-Métis Ethnicity in Sandwich Bay

There is no one definition of ethnicity. Jones (1997:84) suggests that ethnicity may be associated with "culturally ascribed identity groups, which are based on the expression of a real or assumed shared culture and common descent" (Jones 1997:84). A consciousness of difference is necessary to form and to maintain an ethnic group. The ethnic group must be perceived as different both by its members and by people who are not members of the group. Ethnicity is an ever-changing and socially adaptive mechanism to cope with changing economic, social, and political circumstances (Burley et al. 1992; Jones 1997).

The Inuit-Métis are primarily the descendants of Inuit women and men from the British Isles who came to the coast of Labrador during the late eighteenth and early nineteenth centuries to work at British fishing and trading stations. The first generation of people with ethnically mixed heritage considered themselves neither European nor Inuit, and often married others of mixed ancestry (Kennedy 1997). Ethnic endogamy reinforced ethnic consciousness, and the ancestors of contemporary

Inuit-Métis appear to have been considered distinct by the Inuit and the Europeans. This said, we know more about the process in northern Labrador where, for example, Moravian missionaries recorded that Inuit referred to peoples of mixed ancestry as Kablunângajuit, meaning "partly white" (Kennedy 1997:8). Similarly, Europeans and Americans who visited the coast of Labrador referred to them as "mixed" or "half-breeds" in their journals and censuses (e.g., O'Hara 1870, Rompkey 1996). During the recent era, the term "Métis" was first applied to ethnically mixed communities in Labrador in 1975. Prior to this, these people referred to themselves and were often referred to by others as "Settlers," "Liveyeres," or Labradorians, and they were reluctant to acknowledge their Inuit heritage (Kennedy 1997). The recent shift from Settler to Métis indicates a change in the way the Inuit-Métis acknowledge their identity (Kennedy, chapter 11). This shift also changes the way the Inuit-Métis portray their identity to others. Finally, it is not known how people of mixed Inuit and European heritage understood their ethnicity during the nineteenth century, but historical documentation suggests that both the community and visitors to it saw them as distinct from their Inuit and European neighbours.

Living Seasonally in Sandwich Bay

Although George Cartwright established a post at what would become Cartwright in 1775, most Europeans came to Sandwich Bay during the mid-nineteenth century as Hunt and Henley Company employees (Fitzhugh 1999:140). The company began its ventures there in 1836. Their primary interest was in the salmon fishery, first pickling and later canning salmon at Eagle River and Paradise River. Their Sandwich Bay ventures also included posts at Cartwright, Pack's Harbour, and Dumpling Island (Fitzhugh 1999:140; Kennedy 1995:100). The majority of these Europeans were single males, many of whom eventually married local Inuit women, giving rise to the local Inuit-Métis community.

Traditionally, Sandwich Bay residents were largely self-sufficient, moving seasonally between two or three locations each year: a winter location, a salmon-fishing station, and a cod-fishing station (salmon fishing may have been carried out in summer from the family's winter home, the summer cod-fishing location, or in an entirely separate location). For the purpose of this discussion, Inuit-Métis sites have been separated into two groups: cold-season occupation sites and warm-season occupation sites. If salmon fishing was carried out at the same location as a winter location, it is considered a cold-season occupation site. If salmon fishing occurred at a cod-fishing location or a separate location, it is considered a warm-season occupation site.

Families built their winter houses in heavily sheltered bays or coves, near timber, game, and fur-bearing animals. Families occasionally planted a garden of potatoes and greens near their winter homes, then moved to their salmon-fishing stations, where they stayed until the end of July. The salmon stations were mostly located within the bay, near rivers, or farther out the bay from their more sheltered winter locations. After the salmon season, families would move to their cod-fishing locations, which were usually located on the islands outside of the bay. Families would remain at these stations until late September or early October, when they would return to their winter locations (Kelvin 2011:53–54).

Families harvested sufficient local resources to survive and to trade with local merchants. Furs trapped during winter were traded on a credit/debit system, as were salmon and cod caught during summer. Through this system people in Sandwich Bay had access to European goods and food, valuable resources they could not procure from the land (Kennedy 1995:102). This way of life was practised in Sandwich Bay until the beginning of the twentieth century, when a variety of changes, including an epidemic of Spanish influenza, the introduction of formal education, and government-sponsored resettlement programs, altered settlement patterns and caused rapid changes in Sandwich Bay society.

Inuit-Métis Archaeological Sites

To date, only one known Inuit-Métis sod dwelling has been excavated, at North River in Sandwich Bay (FkBg-24; Figure 1). In 2010, local informants described another 12 Inuit-Métis settlements, including three warm-season habitation sites and nine cold-season sites (Kelvin 2011). A search of the Newfoundland and Labrador archaeological site database indicates that these sites had already been recorded by archaeologists as historic period settlements, yet no ethnicity had been ascribed to the occupants. Kelvin (2011) recorded a further three Inuit-Métis cold-season sites during an archaeological survey undertaken in the summer of 2010 (for a full list of the sites, see Table 1).

Table 1. Possible Inuit-Métis Sites in Sandwich Bay.

Site Name	Borden Number	Site Description
Isthmus Bay 2	FkBd-08	-6 sod houses -mid-nineteenth century
Cape North 1	FkBd-05	-3 sod houses
Snack Cove 4	FkBe-23	-rectangular foundations sodded over -historic
North River 1	FkBg-31	-sod house -nineteenth century
Sandy Cove 1 (Hare Harbour)	FkBe-25	-sod house -nineteenth century
Jackie's Point 1	FkBg-32	-sod house -nineteenth century
Porcupine Strand 19	FkBg-25	-sod structure -historic
Porcupine Strand 20	FkBg-26	-2 rectangular sod structures -historic
Porcupine Strand 21	FkBg-27	-rectangular sod structure -historic

Note: The table is divided into warm-season habitation sites (top three locations) and cold-season habitation sites (bottom six locations). Information taken from Site Record Forms on file at the Newfoundland and Labrador Provincial Archaeology Office.

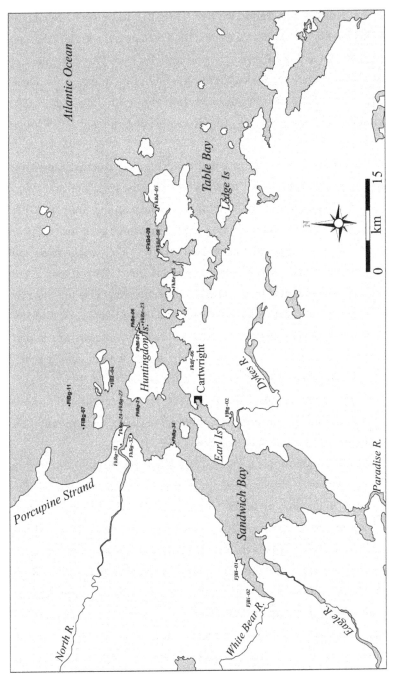

Figure 1. Map of Sandwich Bay indicating sites of historical importance to the Inuit-Métis: Inuit-Métis, Inuit, and possible migratory fishermen archaeological sites.

The North River, Sandwich Bay (FkBg-24) house site excavated in 2007 by Matthew Beaudoin was inhabited by a mixed couple. Ethnohistorical and genealogical research conducted by Patty Way indicates that FkBg-24 was occupied during the winters and salmon season by Charles Williams (d. 1879), who immigrated from Plymouth, England, in 1830, and his wife Mary, who was of Inuit and Scottish descent (Beaudoin et al. 2010).

Excavation of FkBg-24 revealed a rectangular structure measuring 10 m x 4 m, a sawpit located 10 m northwest of the structure, and a midden located just outside the structure's entrance on the south wall. The structure contained a single open room with a stove platform and storage pit. The floor and walls were wooden, most likely made from split logs. The roof was covered with sod and birchbark. The domestic artifacts recovered suggest traditional Inuit practices that also involved the use of European technologies. For example, Beaudoin et al. (2010:156–157) propose that the high number of hollowware ceramics in comparison to flatware ceramics indicates a liquid or stew-based diet like that of the Inuit. The excavation of this site suggests that the architecture, features, and material culture assemblages associated with Inuit-Métis sites might differ significantly from those associated with Inuit and European archaeological sites (Beaudoin et al. 2010).

An additional hint is derived from geographic location. According to the interviews Kelvin carried out in 2010, winter locations were chosen based on the amount of shelter the area provided and the resources available in the area (Kelvin 2011). Access to traplines, game, and firewood was vital to winter survival. Families also wanted to be sufficiently spaced to reduce pressure on local resources. The archaeological evidence appears to support this as all of the cold-season occupation sites identified in Table 1 are located in sheltered areas of the bay and have access to abundant firewood, game, and traplines. Even the larger settlements such as Dove Brook had a small enough population to be sustained by the available resources. There also appears to be a trend for choosing settlement locations close to small brooks or rivers.

Isthmus Bay 2 (FkBd-08), Cape North 1 (FkBd-05), and Snack Cove 4 (FkBe-23) are identified in Table 1 as possible warm-season Inuit-Métis sites. The location of these sites supports the notion that the Inuit-Métis inhabited outer islands and regions of the bay during the summer to participate in the cod fisheries. Most of these sites consist of multiple houses in proximity to each other, reflecting the co-operative nature of the salt cod fishery.

Both cold-season and warm-season settlement locations were passed down through the family—although there is no apparent pattern for inheritance (Davis 1981:11; Patty Way, personal communication, Cartwright, Labrador, July 23, 2010). Many cold- and warm-season sites that were occupied during the nineteenth century are still used today by the original families' descendants, which has been helpful in identifying possible locations of Inuit-Métis sites. However, this may also limit access to sites, and in some cases residents may have built over previous habitations.

Many interviewees stated that their ancestors lived in log or wooden houses that were insulated by sod and moss (Kelvin 2011), descriptions supported by archaeological evidence. As previously stated, FkBg-24 was a wooden structure made from split logs, with sod used as insulation. Test pits taken from Structure 1 at FjBi-02 revealed large amounts of decomposing wood, indicating that the structure was probably made from wood, similar to FkBg-24. The presence of a sawpit on each of these sites suggests the importance of wood for the construction of the house, with scraps used for kindling. The structures at FjBi-02 and the structure at FkBg-24 were all rectangular in shape, as were several of the structures described in Table 1.

To date, no warm-season Inuit-Métis occupation sites have been examined in detail, so it is not known if or how these sites differ archaeologically from cold-season occupation sites. During interviews it was indicated that the winter home was seen as the family's permanent residence, so more time and resources were put into the construction of the winter home. Furthermore, families would bring all their possessions when they moved between houses; consequently, the artifact assemblage may not differ greatly between cold- and warm-season habitations. Although some artifacts may indicate seasonal activity, it is likely that faunal remains and site location would be the greatest indicators of seasonality.

The information gathered in the 2010 interviews, archaeological survey, and testing confirms many of the assertions made by Beaudoin et al. (2010). It is therefore likely that the location of occupation, shape, and construction of residence, as well as associated features, may be used to define Inuit-Métis settlements (Kelvin 2011). Furthermore, the information provided during interviews suggests that the seasonality for each occupation can probably be ascertained based on the location of the site within the bay.

Discussion

Although Sandwich Bay's cultural landscape was diverse during the nineteenth century, the Inuit, Inuit-Métis, and migratory fishermen were in constant contact with one another. An intense, mutual appropriation of material culture has resulted in similar archaeological assemblages; however, it appears each group remained ethnically distinct and this may be represented in the archaeological record (Table 2).

The Inuit in Labrador traditionally settled in outer bays and on exposed outer islands. They lived in semi-subterranean sod dwellings during the cold season and conical skin tents during the warm season. Inuit sod houses contained a single room with a flagstone floor and a sleeping platform that ran along the back wall. The walls and roof were made of sods that were supported by wood and/or whalebone. The entrance was a long, narrow, paved passage, known as an entrance tunnel, which sunk below the house floor to prevent cold air from entering (Kaplan 1985; Rankin, chapter 2). Although there were changes to Inuit house construction and settlement patterns prior to the nineteenth century, some of the most dramatic changes occurred during the nineteenth century.

Table 2. Comparison of Inuit-Métis, Inuit, and Migratory Fishermen Settlement Patterns and Architecture.

Warm Season		
	Inuit-Métis	**Inuit**	**Migratory Fishermen**
Settlement pattern (geographic location)	Outer islands and headlands of the bay	Outer islands and headlands of the bay	Outer islands and headlands of the bay
Architecture and construction materials	• Rectangular shape • One room • Semi-subterranean • No entrance tunnel or sleeping platform • Wooden walls and floor, and frame covered with sod • Not as much time and money put into construction as winter houses • Possible fishing bawns on premise	• Large rocks and boulders holding down skin tent, which is supported by wooden tent poles	• Wooden frame and walls covered in sods • Ground level • Wooden, paved stone, or packed dirt floor • May have multiple rooms • Most likely would contain fishing bawns on premise • No entrance tunnel or sleeping platform

Cold Season		
	Inuit-Métis	**Inuit**	**Migratory Fishermen**
Settlement pattern (geographic location)	Inner sheltered areas of the bay	Possible shift during the nineteenth century from outer islands and headlands toward inner parts of the Bay	Migratory fishermen moved back to their homes at the end of fishing season
Architecture and construction materials	• Rectangular shape • One room • Semi-subterranean • No entrance tunnel or sleeping platform • Wooden walls and floor, and frame covered with sod • More time and money put into construction of these houses compared to warm-season houses • Saw pit	• Oval-rectangular shape • One room • Semi-subterranean • Entrance tunnel • Sleeping platforms • Paved stone floor • Wood and whalebone frame covered with skins and sod	

Further complicating the archaeological record, nineteenth-century Inuit sites in Labrador are highly variable, with many indicating the adoption of European architecture and changes in settlement pattern (Kaplan 1983; Kleivan 1966). There are over 100 nineteenth-century Inuit sites in total recorded in every coastal region of Labrador (Kaplan 1983:299). Although nineteenth-century Inuit houses contain some traditional Inuit artifacts, European materials dominate assemblages (Kaplan 1983:244). The archaeological record indicates that sod-house architecture was highly variable at this time, ranging from traditional Inuit design to a conventional European layout (Kleivan 1966:33–42). Currently, the nineteenth-century Inuit are under-represented in Sandwich Bay's archaeological record. However, Lambert de Boilieu's 1861 journal (Bredin 1963:103) indicates that during that time some Inuit in Sandwich Bay were living in sod houses with traditional architectural components and that they may have changed their settlement patterns. Instead of residing on islands and outer headlands during the winter, the Inuit may have located in inner parts of the bay, similar to the Inuit-Métis, which may explain the lack of recorded nineteenth-century sites. This change in settlement pattern may represent a new reliance on trapping, similar to what has been recorded in other regions of Labrador (Kaplan 1985:362).

Migratory fishermen from the United States, France, and Newfoundland came each summer to fish, and the most important of these fisheries was the stationer fishery from Newfoundland. Newfoundland fishers built "rooms" along the coast of Labrador on outer islands and headlands, in similar places to Inuit-Métis summer settlements. They also borrowed aspects of well-adapted Inuit sod-house construction for their tilts.

Fishermen's tilts retained a traditional European rectangular shape. The fishermen's rooms varied depending on the size and composition of crews using them. The smallest stations contained at least a bunk and cookhouse, a stage for processing fish, and a natural or man-made bawn for drying fish. Larger stations may have also included a separate bunkhouse for the skipper, a separate cookhouse, a salt store, and an attached store selling fish and general supplies (Lewis 1988:70–71). Separate rooms or room divisions denote the importance placed on the distinction between personal and communal space in European-based cultures. Fishermen's tilts also do not contain an entrance tunnel and were not, like Inuit houses, semi-subterranean. The reason may be that the fishermen usually resided in Labrador during the summer and did not need the insulation of a semi-subterranean dwelling or the benefits of the cold trap and entrance tunnel.

Little archaeological investigation has been conducted on nineteenth-century migratory fishermen sites in Labrador. Two excavated migratory fishery sites, Degrat Island (EjAu-05) and Saddle Island (EkCb-01), revealed rectangular structures built out of stone, wood, and sods (Auger 1993; Burke 1991; Tuck 1984). Although similar to Inuit sod houses, the archaeological remains of fishermen's tilts reflect a European construction style.

The architecture of Inuit-Métis houses contains aspects of both Inuit and European construction styles; however, Inuit-Métis houses more closely resemble the European design. They are semi-subterranean, rectangular-shaped, single-room dwellings made of wood, which are then covered with sod for insulation. There appears to be no entrance tunnel or sleeping platforms. Sites may also include sawpit and garden features. Beaudoin (2008:149–150) suggests that the European-style house design observed at FkBg-24 is likely because a European man constructed it. He also suggests that the artifact distribution and spatial analysis of the structure's interior reflects traditional domestic practices of Inuit women because this space would be considered a woman's workspace (Beaudoin 2008:149–150). However, as FkBg-24 is the only excavated Inuit-Métis house, it is not known if it is fully representative of the Inuit-Métis.

The ancestors of the Inuit-Métis had a specific settlement pattern, residing in sheltered areas of the bay during the winter and outer islands and headlands during the summer. Migratory fishermen also settled on outer islands and headlands during the summer, but would return to

Newfoundland for the winter. The Inuit traditionally settled only on outer islands and headlands of the bay for both warm and cold seasons. As the Inuit lived in skin tents during the summer it would appear that only warm-season Inuit-Métis and migratory fishermen sod houses and cold-season Inuit sod houses would be found in outer regions of the bay. Analysis of faunal remains indicates the season of occupation and helps determine if the dwelling's occupants were Inuit. This also suggests that only cold-season Inuit-Métis sod houses would be found within the sheltered areas of the bay. However, documentary evidence indicates that the Inuit in Sandwich Bay, as they were elsewhere in Labrador, may have been shifting their settlement patterns during the nineteenth century and residing within the bay. This complicates the once-clear distinction between Inuit and Inuit-Métis settlement patterns.

Conclusion

Although the characteristics of the Inuit-Métis sites recorded in 2010 appear to support Beaudoin's (2008) conclusions, these observations are preliminary and further investigation and excavation are needed to verify that the Inuit-Métis can be identified as a distinct ethnic population in the archaeological record. An excavation focused on an Inuit-Métis summer house should also be conducted to see how construction and artifact assemblages differ based on seasonality. In addition, more research associated with nineteenth-century Inuit and migratory fishermen in southern Labrador is required to establish a better comparative dataset.

Currently, identifying the ethnicity of the occupants of a nineteenth-century Labrador sod house based solely on archaeological information is, at best, difficult. Studying the history of the Inuit-Métis requires a holistic approach that uses archaeology, archival research, oral histories, and community knowledge. Only through such an approach can researchers better understand the ethnicity and identities of past peoples. Information gained during interviews undoubtedly led our archaeological investigation. The interviews provided context to the archaeological sites that could not be gained through excavation.

References Cited

Auger, R.
1993 Late-18th-and Early-19th-Century Inuit and Europeans in Southern Labrador. *Arctic* 46(1):27–34.

Beaudoin, M.
2008 Sweeping the Floor: An Archaeological Examination of a Multi-Ethnic Sod House in Labrador (FkBg-24). Unpublished Master's thesis, Memorial University of Newfoundland, St. John's.

Beaudoin, M., R. L. Josephs, and L. K. Rankin.
2010 Attributing Cultural Affiliation to Sod Structures in Labrador: A Labrador Métis Example from North River. *Canadian Journal of Archaeology* 34(2):148–173.

Bredin, T. F. (editor)
1969 *Recollections of Labrador Life.* Ryerson Press, Toronto.

Burke, C. A.
1991 Nineteenth Century Ceramic Artifacts from a Seasonally Occupied Fishing Station on Saddle Island, Red Bay, Labrador. Unpublished Master's thesis. Department of Anthropology, Memorial University of Newfoundland, St. John's.

Burley, D. V., G. A. Horsfall, and J. D. Brandon
1992 *Structural Considerations of Métis Ethnicity: An Archaeological, Architectural, and Historical Study.* University of South Dakota Press, Vermillion.

Davis, J.
1981 Davis' of Sandwich Bay. *Them Days* 6(4):4–23.

Fitzhugh, L. D.
1999 *The Labradorians: Voices from the Land of Cain.* Breakwater, St. John's.

Jones, S. (editor)
1997 *The Archaeology of Ethnicity: Constructing Identities in the Past and Present.* Routledge, London.

Kaplan, S. A.
1983 Economic and Social Change in Labrador Neo-Eskimo Culture. Unpublished Ph.D. thesis. Department of Archaeology, Bryn Mawr College, Bryn Mawr, Pennsylvania.
1985 European Goods and Socio-Economic Change in Early Labrador Inuit Society. In *Cultures in Contact: The European Impact on Native Cultural Institutions in Eastern North America, A.D. 1000–1800,* edited by W. Fitzhugh, pp. 45–70. Smithsonian Institution Press, Washington, D.C.

Kelvin, L. E.

   2011 The Inuit-Metis of Sandwich Bay: Oral Histories and Archaeology. Unpublished Master's thesis, Department of Archaeology, Memorial University of Newfoundland, St. John's.

Kennedy, J. C.

   1995 *People of the Bays and Headlands: Anthropological History and the Fate of Communities in the Unknown Labrador*. University of Toronto Press, Toronto.

   1997 Labrador Metis Ethnogenesis. *Ethnos* 62(3–4):5–23.

Kleivan, H.

   1966 *The Eskimos of Northern Labrador: A History of Eskimo–White Relations 1771–1955*. Norsk Polarinstitutt, Oslo.

Lewis, R. M.

   1988 Labrador Fishery: An Anthropological and Historical Study. Unpublished Master's thesis, Department of Anthropology, Memorial University of Newfoundland, St. John's.

Newfoundland and Labrador Site Record Forms

   On file, Provincial Archaeology Office, Department of Tourism, Culture and Recreation, Government of Newfoundland and Labrador, St. John's.

O'Hara, J.

   1870 A Census of the Labrador Coast from Nain to Sandwich Bay Not Including Moravian Settlements.

Rompkey, R. (editor)

   1996 *Labrador Odyssey: The Journal and Photographs of Eliot Curwen on the Second Voyage of Wilfred Grenfell, 1893*. McGill-Queen's University Press, Montreal and Kingston.

Tuck, J. A.

   1984 1984 Excavations at Red Bay, Labrador. *Archaeology in Newfoundland and Labrador Annual Reports* 15:224–227.

CHAPTER 7

The Story of William Phippard

Patricia Way

For centuries, two peoples, the Inuit (formerly "Eskimos") and the Innu (formerly called Montagnais and Naskapi "Indians"), inhabited Labrador. Following 1763, men from Europe came to Labrador to work in the fishery. Some remained and married. Unions between these men and Inuit women produced a "mixed" category of people. These "half-breeds" or "mixed breeds" living south of what is now Nunatsiavut organized as Metis in the 1980s. Today, most self-identify as Métis, Inuit-Métis, or as southern Inuit, and are members of NunatuKavut Community Council (see Kennedy, chapter 1). These people have a culture incorporating both European and Inuit elements. This chapter will address what we know about the first European and Inuit union, who they were, and what became of any children.

Inconsistent historical records in south and central Labrador hindered answers to these questions. With the exception of the Moravians in northern Labrador (Rollmann, chapter 9), the records kept by institutions in southern and central Labrador are incomplete and have complicated efforts to reconstruct social history. Travelling clergy helped, but they rarely visited, and they created, at best, a sporadic documentary trail. Headstones existed in some graveyards, yet few could afford them. Instead, one encountered weather-worn wooden markers, now devoid of names or dates, in short, a lost history. Oral tradition was stronger in some families than in others. A few families kept Bibles where family members recorded the names of their ancestors in the opening pages, and these can be helpful. Since 1975, *Them Days* magazine added to our knowledge by publishing Labrador's oral history.

During the past few decades, I shared my passion for genealogy with Bernard Heard, Sr., and Jason Curl, constantly searching for documentation. Academic researchers have also helped. For example, in 1979 and 1980, Dr. John C. Kennedy hand-copied all Battle Harbour births, marriages, and deaths between 1880 and 1980, supplemented with existing data from the Newfoundland archives from 1850 to 1879. In the course of his fieldwork, Kennedy also visited most southern Labrador cemeteries and copied tombstone inscriptions. This information was used to create a computerized database, which he loaned to me. Similarly, Dr. Hans Rollmann has shared Anglican and Moravian documentation that has helped answer many questions. Finally, under the CURA program, I have visited and investigated the Hudson's Bay Company archives at Winnipeg, fulfilling a lifelong dream. These sources of information have combined to enable the following genealogy of William Phippard, his Inuit partner, Sarah, and their Inuit-Métis descendants.

European Settlement

By the last decades of the eighteenth century, British policies and events reduced the incidence of violence between Europeans and Inuit (Crompton, chapter 5). Policies such as the 1765 treaty between Governor Palliser and Inuit at Chateau Bay, the establishment of the first Moravian post at Nain in 1771, and the positive influences of George Cartwright, who arrived in Labrador in 1770, all reduced violence and made permanent European settlement possible.

The first two Englishmen known to have "settled" in Labrador were William Phippard and John Newhook [Knocks/Nooks] (see Zimmerly 1975). Like other European males, the two came to Labrador to work for British companies that operated there after 1763. According to Lydia

Brooks Campbell (1818–1905), herself of mixed ancestry (Stopp, chapter 8), these two men:

> were given provisions and were promised to get picked up the next year, but the people never came back for three years, as my father told us, for he saw them when he came from England. They went to a place in which there was a river and plenty wood and that river was called English River to this day. The Indians (Mountaineers) and Eskimaux was at war with each other then and [but] they [presumably, the Inuit] was kind to the whites. As their clothing was worn, they went to the Eskimaux (for they was plentiful at that time) and got seal skin clothes from them and meat to eat. When the white men came back to see if they was dead or alive, they found them dressed like the natives about here at that time. When they went on shore and these two, William Phippard and John Nooks, went to meet them, the sailors and whoever went ashore, they thought it was savages and they got afraid until they called out and said it was friends instead of foes. They stayed a few days with them but bid farewell to them again [Campbell 2000:26–27].

Lydia Brooks Campbell told the Rev. Arminius Young about the circumstances surrounding Phippard's union:

> In 1780 the first two white men . . . settled in Hamilton Inlet . . . when a vessel came to pick them up, they declined the offer . . . [they] had by this time acquired, in part, the Eskimo language . . . . They made up their minds to start life there in true Eskimo fashion, consequently they left English River where apparently they were living alone; and settled in Double Mer, a small Eskimo settlement on the north side of the Bay. There they made the acquaintance of a[n] . . . Eskimo widow and her daughter, a young woman. Phippard and the older woman decided to

unite their fortunes, while Newhook, being the younger of the two, was looked upon with favour by the daughter; a double marriage was the result . . . no doubt Phippard and Newhook accepted the Eskimo custom of marriage. . . . Phippard's wife had had two sons (besides the daughter who had married New-hook) by her first husband. Several years after the marriage, when the sons had grown up and a number of white men had settled around the Bay, Newhook with the two lads started on a trip . . . to Kenemich to purchase some nails for the building of a boat. For some unknown reason the two lads turned upon Newhook and killed him. Thus it was that one of the first two Englishmen who settled in Labrador met his death on a hill on the south side of Hamilton Inlet now known as Newhook's Hill [Young 1916:11–13].

Campbell described the same events in her diary:

When I was eleven years old [ca. 1829], my father took me to live with an old Englishman by the name of John Whittle, and his wife was blind and lame. . . . I used to listen to her talk about her young days. She was a native of this country and before John Whittle took her, she was married to one of the first Englishmen that visited this country [John Newhook], but as the Eskimaux were not civilized at that time, her half-brothers killed him while crossing from Double Mer through the woods . . . the other man [William Phippard] was left with his wife and this poor man's wife and her little boy. The little half-breed boy died when he was playing outdoors [Campbell 2000:38–39].

Thus Newhook met his end and his only child died shortly thereafter. William Phippard may therefore be considered the first surviving European who chose to remain in Labrador, take an Inuit spouse, and produce mixed offspring who remained in Labrador. Both Campbell and Young make it clear that after the three years had passed, an opportunity was given to the men to leave if they wished, but both chose to stay. The decision of Phippard and Newhook to remain in Labrador differs from the opinion of Sir Patrick McGrath, who, when discussing Phippard and Newhook, claimed that "their existence was forgotten, and they were forced to become permanent settlers, so to speak" (McGrath 1925:4).

Phippard spent the rest of his days in Double Mer, near Rigolet (see Figure 1 for this location and other places mentioned in text). Some years later, Lydia Brooks Campbell told Rev. Arminius Young that:

> Brooks . . . [Lydia's father] . . . who had recently come to Labrador [ca. 1806] called to see Phippard, then an old man. He found him sitting in the sun, with the Bible in his hand, with tears in his eyes in a very lonely and despondent mood. He too soon passed away [Young 1916:13–14].

Who was William Phippard? An interview on July 12, 1894, by Rev. F. W. Colley with Phippard's grandson, William Phippard III, provides a partial answer. Colley observed:

> It took us two or three hours to get to Shoal Bay Island, but my time was pleasantly occupied in listening to old Phippard, who is quite a character in his way. His grandfather, like the English grandfathers of most of the natives, had a "power of money"; was "high-learned"; spelt his name "Pippard"; lived in the Isle of Wight; ran away from home; and was the first Englishman who settled north of Battle Harbour [Colley 1894:1–12].

Phippard's description of his grandfather may simply illustrate how legendary accomplishments of ancestors increase with each telling, or alternatively, confirm that Phippard's wealth and education exceeded that of the Labrador people of his time.

The first William Phippard came to Labrador with the entrepreneur Jeremiah Coghlan sometime after 1763. In 1765, Coghlan began a sealing enterprise in southern Labrador with Thomas Perkins, and in 1767 he entered into a salmon partnership with Perkins, George Cartwright, and Lt. Francis Lucas.[1] Lucas drowned in 1770 and the partnership dissolved by 1773. After that, Coghlan and Cartwright headed separate enterprises and their cod-fishing, fur-trapping, sealing, and salmon crews steadily moved northward to Sandwich Bay.

By the time William Phippard worked for Coghlan, he was in charge of the cod fishery in Porcupine Bay, as was the case in the summer of 1778 (Stopp 2008:18–21). However, a John Wrixon is also listed as heading stations for Coghlan in 1777 and in 1778, the year Wrixon perished. Cartwright recorded on July 31, 1778:

> Mr. Daubeny [head clerk of George Cartwright] . . . had been to Sand Hill Cove and . . . was informed by those people, that on the eighteenth of May last, a flat having been left carelessly upon the ice, near their winter house, it was carried away when the ice broke up; and that John Wrixon with one of his people got upon a pan of ice with an intent to follow it; but they had not been heard of since [Cartwright 1792:II:352].

John Wrixon is mentioned, as it appears that William Phippard was working with him some years prior to 1778. Wrixon was by then an experienced Labrador hand who had taught George Cartwright to trap (Stopp 2008:57). Phippard and Wrixon had been partners. Thus, on June 18, 1779, Cartwright "got eight beaver skins and three wolverines from him [Phippard], in balance of a debt, which his late partner John Wrixon had contracted" (Cartwright 1792:II:451).

For two winters (1777–1778 and 1778–1779) previous to settling in Groswater Bay, William Phippard and a crew of four men overwintered there to trap and trade, presumably on behalf of Coghlan. Phippard was often mentioned by Cartwright when he stopped at Sandwich Bay when travelling north and south. For example, on June 13, 1778, Cartwright wrote, "when the [shallop] *Beaver* last got to the stage, William Phippard and his crew were there in their way from Ivucktoke Bay (Groswater) to Black Bear Bay; and … they had killed but very few furs last winter" (Cartwright 1792:II:330). Similarly, on September 9, 1778:

> At noon, we saw a shallop coming in here [Sandwich Bay] from the southward. Fearing a privateer's crew might be in her, I armed all my people with guns, sticks or stones, and placed them in ambush behind one of the window-leaves of the stage; but it proved to be William Phippard; who is going with four hands to winter in Ivucktoke Bay. [And on] … September 10, 1778—Early this morning, Phippard sailed for Ivucktoke [Cartwright 1792:II:369–370].

It was through Phippard that Cartwright learned the fate of the Inuit woman Caubvick, one of a group Cartwright brought to England in 1773, with the result that she returned, the only survivor of smallpox. In Cartwright's words, on Sunday, March 28, 1779:

> Mr. Daubeny returned (from Sand Hill) and one of Mr. Coghlan's men with him. … brought with him a medal, which William Phippard had picked up last year among the Indian [Inuit] baggage, which they found on the island in Ivucktoke Bay, where they saw so many dead Eskimaux. As I well remember this medal (for it belonged to a brother of mine who gave it to one of the Eskimo Indians whom I had in England) I am now no longer in doubt respecting their persons, or the cause of their death. I am certain that they must be the same that I was acquainted with; that Caubvick must have retained the infection in her hair which she kept in a trunk; and that the smallpox broke out amongst them in the winter, and swept them all off [Cartwright 1792:II:424].

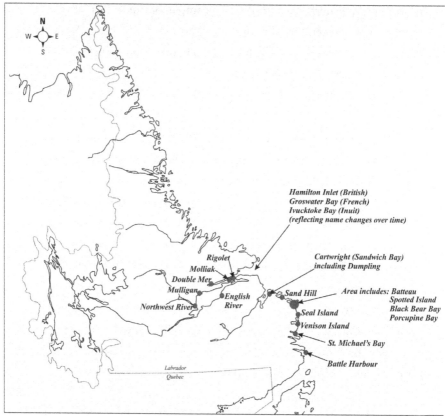

Figure 1. Places mentioned in text.

Prior to settling in Groswater Bay, Phippard was busy learning about the area. For example, on June 18, 1779, Cartwright wrote:

> this afternoon William Phippard and his crew arrived from Ivucktoke Bay, on their way to Sand Hill Cove. He informed me that they had killed but twenty-six beavers, twenty-two martens, six white foxes and three wolverines. . . . He saw the ruins of three French settlements and found several beaver houses. . . . One of the Indians [Inuit] drew him a chart of that Bay, upon birch rind; it is very large, and contains several rivers, islands, and smaller bays [Cartwright 1792:II:451–452].

By 1792, Phippard and his crew "had bought a good deal [of fur] from seven families of Mountaineer Indians which they met with here; and that they could have got much more, had they been provided with some goods and spirituous liquors" (Cartwright 1792:II:352).

Second Generation

The only known child of William Phippard and his Inuit wife Sarah was their son, William Phippard, Jr. (Figure 2). Hudson's Bay Company post journals from North West River make reference to him. For example, on Friday, March 24, 1837:

> In the evening arrived William Blake and William Phippard, planters from Double Mer. The one is fitted out by D. R. Stewart and the latter by Mr. Brownson. They are on a visit to their friends. No great hunt this year among the planters. Foxes are scarce.

Five days later, on March 29, 1837, the post journalist observed, "Phippard and Blake off." By this time, William Phippard, Jr,. was a married "planter," although little is known about his wife, Elizabeth, except that she was an Inuk. Elizabeth's name is listed on some of the baptismal records of their children. Her ethnicity is further confirmed in the aforementioned interview between Rev. F. W. Colley and William Phippard III, son of William Phippard, Jr., and Elizabeth, who informed Rev. Colley that, "his mother and his grandmother were both Eskimo" (Colley 1894:1–12).

The reference to poor trapping of foxes in 1837 may have been the result of the increasing Inuit-Métis population in the central Labrador area. Increased pressures on resources required families to move further afield to survive (Zimmerly 1975). Temporarily poor trapping probably explains why William Phippard, Jr., and his family moved south to the less inhabited Black Bear Bay area of southern Labrador. William's father may have spoken fondly of his years spent in southern Labrador, then largely virgin territory. Whatever the reason, no further

Marriage

references are found to the Phippard surname in the Groswater Bay area following the move of William Phippard, Jr., south in the 1840s.

Third Generation

The first child of William Phippard, Jr., and Elizabeth was Sarah Phippard, whose existence is first confirmed with her marriage to John Blake, August 12, 1850, recorded as marriage number seven in the books of the then newly established Church of England at Battle Harbour. Sarah and John were married in the Rigolet area but recorded by the travelling Rev. Henry Disney that summer. The Church of England record notes that Sarah and John had been previously united in the "manner of the country" by Ambrose Brooks until a church representative was accessible. The Rev. Disney and Captain George Goodridge witnessed the 1850 church union. Although Sarah's birthdate is unknown, her tombstone reads: "Died March 14, 1887, Age 72," meaning she was born in 1814 or 1815. The headstone of John Blake, Sarah's husband, reads: "Died May 24, 1885, Age 73." The dates of these family members are contained in the Blake family Bible, presently in the care of the Alvin Blake family of North West River. Death dates are from headstones at Graveyard Point, Mulliok Arm (Blake 2010:148–149).

The second child of William, Jr., and Elizabeth was Mary Phippard, who would later marry Thomas Reeves, the first Reeves in Labrador. Mary's family name was previously unknown as the birth records of her children (the first as early as 1830) listed the parents as "Thomas and Mary Reeves." However, in 2009, Dr. Hans Rollmann shared some previously unseen records found at the Anglican w in St. John's that identify Mary Reeves's maiden name. In 1848, Bishop Feild of the Church of England had gone to Dumplin(g), Labrador (near Cartwright), where he was the first clergyman to perform baptism and marriage sacraments in more than 20 years. In previous brief visits, Methodist ministers Rev. Thomas Hickson (1824), Rev. Richard Knight (1826), Rev. George Ellidge (1826), and Rev. William Wilson (1828) had baptized and married

Methodist

some of the people, but by 1848 many more awaited these sacraments (Burry 1964:22). Thus, Bishop Feild baptized and married a large number of people on August 21 and 22, 1848, at Dumplin(g), and one such baptism was that of Mary Phippard. Now married years later, Mary Phippard and Thomas Reeves were listed as "previously united" in the "country manner."

Margaret Phippard, third daughter of William, Jr., and Elizabeth, was also baptized that day by Bishop Feild, before marrying widower James Sutton. Margaret and James Sutton had one daughter, Anne Sutton, born by 1848 and baptized then by Feild. However, there are no other known descendants of Margaret Phippard, so any other children likely died young or were otherwise not recorded.

The fourth daughter, Hannah Phippard, was born around 1830 at Double Mer and was a long-time spinster. Initially, Hannah worked as a single girl at Dumplin(g) (1848), where she too was baptized by the Bishop and recorded as the daughter of William and Elizabeth. Hannah was single when births were recorded at St. Michael's Bay (1855), Venison Islands (1856), and Batteau (1865). Somewhere between 1866 and 1869, Hannah met and married widower Isaac Whittle of Spotted Islands. The couple's first child together was born in 1870. Widow Hannah Phippard Whittle died of old age, and was buried at Black Bear Bay, January 13, 1904 (Battle Harbour No. 285).

William, Jr., and Elizabeth's oldest son, John, was born at Double Mer, between 1826 and 1830. Conflicting death records explain John's wide range of possible birth years. John Phippard either died on December 21, 1896 (Battle Harbour No. 197) at Black Bear Bay, aged 70, or was buried there on January 2, 1897 age 66 (Battle Harbour, unnumbered record). In any event, John married Margaret (surname unknown), who was born at Seal Islands around 1827, and died and was buried there on March 8, 1905, age 78 (Battle Harbour No. 339). There are no known descendants.

The second son of William, Jr., and Elizabeth Phippard was William Phippard III, born at Groswater Bay between 1837 and 1842. This range

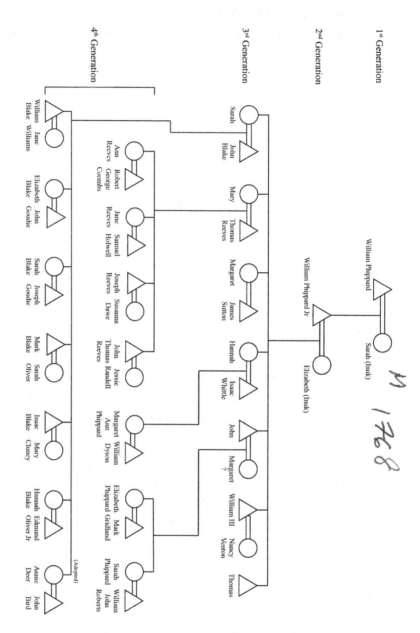

Figure 2. Partial genealogy of William Phippard: First–third generations complete; fourth generation, those with descendants only. (Courtesy of Peter Ramsden)

of birth dates is rooted in a discrepancy in documentary evidence of extant marriage and death dates. William III is the grandson of the original William Phippard, and was the one who was interviewed by the Rev. F. W. Colley. William III married Nancy Venton (daughter of Robert of Flat Island, Newfoundland) on August 20, 1887, at Seal Islands, at age 45, according to the records (Battle Harbour No. 59). He died August 16, 1907, Batteau, listed as age 70, which indicates the earlier (1837) birthdate (Battle Harbour No. 388).

Death records date the birth of the third and final known son of William, Jr., and Elizabeth Phippard, Thomas, to around 1855. Recorded as a fisherman, Thomas died in 1895 at Black Bear Bay, age 40 (Battle Harbour, unnumbered record). No further information is known. Given his approximate date of birth, it is likely that Thomas was a child born when his parents were considerably older or that he was the child of a sibling being raised by grandparents. Before proceeding to the fourth generation, note that the surname Phippard later disappears from Labrador because even by the third generation, only William III, who married a Newfoundland woman named Nancy, had the Phippard name.

Fourth Generation

Sarah Phippard and John Blake had five children born between 1832 and 1850. The couple was officially married in 1850. The first of five children was William Blake (b. March 12, 1832), who later married Jane Williams around 1857. William died February 11, 1901, aged 69, with descendants. Next was Elizabeth (Betsy), born July 12, 1840, who married John Goudie about 1864, with descendants. Sarah Phippard and John Blake's third child was John Blake, Jr., born November 3, 1842. John Blake is occasionally mentioned in HBC documents. For example, on January 3, 1865, the *Rigolet Post Journal* records that "All cruisers [visitors] left except John Blake Jr. and Thomas Groves, Jr." However, John died young. His headstone in Mulliok Arm (Graveyard Point) reads: "John Blake, son of John and Sarah Blake died March 12, 1872, Age 30" (Blake 2010:149). Today, however, this John Blake is occasionally confused with his nephew John Blake (b. 1858), son of his older brother, William.

Sarah (Sally), Sarah and John Blake's fourth child, was born June 19, 1845. Around 1872, Sarah married Joseph Goudie. She died May 17, 1916, with descendants. Mark Blake (b. September 29, 1847, d. November 14, 1881), Sarah and John Blake's fifth child, married Sarah Jane Oliver, with descendants. A sixth child, Isaac Blake (b. September 24, 1850), married a Newfoundlander, Mary Cluney, around 1880. Isaac died January 13, 1910, age 59, with descendants. Sarah and John Blake's seventh child Rebekah/Rebecca, born November 1, 1852, married Peter Michelin, with descendants; and their eighth child, George Blake, born January 21, 1855, married the widow, Ellen Chiquak/Shiwak, in 1878. Ellen's maiden name is unknown; she died in 1888. There are no known descendants. Sarah and John Blake's final child, Hannah, was born February 14, 1857. Hannah married Edmund Oliver, Jr., and she died on March 10, 1925, age 68, with descendants.

John Blake and wife Sarah Phippard also adopted and raised Annie Deer (January 27, 1840, to October 9, 1905). Annie married John Bird of Sandwich Bay in 1859 and the couple had a large family. Annie's birth record is recorded in the Blake family Bible as a niece from the Blake side whose mother had died. HBC records confirm the connection between the Deer and Blake families. For example, on March 2, 1840, the *Rigolet Post Journal* notes that "William and John Blake accompanied by John Deer, their brother-in-law, arrived bringing with them the body of Betsy Blake for interment." This previously unnamed Blake sister, wife of John Deer, may well have been called Esther, based on the fact that Annie's first daughter was so named; that there is no history of that name in the Bird family; and that such honour was usually reserved for a grandmother. A daughter born to Annie's brother, George Deer, was named Kitty Esther.

The large number of descendants of Sarah Phippard and John Blake illustrates that William Phippard is the ancestor of many in the central Labrador region today through his granddaughter Sarah.

Continuing with children from the third generation—that is, William Phippard's grandchildren—we note that most of the children of Mary Phippard and her spouse Thomas Reeves were born prior to their official marriage at Dumplin(g) in 1848, and these children were baptized then. The couple's first child, Ann (born around 1831, based on her headstone in Cartwright), married Robert George Coombs, the first Coombs in Labrador. Thus, all Coombs descendants have Phippard ancestry. Mary and Thomas's second child, Jane, married Samuel Holwell (1832–1903, headstone at Spotted Islands). This couple also had many descendants. A third child, Elizabeth, was baptized in 1848 but there is no further information regarding her. A fourth child, Joseph Reeves (1841–1893), was baptized in 1848. Joseph married Susannah Dawe from Newfoundland and left descendants. Mary and Thomas's fifth child, George Reeves, was also baptized in 1848 at Dumplin(g), although we know nothing more about him. Mary and Thomas's youngest child, John Thomas Reeves, was born February 6, 1860. He first married Jessie Rendell, then Mary Ann Martin of Sandwich Bay, and finally, Susannah Jane Williams Winters, a widow of Sandwich Bay. He left descendants.

Hannah Phippard, William and Elizabeth's fourth child, had several children prior to marriage, with unknown fathers. These children include Sophie Phippard, born on May 27, 1855, in St. Michael's Bay. Little is known of Sophie after she was received into the Anglican Church in 1861 (Battle Harbour No. 423). Mary Phippard was born to Hannah the next year at Venison Islands, September 21, 1856. Mary either died in infancy or was raised by another family, perhaps taking their family name. Hannah's third daughter, Margaret Ann Phippard, was born on July 11, 1865, at Batteau (Battle Harbour No. 673). Her mother's marriage to Isaac Whittle later resulted in Margaret Ann being raised as a Whittle. Margaret Ann married William Dyson, the oldest son of Labrador's first Dyson. Thus Hannah has many Dyson descendants today. Isaac Whittle and Hannah had five children together. These include Rebecca Whittle, baptized August 12, 1870, at Spotted Islands (Battle Harbour No. 791). Rebecca died March 3, 1892, at Seal Islands (Battle

Harbour No. 146). Rebecca's daughter, Elizabeth Whittle, age three, also died at Seal Islands on May 17, 1892 (Battle Harbour No. 150). Hannah and Isaac's second child, William, was born December 4, 1870, at Spotted Islands and received into the church on March 16, 1873 (Battle Harbour No. 880). William married Mary Ann Holwell on April 21, 1901, at Spotted Islands (Battle Harbour No. 123) and they had a daughter, Sarah Jane Whittle, who died August 19, 1916, at the age of 15 (headstone in Spotted Islands cemetery). Mary Ann died March 5, 1905. Following Mary Ann's death, William Whittle married Louisa Keefe and a son, John Thomas Whittle, was born July 10, 1909, at Black Tickle (Vital Statistics No. 10, p. 500, Reel 8 1909). No more is known about William and Louisa's offspring, suggesting that their son died young, leaving no descendants. Hannah and Isaac's third child, Thomas, was born in 1881. Thomas married Ellen Leary of Carbonear at Venison Islands on September 8, 1904 (Battle Harbour No. 156). Nothing more is known of Thomas and Ellen. Hannah and Isaac's fourth child, Elizabeth, was born at Black Bear Bay, where the family was wintering. No more is known of Elizabeth. Hannah and Isaac's final child, John, fails to appear in church records but his death is described by Newfoundlander Greta Hussey in her memoir:

> One of the first few years [early 1920s] that Pop was fishing from his own room in Batteau, he had a Labrador man by the name of Johnny Whittle fishing with him. The next spring . . . we learned that he had died shortly before. Although it was May at the time of his death, the weather was so bad that they had to bury him in Batteau. This nobody liked to do because of the Huskies. A blizzard was raging and the ground was frozen so hard that it took two or three days to get the grave ready. Aunt Charlotte Dave [as there were several Charlotte Dysons in Batteau, this Charlotte Dyson, wife of David Dyson, was referred to using his first name] gave her white cotton print dress to cover his casket. The men dug in shifts. Because of the frost

and the type of ground, the grave had to be built up and piled with stones like a cairn to keep the dogs away. The burial service was read to him by Ralph Barrett who was teaching there at the time. The dogs finally did get around to digging out the grave and his body had to be reinterred [Hussey 1981:91].

John Phippard and Margaret had seven children. Their first, Thomas, was born on September 14, 1854, and baptized in Porcupine Bay on March 1, 1864 (Battle Harbour No. 570). Thomas died on March 1, 1894, at Black Bear Bay. We know of no descendants. John Phippard and Margaret's second child, Elizabeth, was born around 1857 though no birth or baptismal record survives. Elizabeth was married on July 6, 1883, aged 26, at Black Bear Bay to widower Mark Cridland (Battle Harbour No. 9). While Elizabeth and Mark had several children, the only descendants are through her daughter, Agnes Cridland, who married Joshua Dyson of Batteau. Elizabeth died in Black Bear Bay on January 30, 1906 (Battle Harbour No. 356). John Phippard and Margaret's third child, Sarah, was born Feb 17, 1861, and baptized March 1, 1864, in Porcupine Bay (Battle Harbour No. 571). Sarah married William John Roberts on August 31, 1884 (Battle Harbour No. 38), and had two known children: Charlotte Roberts (1889–1913) and Leonard Roberts (1890–1975) (Figure 3), through whom her only living descendants come. Sarah died in the 1890s, leaving young Leonard orphaned. Phippard and Margaret's fourth child, William Phippard IV, was born on August 20, 1864, and baptized March 11, 1866, at Batteau (Battle Harbour No. 669). However, William IV died of tuberculosis, June 1, 1894, with no known descendants. John Phippard and Margaret's fifth child, Mary Ann, was born January 10, 1867, and baptized at Batteau on March 16, 1873 (Battle Harbour No. 881). No further information is known so she likely died young. John Phippard and Margaret's sixth child, Esther Phippard, was born April 15, 1870, at Batteau and baptized on March 16, 1873 (Battle Harbour No. 882). Esther married Martin Delaney at Barton Green's house on Seal Islands, on January 28, 1890 (Battle Harbour No. 68).

There are no known descendants. John Phippard and Margaret's seventh known child, Abram, was born January 5, 1873, at Batteau and baptized on March 16, 1873 (Battle Harbour No. 883). Nothing more is known about him.

Referring again to the third generation, William Phippard III and his wife Nancy had only one known child, John Phippard II, born around 1879, who married Agnes Kate Delaney on May 26, 1901 (Battle Harbour No. 124) at Seal Islands. John Phippard II died of cancer on March 22, 1932, at Mussel Brook. His wife, Kate, died on May 4, 1950, at

Figure 3. Leonard Roberts of Seal Islands, 1929. Roberts (1890–1975) was the great-great grandson of William Phippard and his Inuit wife Sarah. (International Grenfell Association Photograph Collection, Fred Coleman Sears photographs, VA 112-5/F. C. Sears. St. John's: The Rooms Provincial Archives Division)

Batteau (Anglican records, Cartwright). They raised an orphan, Michael Dyson, who did not change his surname though he was locally referred to as "Micky Phippard."

Thus, Kate was the last living person to actually use the Phippard name. Although use of the surname Phippard in Labrador died with Kate in 1950, the descendants of the original William Phippard and Sarah number in the thousands and are their legacy. Some of William and Sarah's descendants married Newfoundlanders employed in the fishery, and most married either Inuit or part-Inuit like themselves, but either way, they helped to build Labrador's Inuit-Métis population. While William and Sarah's story is unique in being first, it resembles that of many other European men and their families in settling Labrador. We know more now about the story of William Phippard and that first marriage to a Labrador Inuit spouse than ever before. Remaining questions await future research.

Note

1. In his journal, Cartwright (1792:I:1) dates this partnership to March 30, 1770, although some kind of earlier partnership may have existed.

References Cited

Blake, Max
    2010 *Eskimo Bay, Labrador*. Transcontinental Press, St. John's.

Burry, Rev. Lester L., B.A., D.D.
    1964 Pioneering Church Work in Labrador. *The Daily News*, 4 September. St. John's.

Campbell, Lydia
    2000 *Sketches of Labrador Life*. Killick Press, St. John's (Reprint from *The Evening Herald*, St. John's, Dec. 1894, Feb. 1895, and May 1895).

Cartwright, George
    1792 *A Journal of Transactions and Events During a Residence of Nearly Sixteen Years on the Coast of Labrador*. 3 vols. Allin and Ridge, Newark, England.

Colley, Rev. F. W.

1894 Work in the Sandwich Bay Mission, Labrador: Summer of 1894. In *The Church in Newfoundland*, Occasional Paper, No. 41. Church of England, Diocese of Newfoundland. Centre for Newfoundland Studies, St. John's.

Hudson's Bay Company (HBC)

1837 Journal of Transactions and Daily Occurrences. North West River, Labrador, B153. Manitoba Provincial Archives, Winnipeg.

1840 Journal of Transactions and Daily Occurrences. Rigolet, Labrador, B183. Manitoba Provincial Archives, Winnipeg.

Hussey, Greta

1981 *Our Life on Lear's Room, Labrador*. Robinson-Blackmore, St. John's.

McGrath, Sir Patrick T.

1925 Memorandum in Reply to the Canadian Case. Section V. Settlement of Hamilton Inlet. Labrador Boundary Dispute. Carton 11. Provincial Archives of Newfoundland and Labrador.

Rooms Provincial Archives Division—Birth, Death and Marriage Records. St. John's, Newfoundland.

Stopp, Marianne

2008 *The New Labrador Papers of George Cartwright*. McGill-Queen's University Press, Montreal and Kingston.

Young, Arminius

1916 *A Methodist Missionary in Labrador*. S. and A. Young, Toronto.

Zimmerly, David W.

1975 *Cain's Land Revisited*. Institute of Social and Economic Research (ISER), Memorial University, St. John's.

CHAPTER 8

"I, Old Lydia Campbell": A Labrador Woman of National Historic Significance

Marianne P. Stopp

I, old Lydia Campbell, seventy-five years old, I puts on my out-door clothes, takes my game bag and axe and matches, in case it is needed, and off I goes over across the bay, over ice and snow for about two miles and more, gets three rabbits some days out of twenty or more rabbit snares all my own chopping down . . . and you say, well done old woman [Campbell 2000:14].

In 2009, the Canadian government, on the recommendation of the Historic Sites and Monuments Board of Canada (HSMBC), designated Lydia Campbell (1818–1905) as a person of national historic significance. Since 1919, the HSMBC has provided advice to the federal government on the commemoration of places, people, and events that have marked and shaped the country's history.[1] This chapter presents Lydia Campbell's place in the Canadian historical landscape. One of Labrador's best known and most cherished foremothers, "Aunt Lydia" is known for her chronicles of Labrador history and life and is "held in high regard as a notable matriarch and transmitter of Labrador memories" (Hart 2000). Through her writing and through oral traditions passed down by her many descendants, Lydia Campbell has long been an iconic figure and a touchstone to Labrador's Inuit, Anglo, and, more recently, its Métis past.

Biographical Details

Born Lydia Brooks on November 1, 1818, Campbell lived all her life in the area of Double Mer in Groswater Bay. Her mother was an Inuk whom we know only as Susan (Baikie 1976:12). Her father was an Englishman named Ambrose Brooks[2] who arrived in Hamilton Inlet around 1800 to escape British press gangs during the Napoleonic Wars (Campbell 2000:ix, 42). Ambrose and Susan Brooks were among the earliest of the documented cross-cultural unions that came to characterize the *métissage* of south-central Labrador. Hamilton Inlet in the late eighteenth and early nineteenth centuries was inhabited by Innu, Inuit, and a small number of European men who worked for French-Canadian and Anglo merchant outfits.[3] Some of these men had partnered with Inuit women and a few of these unions can be identified in the historical record.[4] The number of European men remained relatively small until the opening of the Hudson's Bay Company (HBC) at North West River and Rigolet in 1836. Campbell's way of life followed a seasonal pattern typical of the region, whereby families had winter homes away from the coast and closer to sources of wood and trapping areas, then moved during the spring and summer months to the mouths of salmon rivers or to the mouth of the inlet for the cod fishery and sealing.

The youngest of three daughters, Lydia Campbell (Figure 1) grew up speaking English and Inuttitut. Ambrose Brooks, a minister's son, taught his daughters to read English using family letters and the few texts in his possession, which were the Bible and the *Church of England Book of Common Prayer*. Brooks was one of the first Europeans south of the Moravian stations to teach his children to read, also passing on to them a strong Christian faith (Young 1916:14).[5] From the many Christian references in her writing, it is clear that Campbell's faith remained a guiding influence throughout her life. Susan passed Inuit skills to her daughters, including

Figure 1. Lydia Campbell (far right) wearing her trademark eyeglasses, with husband Daniel Campbell and daughter Margaret (Campbell) Baikie. (Courtesy of *Them Days*, Flora Baikie collection, May 2008)

resource-harvesting techniques such as trapping, shooting, and fishing, medical knowledge, and processing techniques such as skin-clothing manufacture and food preparation. These were skills that stood Lydia and her sister Hannah in good stead throughout their very long lives (the eldest daughter, Elizabeth, born around 1808, drowned in a boating accident).

Lydia Campbell married twice. At the age of 16 she was wed against her wishes to a Labradorian of Inuit-Anglo descent named William Blake, Jr., whose father had come to Labrador in the 1780s. Lydia had five children with Blake, one of whom, Thomas, continued the family name. Following Blake's death in 1845, she lived alone with her children for three years. In 1848, she married Daniel Campbell who arrived in Labrador in 1844 from South Ronaldsey, Orkney, to work a five-year contract as cooper for the HBC at Rigolet (HBC B.183/1/1-36, entry for 24 July 1845; Powell 1986:41–43).[6] The two were married by the recently arrived HBC clerk, Donald A. Smith. They had six children, two of whom, Margaret and John, continued the Campbell family line.

In addition to her biological children, and in a benevolent tradition common along the Labrador coast, Lydia and Daniel also raised two informally adopted children. The first was an Inuk named Lemuel George, who died tragically at the age of 10. The second, Hugh Palliser, was taken in when Lydia and Daniel were in their seventies. Hugh took the Campbell name and also has a line of descendants. Daniel Campbell agreed to work with the HBC for another two years after his marriage to Lydia, and in about 1851 he became a fully independent Liveyer, or permanent resident. He occasionally took work thereafter with the HBC (Baikie 1976:31) but chiefly fished and trapped, selling his catches back to the post. Movement was central to the Campbells' way of life and they had homes in Double Mer, Cul de Sac, and later Mulligan, as well as fishing premises at Black Island, Tinker Harbour, and Burntwood Cove. Daniel Campbell was nicknamed "the Flying Dutchman" for his frequent travels around the inlet and between the HBC posts at North West River and Rigolet (HBC B.153/a/1-44, 13 Jan. 1870). Daniel and Lydia celebrated their "Golden Wedding" with a dance at North West River on September 13, 1898. Daniel Campbell died on August 12, 1900. Lydia was active into her eighty-seventh year, passing away at home on April 29, 1905. She is buried at Mulligan (Way 2006).

The Historical Importance of Lydia Campbell

Lydia Campbell's importance to Canadian history is anchored in her literary contributions. These form a valuable chronicle of the life of a woman of mixed descent but also of a way of life typical of Labrador in the late eighteenth and the nineteenth centuries. Viewed in the broader context of northern Canadian fur-trade society of that time, Campbell's life provides a rare, documented glimpse of Aboriginal women whose alliances with European men created a unique and widespread northern culture. In the context of Labrador's current politics of ethnicity, today's descendants of Campbell can be found among both the Labrador Inuit population of northern Labrador (Nunatsiavut Government) and the Labrador Métis of southern Labrador (NunatuKavut Community Council).

In the remaining text, references to "Settlers" or people of "mixed descent" will be used interchangeably to refer to this emerging Anglo-Inuit population in Hamilton Inlet. The following sub-sections consider Campbell's contribution to historical narrative, her literary contributions, her role as a cultural mediator in Hamilton Inlet, and her own perceptions of ethnicity.

Lydia Campbell as Chronicler and Memoirist

Campbell was the first born-and-bred Labradorian to write a memoir of her life in Labrador.[7] In 1894, at the age of 75, she was approached by Arthur Charles Waghorne, a Newfoundland clergyman visiting Hamilton Inlet, to write about her life, which he subsequently published in 13 short instalments entitled *Sketches of Labrador Life by a Labrador Woman* (henceforth *Sketches*) in *The Evening Herald*, a newspaper in St. John's, Newfoundland.[8] She became relatively well known beyond her Hamilton Inlet homeland thereafter. First read by an urban public, *Sketches* was written in a style that reflected Campbell's homegrown education and her Labrador English. Her writing contains "both light and dark, and significant glimpses of the native inhabitants" (Hart 2000). Foremost, it gives a rare, contemporary glimpse of colonial life spanning a time of pervasive culture change. It also reveals a resourceful, pious woman who straddled European and Inuit worlds using the beliefs, knowledge, and skills of both, sometimes in innovative ways:

> There has been many strange things happening to us in this world . . . one day as I was getting myself and children, 2 little uns . . . to see my rabbit snares, I put my little baby . . . on the bed. It rolled on to the floor and stund itself for a little while. I got a fright

> because she was not christened. So I took the book and baptized
> it with my . . . outdoor clothes on, and my Sarah, 5 years old,
> standing by. . . . When she . . . was all right . . . I took it on my back,
> and lead the other by the hand with my axe, through the snow, to
> my rabbit snares and got a few rabbits [Campbell 2000:35].

In Labrador, history has been passed through the generations in the form of oral narratives conveyed in personal stories that come together as family and community memory. In its structure and level of detail, *Sketches* reflects oral narrative put to paper. It finds its roots both in Campbell's Inuit background and also in the strong oral traditions of her English father. Although it is a relatively short document, *Sketches* is enriching to the people of Labrador because it is a unique first-hand account of a part of their history. It contains minutiae of ancestors' lives that resonate with experiences still in living memory, especially details often absent in formal histories but specific to Labrador life, such as Campbell's description of an old way of catching trout when winter ice has formed:

> and when the ice comes on the rivers . . . then is what we calls
> trouting. Our grandchildren comes from their homes to gather
> here. Then the ice is alive with trout, fine large ones and little
> ones. What fun following the trout as the tide rises or the falling
> water, all chopping ice as hard as they can [Campbell 2000:15].

Labradorians of mixed descent such as Lydia Campbell and her Anglo-Inuit family introduced an entirely new way of life to Hamilton Inlet. They combined traditional seasonal resource practices such as sealing and salmon fishing with the trapping and gardening of a mercantile economy; they blended traditional Inuit foods and preparations with European fare and vegetables; European religious and social traditions were combined with Inuit ways; and traditional clothing, equipment, and housing styles were integrated with the European. These remain elements of life today made rich by their record in Campbell's early writing.

Campbell witnessed tremendous social and environmental changes in Hamilton Inlet and *Sketches* provides glimpses of these, including candid observations about the impacts of alcohol upon the local population and perceptible shifts in human (and animal) populations:

> The times have changed now from them times that I have been writing about. The first time that my dear old father came from England what few whites was here they was scattered about . . . no one to see for miles but Eskimaux and Mountaineers [Innu] and they was plentiful . . . where are they now? [Campbell 2000:49].

Elements of formal Labrador history are confirmed in *Sketches*, where we learn of the earliest Englishmen in Hamilton Inlet who settled there with Inuit wives. This was oral history knowledge passed down from her parents, who knew William Phippard and John Newhook, whom Campbell calls "John Knocks":

> There were landed here some people looking for a place [and] given provisions and were promised to get picked up the next year, but the [ships] never came back for three years, so my father told us, for he saw them when he came from England . . . they went to the Eskimaux (for they was plentiful at that time) and got seal skin clothes from them and meat to eat. When the white people came back to see whether they was dead or alive, they found them dressed like the natives about here at that time . . . these two, William Phipperd and John Knocks [Campbell 2000:26; 1989:62].

This same information is found in Captain George Cartwright's journal for 1778 (1792: entries for September 9 and December 24, 1778).[9] Anglo–Inuit unions began somewhat earlier south of Hamilton Inlet; several of Cartwright's men had Inuit wives in the 1770s. Cartwright himself may have fathered a son by an Inuit woman sometime before 1786, as discovered in Moravian archival material (Stopp 2008:30, 73).

Campbell's writing is a straightforward account of the daily lives and concerns of nineteenth-century colonial Labrador, especially of its women. Historical references to Inuit women's lives at the cusp of the European settlement period are brief but illuminate elements of family and gender relations within Inuit society at a time when Inuit women may have been choosing to establish unions with European men. The reasons for this may be found in Inuit society itself, where associations with Europeans held advantages (for Inuit women and men), and where elemental changes in power structures due to European arrival may have marginalized women's roles in Inuit society. Campbell's account of the runaway Inuit girl cared for by European trappers is reminiscent of others found in Labrador documents. Two examples include that of the Inuit woman Mikak, whose treatment at the hands of Tuglavina is revealing and not unusual for its time, and the account of an Inuit girl-servant who fled her Inuit family to find a better life working for George Cartwright (Campbell 1989:56–57; Cartwright 1792: entry for 7 December 1770; Stopp 2009:52–53).[10]

For her readership in distant St. John's, Campbell's descriptions of life in the inlet counterbalanced, and perhaps at times corrected, prevailing perceptions of backwardness and deprivation as presented by many period visitors to Labrador. Their assessments of thriftlessness and the lack of "get up and go" of Labrador's people were generally based on superficial observations made from ship's deck or during brief disembarkations at community wharves (e.g., Packard 1891). A prevailing absence of close knowledge of Labrador society prevented understanding of the impositions of an unforgiving merchant system that had been in place since 1763, but also of the abilities and innovations of its people who lived self-sufficient and productive lives (Kennedy 1995:94). Campbell showed the outside world that perceived hardships were managed through a range of skills and practices rooted in traditional ways, and that woman in these contexts had relevant skills and were capable actors. One such example described her resourceful older sister Hannah Michelin:

> I have known [Hannah] fighting with a wolverine . . . she had neither gun nor axe, but a stout little stick, yet she killed it after a long battle. . . . She brought up her first family of little children when their father died, teached all to read and write in the long winter nights, and hunt . . . in the day. . . . She would take the little ones on the sled, haul them over snow and ice to a large river, chop ice about three feet thick, catch about two or three hundred trout . . . and haul them and the children home perhaps in the night [Campbell 2000:7–9].

Campbell also recorded observations of Innu and Inuit life that stand alongside George Cartwright's as invaluable, early first-hand, ethno-historic accounts. One tells of "the Eskimaux's notion about the flood, handed down from generation to generation." Another is of an Innu belief in spirits at Churchill Falls, and several entries refer to the old way of life of both peoples:

> Their [Innu] tent was made of deerskin and birch bark and . . . 7 feet long and about the same width; a ridge of snow covered with [fir] branches for their pillows around the tent: all looking so happy with deers [sic] meat stuck up on scivers [skewers] made of wood [Campbell 1989:59].

> I have seen fifteen, as far as twenty, Eskimos seal skin tents in my time scattered here in little groups not far from each other, five or six tents together and such a bustle, women cleaning seal skins and covering kayaks, their little boats. The men out on the water after a large school of seals, throwing their darts at the end of their houliack harpoon strap [Campbell 2000:50].

Campbell's Literary Contributions

The benefits of Lydia Campbell's education were passed to her children, grandchildren, and adopted children, whom she taught to read and write. Her sister Hannah also educated her family, and together this small population of literate individuals grew to influence broader aspects of Hamilton Inlet society. It is also worth noting that relatively well-educated Inuit from the Moravian missions moved to Hamilton Inlet in the 1820s whose learning and Christian conviction stood them in good stead for HBC employment (Rollmann 2008, 2010).

Literacy held social and economic value in Hamilton Inlet. Those who could read, write, and/or understand basic arithmetic could manage economic relations both as Liveyeres and as employees of the growing numbers of merchant firms that arrived after 1830 such as Nathanial Jones, David Ramsay Stewart, Hunt and Henley, and the HBC. A legacy of literacy followed Lydia Campbell's son, John Campbell, for the span of his lifetime. He moved to St. Michael's Bay as an adult and was one of the few literate individuals along the southern Labrador coast. Upon his death in 1935, the church in his summer fishing community of Square Islands had to close because there was no longer anyone who could read the liturgy (Way 2006:33).[11] The literacy of Hamilton Inlet's residents was noted by a number of nineteenth- and early twentieth-century visitors to the area, and it was known as one of the few places in the British colonies where residents were not only versed in the Christian liturgy without ever having met clergy, but were remarkably literate despite the absence of teachers (Wallace 1932:284–285; Young 1916:14).[12]

Lydia Campbell pioneered a way of writing about Labrador that is both history and personal memoir (Buchanan 1986). Her efforts inspired many later Labradorians to set down reminiscences as a form of historical record, beginning with Campbell's own daughter, Margaret Baikie, whose *Labrador Memories—Reflections of Mulligan* (1976) was written around 1918 and covers the years as far back as 1846. Perhaps it is not by chance that other Labrador memoirists who have written in Campbell's genre also happen to be descendants. Campbell's great-granddaughter,

Elizabeth Goudie, published *Woman of Labrador* in 1973, winning the 1976 Canadian Book Award. Goudie is also featured in the National Film Board's *A Family of Labrador* (1978) and received an honorary doctorate from Memorial University of Newfoundland in 1975. A great-grandson, Benjamin Powell of Charlottetown, Labrador, has published numerous volumes of Labrador stories and is a recipient of the Order of Canada. Doris Saunders, great-great granddaughter of Campbell and editor of *Them Days* for nearly 30 years, compiled one of the largest collections of oral history and genealogical information about Labrador, earning her an Order of Canada and an honorary doctorate from Memorial University of Newfoundland. Many articles published in *Them Days* and other Labrador publications follow Campbell's informal, unstructured style, and use autobiography as a way of documenting the past (Battle Harbour Literacy Council 1998, 1999, 2000; Maggo 1999; White 2004; Montague 2013).

Sketches has been reprinted several times since its appearance in 1894–1895 and continues to be read and studied today as a literary work, as a historical text of the Settler experience, as early autobiography, women's writing, and Aboriginal writing, and as one of the few accounts about and by colonial women who were not of the middle or upper classes (e.g., Ball 1976; Buchanan 1986, 1987, 1991, 1995; Hart 1977, 1982; Hulan 2002; Petrone 1988).

Campbell as Cultural Mediator

Lydia Campbell is representative of the role held by many Indigenous women across the Canadian North who facilitated colonial efforts. These women provided a bridge for European newcomers, at times ensuring the latters' very survival and certainly their eventual successes and, as Brown (2009) emphasizes, their patriarchies. Although largely invisible in formal history, figures such as another northern Métis matriarch, Catherine Beaulieu Bouvier Lamoureux (ca. 1836–1918) from Fort Providence, Northwest Territories, were cornerstones of social development in the North. Like Campbell, Lamoureux remains a cherished icon whose descendants are numerous and whose life story figures large in oral accounts (Stopp and Constantin 2009). Similarly, the young Dene woman Thanadelthur, who helped HBC trader William Stuart negotiate his way through Cree country in 1715, was central to the success of colonial efforts (Coutts 1999; Van Kirk 1980:69), as was Scottish-Woods Cree Charlotte Small, who ensured the success of explorer David Thompson's travels and mapping of immense areas of western Canada and the United States, ca. 1800 (Brown 2007; Van Kirk 1980:97).[13]

For its part, *Sketches* is invaluable for the "teeth" it gives to the premise that Aboriginal know-how and specifically female intervention, bonding, technical skills, and overall local knowledge were vital to European foundations in Labrador. Campbell's daughter Margaret recorded, for instance, that Daniel Campbell "did not know much about trapping. My mother used to go with him to set the traps" (Baikie 1976:2). Campbell (2000:9) noted that the HBC's servants used to get local women to supply them with clothing suited for the Labrador climate, including pants, shirts, flannel slips, drawers, sealskin boots, deerskin shoes, and caps, details that are confirmed in the HBC records for North West River.

A scattering of historical information suggests that Lydia Campbell served as an important point of contact for newcomers and as a cultural mediator between people of the inlet and visitors from elsewhere, especially church representatives. Campbell facilitated the efforts of several missionaries at a time when the Moravian, Wesleyan Methodist, Anglican, and Roman Catholic churches all considered setting up ministries in south-central Labrador (Rollmann 2010). Missionaries were on different occasions directed to Campbell by the people of the inlet partly because her piousness was recognized by all, but also in recognition of her role as an educated elder whose opinion in the context of inlet society was respected. In 1857, Moravian missionary Ferdinand Elsner travelled in April by sledge from Nain to the HBC post at North West River to ascertain whether a mission could be established somewhere in Hamilton Inlet. En route he was directed to the Campbell home in Mulligan where he received Campbell's advice that a mission would be welcomed but that attendance would be compromised by the distances between households. Despite the project's full backing from HBC Chief Trader Donald Smith, who committed £100 per annum to the project, the Moravians eventually decided against the venture, probably having considered Campbell's observations (Zimmerly 1975:81–83).

In August of 1891, Dr. John Clement Parker, a member of the Bowdoin College Scientific Expedition to Labrador, visited "the old lady Mrs. Lydia Campbell" over several days at their summer home on what appears to have been Esquimaux Island (Kennedy 2010). Methodist Reverend Arminius Young became a great admirer of Campbell's, visiting her for extended periods during his two-year stay in Labrador. His first impression of her in 1902, when she was 83, is endearing and enduring:

> At 10 o'clock I noticed boats coming from all directions. From one of them there stepped ashore an old, dumpy and interesting-looking lady. I saw, through the dining-room window, that as she came along she had a word to say to everybody, and everybody had a word to say to her [Young 1916:39].

That same morning, his first Sabbath service in Groswater Bay, Young was given unsolicited advice by Campbell: "Now, my son," she cautioned in her Labrador cadences, "you must go out into the kitchen and talk to the people as the other ministers used to do. . . . If you don't the people won't like you" (Young 1916:39). A previous Methodist incumbent, whose preaching had been emotional and zealous, failed to heed her warning not to "preach like that" in the lumber camps dotting the shore of Hamilton Inlet at that time, "because they will make fun at you if you do." As she had predicted, the lumbermen received that particular gospel "with demonstrations of power and that without any apology. His stay on the coast was short" (Young 1916:32–33).[14]

Lydia Campbell's Observations on Her Ethnicity

Campbell's writing intimates that she placed herself "among the few whites" (Campbell 2000:14) in Hamilton Inlet while recognizing that this group was of mixed descent, as in, "our dear Elizabeth got married to a young half-breed as we was" (Campbell 2000:13). She draws a fine distinction between her bloodline and ways and those of the Inuit of the inlet, describing their way of life as an observer and not as a member participant. Campbell was the first Labradorian to express self-identity and a consciousness of mixed descent in her use of the term "half-breed," limning an awareness that was by then an established part of the social landscape: "Through the snow, to my rabbit snares and got a few rabbits . . . not for want of hunger . . . but for custom. Such was life among the half-breeds of Eskimaux Bay" (Campbell 2000:37).

Campbell has a symbolic (and genetic) role in the formulation of concepts of mixed descent and identity politics, since European patrilineal systems were not readily available to this emerging population and present-day membership inevitably extends back to female roots, albeit often unknown.

The way of life of the small, mixed-descent population of Hamilton Inlet was defined by the fur trade, as in the rest of the Canadian North, distinguishing it from many of the Innu and Inuit of the region who participated in aspects of this economy but who were not tied to it in the same way as families such as the Campbells. Such a way of life included European domestic patterns, social customs, language, religion, skills, and work habits that together resonated with merchants' notions of capability. These were bridging elements that allowed relatively seamless entry into this economy, especially with the HBC when it opened its first posts in Labrador in 1836, later than elsewhere in Canada. At that time the population of Lake Melville area stood at 37 Settlers. Well-known names such as Thomas Groves, George Flowers, John Mason, William Blake, William Mesher, John Mesher, and William Phippard appear in HBC records alongside even earlier French-Canadian names such as Old

Dubais.[15] Most, if not all, were men with Inuit or mixed-descent wives and families but little is known about these women. Such alliances in fact predated the HBC in Hamilton Inlet by about 50 years, but it is quite likely that even earlier ones (with Inuit and Innu women) began when Quebec-based trader Louis Fornel opened a year-round post in 1743, marking the start of 85 years of French traders in the inlet.[16] The resident settler population was described by Reverend Thomas Hickson in 1824, who counted 326 people of whom he considered 60 to be of mixed descent ("half-Eskimos"), 160 "pure Eskimo," 90 European Settlers, and 16 French-Canadian (Tanner 1947:466). It is quite likely that a substantial number of the "pure Eskimo," "European," and French-Canadian inhabitants enumerated by Hickson were in fact of mixed descent.

Early mixed-descent families in Hamilton Inlet emerged as overwhelmingly successful competitors for jobs in the fur trade; as already noted, ethnicity became tied to economic success through employability. These families earned income by provisioning the post, and in resource extraction industries such as trapping, salmon fishing, sealing, and the cod fishery. Success was also tied to resource territory expansion. In a letter tabled before the Boundary Commission, Stuart Cotter (1922), factor at North West River post during the years 1893–1901 and 1904–1906, noted the aggressive expansion of Settler trapping activities on behalf of the HBC into Innu lands. Although trapping had subsided almost entirely by the 1950s, it continued to be an elemental aspect of identity well into the 1980s (Plaice 1990) and remains so today.[17] For the Innu, these traditional territories could never be reclaimed because of further land losses due to the Churchill hydroelectric development, the designation of NATO military camp and training areas (Wadden 1991; Mailhot 1997; Pepamuteiati Nitassinat 2008), and the appearance of fishing and hunting lodges on interior lake systems.

Self-awareness of a distinct ethnicity among the Settler families of Hamilton Inlet is mirrored in the partnerships of French and Anglo fur traders with Aboriginal women across the Canadian North. These partnerships began with the North West Company (NWC) in the Canadian

West in the late eighteenth century and continued after its merger in 1821 with the HBC. The Company's governor, George Simpson, introduced a culture of race awareness and class that differed from the earlier NWC, but by the 1840s he was forced to admit the necessity and advantages of having mixed-descent workers and local women. Lydia Campbell's awareness of her separate ethnicity resembles and finds context in this broader fur-trade society, as does her education. By the 1820s, many offspring of mixed unions were comfortable with a dual heritage that combined knowledge of the backcountry with literacy and Christianity. Diverse cultural ties were expressed in their fur-trade roles as cultural brokers and interpreters and, in time, as teachers, catechists, clerks, small traders, and commissioned HBC officers (Brown 1980a, 1980b; Fuchs 2000; St. Onge et al. 2012).

Despite their education, however, the children of the fur trade struggled against subtle prejudices. While acknowledging their wilderness skills and ability to communicate with Aboriginal populations, the HBC believed mixed-descent men tended towards unruly behaviour. At the same time, mixed-descent women were subject to rigorous and unyielding social expectations and class assessments (Brown 1980a; Goldring 1979).

In Hamilton Inlet the situation may have been somewhat different, at least after 1848 when two of the leading fur-trade families in the district were themselves distinguished by mixed bloodlines. In 1848, Richard Hardisty (ca. 1792–1865) became district chief trader at the Esquimaux Bay post in Hamilton Inlet. The Hardisty family arrived in North West River having canoed and boated their way from distant Moose Factory. Hardisty's wife, Margaret Sutherland (ca. 1802–1876), was the daughter of Scots fur trader John Sutherland (fl. 1778–1813) and Jeanny Sutherland, a literate and capable Swampy Cree woman from Albany District, west of Hudson Bay (Van Kirk 1980:103). The Hardisty family in all respects symbolized the realities of fur-trade society of the mid-1800s, and readily fit into the life of the inlet.

Donald Smith (1820–1914) arrived at the same time as Hardisty and from 1848 to 1852 served as clerk at Rigolet. He became chief trader of the district upon Hardisty's departure in 1852 and chief factor in 1862 until 1868 before moving to Montreal, where he served as chief factor of the vast Montreal Department. Much later he became governor of the HBC (1889) and Baron Strathcona and Mount Royal (1897). While the Hardisty family was still resident in North West River, Smith began a lifelong partnership with Hardisty's daughter, Isabella Sophia Hardisty Grant (Brown 1980a:215; HBC, Biographical Sheets; MacDonald 1996). Isabella had been sent to school in England and was "well equipped to function in her future role as Lady Strathcona" (Van Kirk 1980:233), but she was also a woman of the North, of mixed descent, and at home among the people of the inlet.

Under their regime, Settler families were less affected by HBC prejudices than under previous Esquimaux Bay District factors. The tenor of the HBC journals kept by Hardisty and Smith stand in contrast with those of the first chief trader of the district (1836–1841), Simon Mc-Gillivray, Jr., whose prejudices mirrored those of the Company as a whole and extended to his Orkneymen crew, to rival firms in the bay, and to local families (HBC 1836). Under Hardisty and Smith, the Campbells flourished, as did other inlet families (and the HBC). Smith spent many a night in the Campbell home while travelling up and down the inlet and Lydia's daughters cared for the Smith children (Baikie 1976:5, 12). Campbell was living at Mulligan River in April 1894 when she wrote that, "many is the time that I have been going with dogs and komatik, 40 or 50 years ago with my husband and family, up to North West River, to the Hon. Donald A. Smith and family to keep New Year or Easter" (Campbell 2000:25).

Conclusion

Little is known of the early generation of northern women whose way of life spanned both the Aboriginal and the European. The oral accounts that remain of most of these northern matriarchs emerge from the collective memory of extended family ties that are vast and represent "family history on a grand scale" in the North (Hanks 1999:1). Shared memories are the essence of community and belonging, and are cherished from Labrador to Yukon, but such memories have become increasingly fragile with time. These accounts are found outside formal historiography yet contain valuable glimpses of the northern past, of the central role played by women and their capability, and of an early way of life of Métis peoples that began in female bloodlines (Brown 1980a; Van Kirk 1980; Brown and Peterson 1985; Métis Heritage Association 1998).

Lydia Campbell's life story is thus doubly significant to Canadian history for what it tells us of these early matriarchs. Like their stories, it has been quilted together from oral accounts and limited printed documents. From such sources, we come to appreciate Campbell's contribution to the development of Labrador society, to education, and to passing on an "old way" of life that informs identity today.

Aunt Lydia is a familiar figure in the iconography of the province of Newfoundland and Labrador, and has been recognized in a number of ways. Alongside her many literary reappearances, her role as an esteemed matriarch was reflected in the play *All Lydia's Children*, written and produced in 1987 by young people from North West River for the Labrador Arts Festival. It parodied a familiar afternoon television program through the many and diverse dramas of a small Labrador town.[18] The Lydia Campbell Award for Writing was established by the Newfoundland and Labrador Arts Council in 1985 and is awarded annually to a writer of distinction. The Lydia Campbell Building in Happy Valley-Goose Bay houses the *Them Days* office and archive.

In closing, Lydia Campbell's importance to Canadian history lies in her literary and educational contributions. *Sketches of Labrador Life* represents the beginnings of a literary tradition in Labrador that presents history though autobiography, and provides a pragmatic account of the daily lives, concerns, and beliefs of late eighteenth- and nineteenth-century colonial Labrador as observed by a woman of Inuit and British descent. She is representative of the role held by many Inuit and

Inuit-Anglo women in Labrador and throughout the North, of facilitating colonial efforts through partnerships with European newcomers and through their unique skill-sets needed to carry out the goals of early colonial economy. Campbell's writing and the various oral accounts that exist of her have given the people of Labrador, with their roots in several cultures, a significant part of their early colonial history, in turn affirming self-identification through knowledge of the past.

Notes

1. Directory of Federal Heritage Designations; at http://www.pc.gc.ca/apps/dfhd/default_eng.aspx.
2. Referred to as William Brooks in Young (1916:13). The Campbell family tree has been compiled by Way (2006; chapter 7).
3. These included people of French, Scottish, English, Irish, and/or Orkney descent.
4. Little is known of partnerships between European men and Innu women.
5. From her own account, it appears that Lydia Campbell taught herself to write later in life, and Young (1916:13) further states that for this she used letters from her father's family.
6. An overview of the political and economic circumstances that led to the arrival in Hamilton Inlet of men from the West Country and from the Orkneys can be found in Plaice (1990:23–27).
7. The earliest published account in English of life in Labrador was by Captain George Cartwright, an Englishman who operated merchant stations between St. Lewis Inlet and Sandwich Bay for 16 years and lived there intermittently (Cartwright 1792; Stopp 2008). Unpublished for over a century was Abraham Ulrikab's 1880–1881 account in Inuttitut of his life while in Europe before dying of smallpox (Lutz et al. 2005).
8. Two sources must be consulted for all of Campbell's installments: Campbell (1989) and Campbell (2000). Campbell had once before written a memoir at the request of a Reverend A. A. Adams, "but he lost it" (Campbell 2000:15).
9. In 1902, only two of the earliest generation of Englishmen were still alive. Joseph Lloyd and Charles Allen had married Inuit sisters (Young 1916:47–48). The bulk of the population in Groswater Bay by this time was Euro–Inuit with a few full-blooded Inuit in the Rigolet area who had originally come from the northern coast.
10. Inuit men also offered females for sale or barter. At least one female Inuk in Cartwright's household was purchased. Cartwright (1792:entry for 16 Nov. 1773) refers to "my slave girl" who ran away for a night to spend time with her

mother. Slavery was still very much a part of British society. Of interest is that George Cartwright's brother, Major John Cartwright, was a leading activist in the anti-slavery movement.

11. Many families in St. Michael's Bay are descendants of Lydia Campbell through John Campbell (author interviews with O. Marshall, S. Campbell, Charlottetown, Labrador, July 2012).

12. See also Judge Sweetland's remarks (Judicial Committee of the Privy Council (JCPC) 1972:1864, No. 529, 1448); Judge Pinsent's remarks (JCPC 1927:1867, No. 529, 1454); Zimmerly (1975:103–105). This was also true in Sandwich Bay as noted by Bishop Feild (1849:19) in 1848, who observed a largely Anglican populace, among whom were many Inuit, who could read the Anglican catechism, write, and speak English.

13. Similarly, the Labrador Inuit woman Mikak (ca. 1740–1795), designated by the HSMBC as a Person of National Historic Significance in 2011, aided British colonial efforts while in England and in Labrador (Stopp 2009).

14. By 1902, several lumber camps operated in Hamilton Inlet belonging to the Grand River Pulp and Lumber Company of Stewiacke, NS, owned by Alfred Dickie, who held leases for nearly 300 square miles of timber along the north and south sides of the inlet (JCPC 1927:1:136).

15. When the HBC opened its posts in 1835–1836, the population of year-round Settlers of European descent in the Lake Melville area consisted mainly of individuals with Anglo names, as well as a few with French names. Some had lived in Hamilton Inlet since 1800 or earlier and had Inuit wives. Names on record of these permanent Settlers were Thomas Groves (at Traverspine), George Flowers, Old Dubais, John Mason, William Blake, William Mesher, John Mesher, William Phippard (known to be at Double Mer), Ambrose Brooks, John Newhook, James Sutton, Charles William, Francis Quirk, Charles Davis, Patrick Sullivan, James Morris, James Goodenough, H. Lucy, Patrick Connors, William Fancy, Jonathon Kennedy, Josh Wills, John Mudge, George Pottle, John Reed, Thomas Broomfield, and Josh Broomfield. There were also merchants and/or their representatives present in the inlet, but these were not considered Settlers and may only have kept summer residency (HBC B153/a/1-11; Anick 1976:667–672; Zimmerly 1975:31–65).

16. The known French establishments began with grants to L. Fornel, followed by his widow M. Barbel (1743–ca. 1755); then an unknown trader ca. 1757; in turn followed by Jacob Pozer (1770s to 1823); Pierre Marcoux (ca. 1785–1799); P. Marcoux and Dumontier (ca. 1799 to ca. 1820s); Flavien Dufresne, who purchased the Pozer properties (1823–1828); Jean Olivier Brunet, who purchased the Dufresne properties in 1828 and sold them a year later to William Lampson and David Ramsay Stewart. The first Englishmen operating in the inlet may have been Jeremiah Coghlan's planters, ca. 1777–1778. Thereafter, English operated

alongside French-Canadian furring and sealing concerns. Robert Collingham began to trade around Rigolet in ca. 1785 (probably in partnership with Pierre Marcoux), and Thomas Bird established a salmon fishery at Kenemish in 1824, followed by several larger merchant concerns.

17. In Plaice's (1990) interesting study of Settler–Innu dynamics and identity, she observed that identity was self-referential and situation-dependent. The study presents a picture of identity just before the growth of the Labrador Métis movement and before "Settlers" began to consider themselves as Inuit. In 1962–1963, Ben-Dor (1966) argued that the ethnic differences between Inuit and Settler in Makkovik might not be apparent to an outsider, but that the distinction was clear to the people themselves. Situational factors included the language one was brought up in, birth location, geography, and the family one was raised in. Over time, mobility or passing from one group to another was possible but was not like "club membership" that actors joined or quit (1966:151). The ethnic divide Ben-Dor (1966) described remained firm when restudied by Kennedy in 1971–1972 (1982).

18. Timothy Borlase, Labrador Institute (retired), and Martha MacDonald, Labrador Institute (personal communications, 7 April 2008).

References Cited

Anick, Norman
> 1976 *The Fur Trade in Eastern Canada until 1870.* Manuscript Report 207. Parks Canada, Ottawa.

Baikie, Flora
> 1976 I Likes to Go Fishing. *Them Days* 1(4):12–14.

Baikie, Margaret
> 1976 *Labrador Memories — Reflections at Mulligan, Happy Valley.* Them Days, Happy Valley-Goose Bay.

Ball, Jean
> 1976 Lydia Campbell. In *Remarkable Women of Newfoundland and Labrador*, edited by St. John's Local Council of Women, pp. 10–16. Valhalla Press, St. John's.

Battle Harbour Literacy Council
> 1998 *Linking the Generations.* Battle Harbour Literacy Council, Battle Harbour.
> 1999 *Our Time, Our Story.* Battle Harbour Literacy Council, Battle Harbour.
> 2000 *Twinelofts and Pantries.* Battle Harbour Literacy Council, Battle Harbour.

Ben-Dor, Shmuel
> 1966 *Makkovik: Eskimos and Settlers in a Labrador Community.* Social and Economic Studies No. 4. Institute of Social and Economic Research (ISER Books), St. John's.

Brown, Jennifer S. H.

1980a *Strangers in Blood: Fur Trade Company Families in Indian Country.* University of British Columbia Press, Vancouver.

1980b Linguistic Solitudes and Changing Social Categories. In *Old Trails and New Directions: Papers of the Third North American Fur Trade Conference,* edited by Carol M. Judd and Arthur J. Ray, pp. 145–159. University of Toronto Press, Toronto.

2007 Charlotte Small (1785–1857). Historic Sites and Monuments Board of Canada Submission Report 2007–13. On file, Parks Canada.

2009 Woman as Centre and Symbol in the Emergence of Metis Communities. In *Rethinking the Fur Trade,* edited by Susan Sleeper-Smith, pp 519–528. University of Nebraska Press, Lincoln.

Brown, Jennifer S. H., and Jacqueline Peterson (editors)

1985 *The New Peoples: Being and Becoming Métis in North America.* University of Nebraska Press, Lincoln.

Buchanan, Roberta

1986 Autobiography as History: The Autobiographies of Three Labrador Women—Lydia Campbell, Margaret Baikie, and Elizabeth Goudie. In *Newfoundland History: Proceedings of the First Newfoundland History Conference,* edited by Shannon Ryan, pp. 73–85. Newfoundland Historical Society, St. John's.

1987 Life into Art: Some Theoretical Approaches to Autobiography and Lydia Campbell's "Sketches of Labrador Life." On file, English Department, Memorial University of Newfoundland.

1991 Country Ways and Fashions: Lydia Campbell's "Sketches of Labrador Life": A Study in Folklore and Literature. In *Studies in Newfoundland Folklore: Community and Process,* edited by Gerald Thomas and John D. A. Widdowson, pp. 289–308. Breakwater, St. John's.

1995 Autobiography as History: The Autobiographies of Three Labrador Women—Lydia Campbell, Margaret Baikie, and Elizabeth Goudie. In *Their Lives and Times: Women in Newfoundland and Labrador, a Collage,* edited by Carmelita McGrath, Barbara Neis, and Marilyn Porter, pp. 67–74. Killick Press, St. John's.

Campbell, Lydia

1989 Sketches of Labrador Life. *Them Days* 14(3):56–63.

2000 *Sketches of Labrador Life.* Killick Press and Them Days, St. John's.

Cartwright, George

1792 *A Journal of Transactions and Events during a Residence of Nearly Sixteen Years on the Coast of Labrador.* 3 vols. Allin and Ridge, Newark, England.

Cotter, Stuart

1922 Letter of Stuart Cotter to Sir Patrick McGrath, 10 April 1922, Provincial Archives of Newfoundland and Labrador, MG-8, Box 15, File 1.

Coutts, Robert
1999 Thanadelthur. HSMBC Agenda Paper 1999–50. On file, Parks Canada.

Feild, Bishop Edward
1849 *Church in the Colonies No. 19, A Visit to Labrador*. Society for the Propagation of the Gospel, London.

Fuchs, Denise
2000 Native Sons of Rupert's Land, 1760 to the 1860s. Unpublished Ph.D. dissertation, Department of History, University of Manitoba, Winnipeg.

Goldring, Peter
1979 *Papers on the Labour System of the Hudson's Bay Company, 1821–1900*, Vol. 1. Manuscript Report 362. Parks Canada, Ottawa.

Goudie, Elizabeth
1973 *Woman of Labrador*. Peter Martin, Toronto.

HBC, Biographical Sheets
Electronic document, http://www.gov.mb.ca/chc/archives/hbca/biographical/, accessed June 6, 2013.

Hanks, Christopher
1999 Francois Beaulieu II: Son of the Last Coureurs de Bois in the Far Northwest. HSMBC Agenda Paper 1999–51. Parks Canada, Ottawa.

Hart, Anne
1977 Sketches of Labrador Life. In *From This Place: A Selection of Writing by Women of Newfoundland and Labrador*, edited by Bernice Morgan, Helen Porter, and Geraldine Rubia, pp. 44–47. Jesperson Press, St. John's.
1982 Sketches of Labrador Life. *Canadian Women's Studies* 3(1):4–9.
2000 Brooks, Lydia. *Dictionary of Canadian Biography*. Electronic document, http://www.biographi.ca/EN/ShowBio.asp?BioId= 40704&query=brooks, accessed September 19, 2013.

Hudson's Bay Company (HBC)
1836 Journal of Occurrences of the Post of Esquimaux Bay. HBC B153/a/1.

Hulan, Renée
2002 *Northern Experience and the Myths of Canadian Culture*. McGill-Queen's University Press, Montreal and Kingston.

Judicial Committee of the Privy Council (JCPC) (Great Britain)
1927 *In the Matter of the Boundary between the Dominion of Canada and the Colony of Newfoundland in the Labrador Peninsula, between the Dominion of Canada of the One Part and the Colony of Newfoundland of the Other*. W. Clowes & Sons, London.

Kennedy, John C.
1982 *Holding the Line: Ethnic Boundaries in a Northern Labrador Community*. Social and Economic Studies No. 27. ISER Books, St. John's.

1995 *People of the Bays and Headlands*. University of Toronto Press, Toronto.

2010 Visitors' Accounts of Inuit-Métis between Cape Charles and Cape Harrison, Labrador. Unpublished Report to Labrador Métis Nation.

Lutz, Hartmut, Alootook Ipellie, and Hans-Ludwig Blohm
2005 *The Diary of Abraham Ulrikab*. University of Ottawa Press, Ottawa.

MacDonald, Donna
1996 *Lord Strathcona: A Biography of Donald Alexander Smith*. Dundurn Press, Toronto.

Mailhot, José
1997 *The People of Sheshatshit*. Social and Economic Studies No. 58. ISER Books, St. John's.

Maggo, Paulus
1999 *Remembering the Years of My Life: Journeys of a Labrador Inuit Hunter*, edited by Carol Brice-Bennett. Social and Economic Studies No. 63. ISER Books, St. John's.

Métis Heritage Association
1998 *Picking up the Threads: Métis History in the Mackenzie Basin*. Métis Heritage Association of the Northwest Territories and Parks Canada, Yellowknife.

Montague, Louie
2013 *I Never Knowed It Was Hard: Memoirs of a Labrador Trapper*, Edited by Elizabeth Dawson. Social and Economic Studies No. 74. ISER Books, St. John's.

Packard, Alpheus S.
1891 *The Labrador Coast: A Journal of Two Summer Cruises to that Region*. H. D. C. Hodges, New York.

Pepamuteiati Nitassinat
2008 Electronic document, http://www.innuplaces.ca/credits.php?lang=en, accessed February 12, 2013.

Petrone, Penny
1988 *Inuit Writing in English*. University of Toronto Press, Toronto.

Plaice, Evelyn
1990 *The Native Game: Settler Perceptions of Indian–Settler Relations in Central Labrador*. Social and Economic Studies No. 40. ISER Books, St. John's.

Powell, Roland E.
1986 Daniel Campbell. *Them Days* 11(4):41–43.

Rollmann, Hans J.
2008 Moravian Education in Labrador: A Legacy of Literacy. In *Symposium 2008: Post-Confederation Education Reform—From Rhetoric to Reality*, edited by Gerald Galway and David Dibbon, pp. 227–236. Memorial University of Newfoundland, St. John's.

2010 Moravians in Central Labrador: The Indigenous Inuit Mission of Jacobus and Salome at Snooks Cove. *Journal of Moravian History* 9:7–40.

St. Onge, Nicole, Carolyn Podruchny, and Brenda Macdougall (editors)
2012 *Contours of a People: Metis Family, Mobility and History.* University of Oklahoma Press, Norman.

Stopp, Marianne P.
2008 *The New Labrador Papers of Captain George Cartwright.* McGill-Queen's Press, Montreal and Kingston.
2009 Eighteenth Century Labrador Inuit in England. *Arctic* 62(1):45–64.

Stopp, Marianne, and Jennifer Constantin
2009 Catherine Beaulieu Bouvier Lamoureux (ca. 1836–1918). HSMBC Supplementary Report 2009-23-A. On file, Parks Canada.

Tanner, Vaino
1947 *Outlines of the Geography, Life and Customs of Newfoundland*, Vol. 2 (*Labrador*). Cambridge University Press, Cambridge.

Van Kirk, Sylvia.
1980 *"Many Tender Ties": Women in Fur-Trade Society in Western Canada, 1670–1870.* Watson & Dwyer, Winnipeg.

Wadden, Marie
1991 *Nitassinan: The Innu Struggle to Reclaim Their Homeland.* Douglas & McIntyre, Vancouver.

Wallace, William S.
1932 *John McLean's Notes of a Twenty Five Years' Service in the Hudson's Bay Territory.* The Champlain Society, Toronto

Way, Patricia
2006 Descendants of Lydia (Brooks) (Blake) Campbell. Unpublished manuscript on file, Parks Canada, Ottawa.

White, Winston
2004 *Labrador: Getting Along in the Big Land.* Flanker Press, St. John's.

Young, Rev. Arminius
1916 *A Methodist Missionary in Labrador.* S. and A. Young, Toronto.

Zimmerly, David W.
1975 *Cain's Land Revisited: Culture Change in Central Labrador, 1775–1972.* Social and Economic Studies No. 16. ISER Books, St. John's

"... That Between Their Church and Ours There Is Hardly Any Difference": Settler Families on Labrador's North Coast Join the Moravian Church

Hans J. Rollmann

In the 1850s the Reed, Lane, Voisey, and Mitchell families, all Settlers from north and south of Hopedale, attached themselves to the Moravian Church. Unions of European men with Inuit women led to an ecclesiastical integration of ethnically mixed Settler families, where before the missionaries had seen their ministry exclusively directed at Inuit. This widened mandate was forced upon the church by the spiritual needs and close proximity of Settlers, who at the time worked for various British and Newfoundland trading companies. Starting in the 1850s, log houses for Settlers were erected in Hopedale in a Settler quarter near the mission complex, in which they lived when visiting Hopedale during the festive seasons and when attending choir and other festivals. Eventually, a separate English-speaking itinerant missionary devoted himself to these families.

Improved relations between Settlers and the mission were likely also aided by economic and social considerations. Helge Kleivan observed that the "transition of the Settlers to an economy based solely on hunting and fishing" as opposed to the earlier trade with Inuit "was an important condition for the improvement of their relations with the mission" (Kleivan 1966:102; cf. Treude 1974:86–89, 93–94; Brice-Bennett 1981:440–451). At the same time, however, the former solidarity between Settlers and Inuit appears to have weakened. Like his fellow Settlers, Amos Voisey could not "bear the idea of leaving this world, with his children growing up in heathenism," and, along with other Europeans, he sought an English education for them (Freitag 1854:3). In the 1880s we observe the establishment of a boarding school for Settler children in Hopedale, alongside the Inuttitut instruction that was available free of charge to them in the Moravian day schools. In the eyes of the missionaries, Settlers became Inuit role models for European housing and subsistence as well as examples of industry and thrift (Kleivan 1966:100–102; cf. Bourquin 1866).

In the following, I am using the German missionary correspondence and other Moravian documents to discuss the process by which Settler families became part of an ecclesiastical institution that for 80 years had seen its ministry exclusively directed at Inuit. While Carol Brice-Bennett has provided some excellent Settler profiles in her book on Hopedale (Brice-Bennett 2003:60–67), this chapter extends the discussion by examining the internal records of the Moravian Church to clarify the religious dynamic arising from the ecclesiastical conditions under which Settler families could be admitted into church membership. The response to the baptism of John and Johanne (Jane) Reed as well as the cases of Amos and Clara Voisey and Leah and Robert Mitchell receive particular consideration. The appendix, "Settlers and Merchants," translates a document from the German from the nineteenth-century transition period, in which frank Moravian concerns about trading companies and the more accepting position of the church towards Settlers are expressed.

Settlers Join the Moravian Church

The regulations governing the Settler presence in church, housing, and trade can be traced in the drafts and prints of several policy documents

(Moravian Policy Documents:13845–13921, MAB). An early draft, titled "Congregational Polity for External Members of the Missionary Settlements of the Moravian Church in Labrador," was submitted in 1855 by the Labrador Mission Conference to the Mission Department in Saxony (Gemeinordnungen 1855c). In the German draft, a brief history of the Moravian Church and its roots in the Czech Reformation of Jan Hus introduces outsiders to the church's origin and past. The Unity of the Brethren is presented here not as a sect or dissenting body but as an "ancient Protestant Episcopal Church," recognized as such in 1749 by the British Parliament and one giving confessional allegiance to the Augsburg Confession of 1530. The church, while not seeking to proselytize among the existing denominations, saw itself nevertheless as an instrument that created the conditions for the spread of Christ's kingdom throughout the world (Gemeinordnungen 1855c:562–563). A sizable section of the document is devoted to explaining church discipline, which is legitimized by proof-texts largely derived from the Pauline epistles (Gemeinordnungen 1855c:563–566). Since Settlers were living dispersed and away from the missionary settlements to which Inuit congregated during the winter months, home devotions were especially encouraged to fill the ecclesiastical void (Gemeinordnungen 1855c:566).

Whenever possible, Settlers were asked to visit the missionary settlement nearby, apparently a mutual desire that led to the establishment of the Settler quarter with wooden houses on Moravian land near the mission buildings (Figures 1 and 2; Gemeinordnungen 1855c:566, 568). Beyond this mutually beneficial relationship, Settlers were not to trade with Inuit in competition with the mission, sell alcohol to them, or build without permission in the Moravian land grant area. Trade with Moravian stores was offered to the Settlers as a voluntary opportunity for the maintenance of the mission. Settlers were encouraged to participate in such support by selling furs to the store at its customary (at times disadvantageous) prices (Gemeinordnungen 1855c:567–568), although also a more general discussion of financial contributions and a general raising of prices for goods bought by the Moravian stores ensued during this

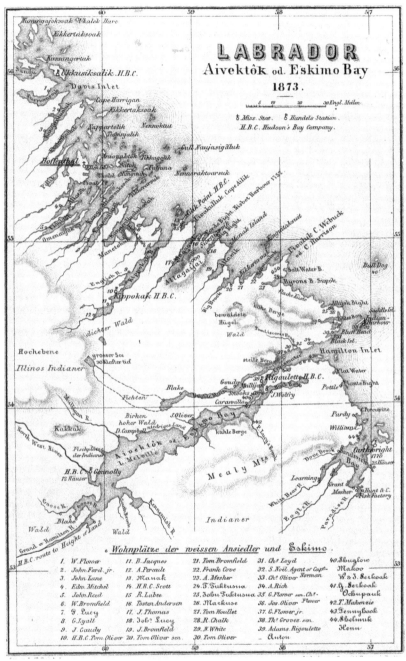

Figure 1. Map with Settler and Inuit locations from Davis Inlet to Sandwich Bay in 1873 by Levin Theodor Reichel. (Courtesy of Hans Rollmann)

period (Elsner 1853a:5–6). Settler children were encouraged to receive a free education in Inuttitut, the language of their mother. Eventually the boarding school established in Hopedale in 1880 through a joint missionary and Settler initiative sought to provide a rudimentary English education for children of these Settlers. Among Moravians, literacy and universal education were of great importance and a necessary tool for religious catechizing and liturgical activities, as well as for the maintenance of trading relations (Gemeinordnungen 1855c:67; Rollmann 2008:227–236; Grant 2003:21–54). In 1870, a more formal "Statute referring to the carrying on of the diaspora work among the Southlanders in Labrador" defined not only the position and activities of the English missionary devoted to the Settlers and Inuit outside the major settlements but also laid out the "Church transactions for the Settlers" that governed the solemnization of marriages and the baptism of adults and infants as well as confirmations. The document also outlined the relationship of the mission conferences in the individual settlements toward the

Figure 2. Settler quarter and school (second building from right) at Hopedale, 1880. (Hermann Jannasch, FS-Mission, Labrador, U2, unnumbered; permission Unity Archives, Herrnhut)

Settlers, including the unique Moravian confessional conversations called "speakings," the participation in Moravian choir festivals, and the degrees to which Settlers could relate to the Moravian Church, ranging from mere church attendance to full membership and participation in the Lord's Supper, or Holy Communion (Instructions 1870).

The closer relationship between Settler families and the mission became a reality through their proximity to the mission and eventual affiliation with the church and the baptisms of their children. Beginning in the 1850s, Hopedale church records and the internal ecclesiastical correspondence from Labrador document this intensified contact with Settler families and a ministry responsive to their religious needs. On March 7, 1853, John, the son of William Reed and his wife Mary, an Inuk, from Cross Water (Groswater) Bay, and Johanne Reed, living in Udjuktok (Ukjuktok) Bay, became baptismal candidates, were shortly thereafter baptized, and their marriage publicly solemnized (KB Hoffenthal, Tauf Candidaten:nos.137 and 138, 36225, MAB; Erwachsene Getaufte:nos.130 and 131, 36244, MAB; Getraute, no.56, 36315, MAB; 1852/53 Hopedale German Diary:38–39; note the fine sketch of the Reed family by Brice-Bennett [2003]:60–62). In April of 1855 John and Johanne Reed became candidates for Holy Communion, to which they were admitted on 20 March 1856 (KB Hoffenthal, Abendmahls-Candidaten:nos.210 and 211, 36276, MAB; Abendmahls-Geschwister:nos.178 and 179, 36294, MAB).

John Reed had come to the attention of the missionaries as an individual who could be relied on as a mediator between the mission and the widely dispersed population and visitors to the north coast.[1] He had established a solid reputation for defending Moravian interests against any criticism. In a letter of July 8, 1851, to the Mission Department of the Unity Elders Conference in Saxony, Superintendent Freitag (1807–1867) wrote that "he defends the Brethren at every opportunity against natives and foreigners and does not permit anyone to speak against them." Reed often visited Hopedale and eventually asked to build a house there, which the Moravians granted with conditions attached in the hope that his house would also accommodate other visitors to the mission (Freitag 1851:[5–6]).

The Mission's decision to admit John and Johanne Reed as baptismal candidates followed considerable discussion because such sacramental practice could set a precedent for others since the family "lived entirely in the manner of the settlers here." And yet ethnicity appears to have been a factor in easing the missionaries' concern over admitting them as church members, for Freitag mentions prominently Reed's own Aboriginal background in his letter to Elder Eugen Reichel of the Moravian Mission Department. Freitag thought that by admitting the Reed family into church membership the missionaries had not "in any way exceed[ed] our authorization and mandate for the Eskimo Nation, for the man is a half-European (*Halbeuropäer*), his father [William] Read [*sic*] an Englishman, his mother an Eskimo, likewise his wife an unbaptized Eskimo" (Freitag 1853b:2; see also KB Hoffenthal, Tauf-Candidaten: nos.137 and 138, 36225, MAB).

To admit John and Johanne Reed into membership, they first had to be baptized, since this north-coast Settler from central Labrador was never properly baptized by any clergyman, nor was his wife, who was born of Inuit parents. At most, as was customary in Labrador, Reed had "water poured on him by a sailor or settler while a flag was being waved" and he was given the name John. This act of naming a child, Freitag informed Reichel, would never have been recognized by Anglicans as a legitimate baptism. That Reed "lives like a European, speaks only English, understands Inuttitut ("eskimoisch") well and thus is viewed as a European" were therefore not sufficient grounds for the missionaries to bar him from the administration of baptism and membership in the church. Importantly, the missionaries believed they had observed in him and his wife a significant moral change, which was attributed by them to the action of the Holy Spirit, who apparently had begun his work already in the couple some time ago. Reed's ethical self-estimate lent credibility to Freitag's observed change. He had been, so Reed related to the Hopedale missionaries, affected by the preaching at Hopedale and turned away from being a drunkard ("Trunkenbold"). In the view of the missionaries, the couple were once "highly immoral people and living in the sins of the flesh," but had in the meantime changed their lives. The description "sins of the flesh" indicated sexual improprieties according to the strict Moravian moral and religious code (Freitag 1853b:2). In confessional conversations with the missionaries, Johanne Reed had spoken candidly about her previous relationships with other men (1852/53 Hopedale German Diary: 38–39). The couple was also literate—he in English and she in Inuttitut—and thus were able to avail themselves of religious literature and follow the liturgical readings (Freitag 1853b:2). An indication of John Reed's literacy

Figure 3. Grave marker of John Reed (1806–1883), Hopedale. (Courtesy of Hans Rollmann)

was demonstrated during their confirmation ceremony on Palm Sunday 1856, when, according to the Hopedale diarist, he "expressed in English the feelings of his heart in a confession of faith composed of Bible verses, which was translated to the congregation," while "his wife answered the questions put to her in the Eskimo language" (1855/56 Hopedale German Diary:12; Figure 3).

The impact that the baptism of John and Johanne Reed had upon the other Settlers reveals much about the religious self-understanding of the English Settlers as well as the Moravian Church as an ecclesiastical institution. Elsner informed the Mission Department that several of the English visitors at Hopedale who had witnessed the baptism said afterwards that what they had seen had convinced them "that between their church and ours there is hardly any difference" (Elsner 1853a:5; Freitag 1853b:10). This recognition was important in that the English Settlers, usually members of the Church of England, recognized in the Moravian Church a kindred institution with which they could identify religiously and socially. It was this ecclesiastical kinship in polity and liturgy among the two Reformation churches that had led in 1749 to parliamentary recognition of the Moravians, the oldest Protestant church, as an "ancient Protestant Episcopal Church." At the time, when the English penal laws were still in operation, only such public recognition had opened the doors to a meaningful presence of this church in the colonies, including British North America, as the vast territory including Labrador was then called. This act of Parliament had made the Moravian Church in England a sister church of the Church of England, a fact that Johann Christian Erhardt cited in his letter of 1750 to Bishop Johannes von Watteville to legitimize such work among the Inuit (Rollmann 2009a:57). And during the summer of 1764, several years before Moravians established themselves in Labrador, Jens Haven had argued in the cabin of the ship of Governor Hugh Palliser, in St. John's harbour, that the Moravians were no sect but a hierarchically governed and legally recognized institution, when he asked the governor to change the reference to him as a "member of the Moravian sect" in the letter of introduction he had just written for him (Haven 1780s:13 [228]).

Sociologically and ecclesiastically, the Moravian Church is not—in the typology created by Max Weber and Ernst Troeltsch—a voluntaristic institution, a "sect," whose character is defined by individual wilful participation and allegiance, but a "church," an objective salvific institution that incorporates individuals already as infants into its fellowship and administers divine grace in the sacraments through validly ordained cultic professionals such as deacons, presbyters, and bishops (Weber 1969:334–343; Troeltsch 1931:331–343). The Moravians stressed this character of the church in the historical part of their policy document for newcomers to the church in Labrador. Consequently, baptism and the Lord's Supper, a shared inheritance of both the Church of England and the Moravian Church, were familiar sacraments for the Settlers wishing to join the church with their children and had deeply ritualistic implications for the Inuit wives of the European settlers. They consequently desired membership in a church that was similar institutionally and liturgically to the one they had grown up in and were already familiar with. And yet, at mid-century, they could not be accommodated religiously by the missionaries since they had not been authorized to admit Europeans into their church (Elsner 1853a:5–6). To convey to the elders at home the depth of emotion that such exclusion from church membership and participation in the sacramental life of the church evoked in Labrador, Elsner described to Reichel the reaction of a frequent visitor to Hopedale, Mary Thomas.

Mary Thomas, baptized by visiting Methodist missionaries in Hamilton Inlet, was the wife of the Makkovik Bay trader Samuel James Thomas, a native of Sussex, England (Andersen 1996:1–2). When she arrived in Hopedale for Easter festivities in 1853, she was particularly taken by the news of the impending baptism of John and Johanne Reed. What troubled her especially was the fact that she would remain deprived from participation in the sacrament of the Lord's Supper. Like Leah Mitchell, whom we meet below, Mary Thomas was a sensitive religious individual, whose own devotional life was nourished by reading the Bible and other devotional literature. During repeated visits to the Moravian mission in Hopedale she had many religious questions about her readings, which she clarified in conversations with the missionaries. Upon the death of her husband, she would even have a moral biographical tract printed of his life, titled *Good Man Thomas* (private communication). Elsner wrote:

> Mary Thomas, a half-Eskimo and wife of a trader [Samuel James Thomas,] who is by no means opposed to us, except that he pays higher prices than we do, was here on Easter. She came soon after her arrival here into our quarters, and upon notification that John Reed and his wife would be baptized, she shed a stream of tears and was unable for approximately a quarter of an hour to speak a word. When she had recovered she said: "Will John Reed now become a member of your church? And will he one day be able to take the Lord's Supper?" When this was affirmed, she once more broke out into tears and told us

that she had just recovered from an emotional upset, during
which she was assailed by such strong doubts, whether a human being, who during her entire life had never partaken of
Holy Communion, could be saved [Elsner 1853a:6–7].

Only later, in 1881, did Mary Thomas attain her much desired confirmation that admitted her to Holy Communion in the Moravian Church
(Labrador 1881:245; Catalogus:[9–10]).

Elsner used the occasion of the 1853 baptism of John and Johanne
Reed, which came to be seen as a precedent and increased the pressure
on the church to accommodate other Settlers as well, to urge the Mission
Department to respond to the religious needs of the presently excluded.
Even if their own membership was not yet possible, Elsner reported, the
Settlers had asked the missionaries to seek at least permission to have
their children baptized. The missionary voiced his own opinion on the
matter to his superiors as follows. "It seems to me," he wrote, "the time
is ripe and we have an obligation to deal with these people. Around us,
their number increases each year. To keep them away from our congregation is neither possible nor right, nor Christian." He implored the elders to consider the consequences of a refusal. Either the unchurched
people would fall entirely into heathenism or, as their numbers increased, they would pay handsomely the visiting Irish Catholic clergy
who arrived annually with the Newfoundland schooners.

The influence of such inadequately served Settlers upon the Inuit
could only be detrimental. But especially the needs of Settler children
demanded a resolution (Elsner 1853a:5–6). The Mission Conference at
Hopedale wrote that Amos Voisey had asked "that we should consider
how he and others in the same situation felt at the thought of leaving
this world and leave behind really heathen offspring" (Mission Conference 1853c:3). Matters were somewhat complicated by the fact that
Moravians only baptized children on the mission field up to age four.
Older children had to wait until age 14 when they could be baptized as
adults, so that some children of Settler unions would remain unbaptized.

The Hopedale Mission Conference had only recently asked the Superintendent in Nain whether children of Settlers, once they had reached the proper age, could be baptized after submitting their request to the traditional practice of casting lots (Freitag 1853b:11–12). Such baptismal practice was operative also in other missionary locales and changed only gradually in response to situations such as had arisen in nineteenth-century Labrador. The subjection of baptismal candidates to the lot would be abolished church-wide in 1869 (Schulze 1901:263). In August of 1852 Superintendent Freitag had already asked the elders whether European settlers belonging to the Anglican Church and who had no opportunity to have their children baptized elsewhere could be baptized (Freitag 1852:7). Finally, in 1854, he acknowledged with pleasure the positive response he had received regarding his questions about the admission of Settler couples such as Leah and Robert Mitchell and about the baptism of Settler children, and on February 11, 1855, he informed Ferdinand Kruth, the leader of the mission in Hopedale, that the questions raised about the Mitchell and Voisey families had been resolved. "There is nothing standing in the way to receive them into the congregation," Freitag wrote, but added that it would only be proper and necessary for them to pay an annual contribution since they also had total freedom of trade (Freitag 1854:[3]; Freitag 1855b:32410, MAB).

The baptism of Settler children in Labrador started in 1855 with the baptisms of Emilie, George, and Samuel Voisey, children of Amos and Clara Voisey, and Mary and James Lean (Lane), children of John and Mirjan Lean (Lane), through Brother August Ferdinand Elsner (1822–1895) (KB Hoffenthal, Zweiter Theil, Eskimoische Kinder:nos. 415–419, 99). This baptism followed a visit in early March of 1855 by Brethren Elsner and Karl Gottlieb Kretschmer (1822–1891) to the family of Amos Voisey at Kangerdlualuk. Upon receiving the missionaries' report, the Mission Conference decided to admit the five adults into the church and baptize the five children (1854/55 Hopedale German Diary:29). The two families arrived at Hopedale on March 30, 1855, on three sledges. The children were baptized together with an Inuit child on the second day of

Easter, when also Robert and Leah Mitchell were admitted into the church (1854/55 Hopedale German Diary:29–30).

Salomo Lean (Lane), a son of James Lane and the Inuk Clara, was born on December 26, 1835, at Kangerdlualuk and, like his brother John, was later baptized by the Anglican Bishop Edward Feild in the south. In 1855 he affiliated with the Moravians at Hopedale and was publicly married there to his Inuit partner Teresia (KB Hoffenthal, Getraute: no.72, 36317, MAB; Catalogus:no.1). In the same year Salomo's unmarried sister Mary became a baptismal candidate and was baptized the following year (KB Hoffenthal, Tauf-Candidaten:no.144, 36226, MAB; Erwachsen Getaufte:no.137; 36244, MAB; 1855/56 Hopedale German Diary:14). Salomo's brother John was born on July 20, 1834, at Nuêrtorvik. He and his wife Mirjan, an Inuit baptismal candidate, were living at Kangerdlualuk. They were received into the Moravian Church in March of 1856 (KB Hoffenthal, Aufgenommene:no.148, 36261, MAB; Tauf-Candidaten:no.145, 36226, MAB; Catalogus:no. 3). Mirjan died at the birth of a daughter in January 1857, and John later remarried three more times (KB Hoffenthal, Heimgegangene:no.315, 36380, MAB; Catalogus:no. 3).

In April of 1857, the already mentioned Amos Voisey, an Englishman born near Plymouth, Devon, in 1817, and at the time living at Kangerdlualuk with his wife Clara, a Moravian Inuk, affiliated with the Hopedale Moravians (KB Hoffenthal, Aufgenommene:no.157, 36262, MAB; cf. *Them Days* 1997). Amos had gone to sea as a 16-year-old and subsequently came to the Nain area on a three-year contract with the British trading firm Hunt to serve the Southlanders that did business with the firm. Eventually he settled in the Davis Inlet area and united with Clara. She had been living with James Lane, but he left her for a younger Inuit woman and took the couple's two sons with him. Amos Voisey lived with Clara and her two daughters and had three more children with her, who were baptized on Easter 1855 (Elsner 1855a:232–234). Clara died in June of that year (KB Hoffenthal, Heimgegangene: no.304, 36379, MAB; cf. Catalogus:no.2). Two months later, Amos married the widow Rahel in a Moravian ceremony (KB Hoffenthal, Getraute:

no.73, 36317, MAB). He became a candidate for Holy Communion in February 1859 and, after some fluctuation in his church commitments, was admitted to communion at Zoar in April of 1868 (KB Hoffenthal, Abendmahls-Candidaten:no.232, 36278, MAB; Catalogus:no. 2; KB Zoar, ZumerstmaligenGenuss des hl. Abendmahls Gelangte:no.4, 200).

Since the linked life stories of the Voisey and Lane families, as told by Amos Voisey and his wife Clara to the Moravian missionary August Ferdinand Elsner, are only preserved in the German manuscript record of 1855, but not in the printed versions of the travel narratives, Elsner's original account, including the missionary's moral judgments, is translated here from the German. The missionary wrote:

> Amos Voisey comes from a village near Plymouth in England. At age sixteen he went to sea, hired himself out to a trading company (Hunt & Co.), which also has branches in Labrador, was sent to the area of Nain to serve there his three years among the often-mentioned so-called Southlanders. At that time, it may indeed have been so with him, as he said, that he lived a life like the foxes and wolves, at least his [later] change of position indicates this. For he got to know the . . . older Newfoundlander James Lean, who had with him as his wife a female by the name of Clara, who had left Nain; and Voisey decided upon Lean's encouragement to settle next to him. And, since Lean was tired of his wife, who had born him two sons and two daughters, and wanted to take a younger one, Voisey took Clara and lived with her in such a marriage as Lean had before him, and she bore him three children. They divided up the children of the first marriage. Lean kept the boys, . . . who were baptized during a visit of Lean to the south by an Anglican bishop [Bishop Edward Feild of Newfoundland and Bermuda], of course without any Christian instruction, and Voisey took over with Clara the two girls, who are now 16 and 18 years of age.
>
> Clara, according to her own narrative, had come in the

following way to such an abominable life. Born in Nain, she received from her father Salomo a more heathen than Christian upbringing; her mother—as defective as it may have been—directed her to the Saviour. She was educated in the school there, progressed in the church's graces, and received Holy Communion. Then it occurred to her brute father (who was under suspicion for murder) to leave the church, although his wife and his two daughters had to follow him entirely against their will. The travel took them to the south, during which they met the above-mentioned James Lean, who asked the father for Clara. The father agreed at once, but the daughter refused her "Yes." The father is then said to have loaded his gun and with the gun directed at her to have extorted her agreement. One can no doubt believe that such circumstances caused Voisey sleepless nights once his conscience had been awakened. His most dearly-loved wish, to have his marriage sanctioned through priestly blessing, has, however, not been fulfilled, for Clara ended her earthly walk, after she had been readmitted to the church, [but] before she could be ecclesiastically married, without violating the written statutes, that were still valid until then. But I believe that as a penitent sinner she found—like the lost son [in the parable]—admission into the mansions of peace [Elsner 1855a:233–235].

Leah and Robert Mitchell

The family of yet another English settler and Inuit woman from Nain, Robert and Leah (Lea) Mitchell (Figure 4), whose many descendants can today be found among north coast and southern Inuit of Labrador, left perhaps the most tracks in the Moravian records. Leah Mitchell, an Inuk from Nain, is a good example of the first generation of Moravian Inuit women who married European men and whose families became part of the Moravian Church in Labrador. Although the missionaries from Hopedale observed as early as 1796 that it was "becoming very popular" for non-Moravian European men living in Makkovik Bay to marry Labrador Inuit wives (1796 Diarium:322), the association of Europeans with the Moravian Church and the formalization of these marriages dates to the 1850s. In the case of Leah Mitchell, we are fortunate to have a photograph of her, one in a series of early Inuit portraits taken on Labrador's north coast and preserved in the archival collection at the Moravian Historical Society in Nazareth, Pennsylvania. It is here reproduced with the permission of the Moravian Archives located in Bethlehem. From the Moravian Church records we are also able to trace the Inuit lineage of Leah's ancestors.

Figure 4. Leah Mitchell (1822–1886). (Moravian Historical Society, Nazareth, Pennsylvania, P-2-22; permission Moravian Archives, Bethlehem, Pennsylvania)

Leah (Lea) Mitchell's maternal grandfather was Matheus, whose Inuttitut name had been Serkoak (Nain Duplicate Church Book, Adult Baptisms, Erwachsen Getaufte:no.42). Both he and his wife Lea, whose Inuttitut name was Pannionijok, were baptized as adults on January 6, 1798, in Nain by the Superintendent of Labrador Missions, Brother Christian Friedrich Burckhardt (1743–1812) (nos.42 and 43). Grandmother Lea had been admitted as a baptismal candidate on January 23, 1795, and her husband was readmitted as candidate on January 6, 1796 (nos.42 and 43). In January 1803 both were admitted to Holy Communion. Lea died on March 7, 1813, in Nain, while her husband survived her until September 12, 1827 (nos.42 and 43).

Leah Mitchell's parents were Daniel and Christina. Christina was the second child but first daughter of Lea and Matheus (Nain Duplicate Church Book, Baptisms:no.27). She was born on May 1, 1801, at Akuliakattak and baptized as the child of Christian parents in Nain on May 17,1801, by Brother Burckhardt, who had also baptized her parents (Nain Duplicate Church Book, Baptisms:no.27). After her marriage (Nain Baptisms:-no.27; Nain Adult Baptisms: no.97) to Daniel, an Inuk from the south, whose Inuttitut name was Kullak, she gave birth to two sons, David, 1819–1864 (Nain Baptisms:no.108), and Moses, 1827–1881 (Nain Baptisms:no.171), as well as two daughters, Lea and Ernestine, 1825–1881 (Nain Baptisms:no. 147). Christina died on January 16, 1829, and was buried in Nain (Nain Baptisms:no.27). Daniel remarried in 1846, taking the Christian Inuk Justine as his wife. He died 10 years later on Paul's Island, where he was also buried (Nain Adult Baptisms:no.97).

Leah (Lea) Mitchell, the second child of Daniel and Christina, was born on April 2, 1822, in Nain and baptized on April 8 by Brother Benjamin Gottlieb Kohlmeister (1756–1844; see Figure 5), the missionary who in 1811 explored Ungava Bay with Georg Kmoch (1770–1857) and whose name is still preserved today as a well-known Inuit surname in Labrador (Nain Baptisms:no.127). Leah's official reception into the Moravian Church took place on January 6, 1837, and she became a candidate for communion on April 4, 1844 (Nain Baptisms:no.127). Two years later,

Figure 5. Benjamin Gottlieb Kohlmeister (1756–1844), Labrador missionary who baptized Leah Mitchell. (Permission Moravian Church House Library, London)

however, in 1846, she left Nain to live with Robert Mitchell, born on July 6, 1812, in the Parish of Stoke Fleming near Dartmouth, Devonshire, whom she bore a son, Edward, on September 17, 1848, while travelling on a boat north of Hopedale (Nain Baptisms:no.127; KB Hoffenthal, Tauf-Candidaten:no.148, 36226, MAB; Erwachsene Getaufte:no.138, 36244, MAB; Figure 6). Edward was later baptized in Hopedale on January 6, 1859 (1858/59 Hopedale German Diary:60). In moving away from Nain and living with a European, she formally severed her ties with the Moravian Church, although the church's piety still remained indissolubly part of her religious self. According to genealogist Patty Way, Edward married Mary Ann Ford (Figure 6), daughter of John Ford of Kingsbridge, Devon, and Mary Ann Summers. John Ford was agent for the Hunt Company (and, later, the HBC) at Paul's Island (Kennedy, 2015).

When Robert and Leah Mitchell moved to Allatorusek and Allatôk Bay, they were unaware that the Moravian missionaries considered these places of habitation as lying within the Hopedale land grant area (on the Moravian land grants, see Rollmann 2009b). In a meeting with them, the missionaries from Hopedale read to Robert and Leah the proclamation of the governor that no one could settle in the land grant area without the permission of the church. Not only had Robert and Leah established themselves there, but also an Inuit family from Kaipokok had come along with them. Upon hearing that they were trespassing on Moravian land, Robert was quite willing to move two bays farther south to Kanigiktok (Kanairiktok) Bay, where William Metcalfe settled. But the Mitchells and the missionaries seem to have reached an agreement for them to stay, since Robert and Leah remained in Allatôk Bay until they died (1850a Hopedale Mission Conference:12161–12162, MAB; 1850b Lundberg:33277, MAB). Also the family of their son Edward and his wife Mary Ann Ford continued to live there after the death of his parents, as did an adopted son, the orphan Jonathan James Pardy

Figure 6. Edward and Mary Ann (Ford) Mitchell. (Photographic Collection of Labrador and Greenland, [M]2031; permission Unity Archives, Herrnhut)

(1859–1930). Pardy was the child of Jonathan Pardy (whose father George had settled in the Cartwright area) and Elizabeth Williams, the daughter of John Williams, who with his Inuit wife lived in the Flatwaters/Tub Harbour area. Jonathan James's father died in his early thirties, leaving behind seven children. The widow, Elizabeth (Williams) Pardy, then married John Winters from the Cartwright area and both moved north with her four youngest children, bringing the surname Winters to northern Labrador. Jonathan James was taken in by the Mitchell family and treated as their own son (1894 German Diary of Hopedale:35798–35799, MAB; private communication Patty Way).

It appears that Leah was a true *Homo religiosus* for whom the community with fellow believers, notably participation in the sacramental life of the church, mattered much. After leaving Nain and joining Robert Mitchell, she suffered greatly under the separation from the church of her childhood, where she had been a candidate for communion. Robert and Leah met when he was likely working for John Ford, the HBC sub-trader at Ukkusiksualik (Labrador 1873:399). After moving to Allatôk and establishing contact with the Moravian Church, it seems that Leah, who is mentioned throughout the Moravian records in complimentary terms, intensified the contact with the Moravian missionaries, which eventually resulted in church membership for her whole family. Ferdinand Elsner reveals in his letter to Brother Eugen Reichel of July 1, 1853, how much church fellowship and communion meant to her. Elsner writes:

> Earlier, she was a candidate for communion in Nain and lost her claim to the church when marrying Robert Mitchell. She said under many tears: externally, I am much better off than earlier. I no longer have to starve and have good clothes, but I am poorer than earlier, for I have lost the community of God's children. I love my husband, but not more than the salvation of my soul. Oh, I have to pay severely for my youthful carelessness of having married him, so that I can no longer return to the church until he dies, which, under the present circumstances, I

can only wish, for Holy Communion appears to me important above everything [Elsner 1853a:6].

It was the case of a spiritually troubled Leah and her supportive European husband Robert Mitchell that—after correspondence with church authorities in Saxony and England during 1852 and 1853—contributed in no small measure to a change in church regulations and policies towards Settlers (Freitag 1852:7; Freitag 1853b:11; Elsner 1853a:5–7). Leah was readmitted to the church on April 9, 1855, the same day that Robert asked to be received into it, which took place on March 24,1856 (KB Hoffenthal, Aufgenommene:no.149, 36261, MAB). The two had their marriage solemnized publicly by Brother Philipp Bubser (1822–1858) on May 28, 1855, at Hopedale (KB Hoffenthal, Getraute:no.71, 36316, MAB; 1855b Freitag:32410, MAB). Both were later admitted to Holy Communion on April 9, 1868 (KB Hoffenthal, Abendmahls-Geschwister:nos.228 and 229, 36297, MAB; 1867/68 Hopedale German Diary:95; Letter of the Hopedale Brethren 1868a:27028, MAB; Ribbach 1868b:1).

In April 1863, the missionary Samuel Weiz (1823–1888) and his wife Adolphine (1830–1903) made a journey with the Hopedale Inuk Philippus to visit the Mitchell family at Allatôk Bay (Figure 7) and left the following narrative of their visit, which was preserved by Bishop Levin Theodor Reichel (1812–1878) as follows:

> Robert's accommodation, a nice spacious log house, is built near the shore; behind it rises a hillside that is abundantly covered with spruce trees. We were greeted cordially by Robert's wife Lea, her son Edward and an Eskimo family, which is staying there for a while. Then we ate a frugal lunch, after which I left soon again with Robert, to climb a pretty high mountain, from where we had a nice view.
>
> My wife had stayed in the meantime with Lea, taught her upon her request to knit correctly the heels in stockings or knit

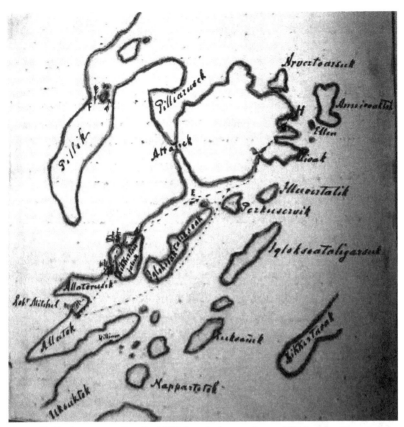

Figure 7. Sledge route taken in 1863 by missionary Samuel Weiz from Hopedale to Robert and Leah Mitchell in Allatôk Bay. (Contained in 1861–1869 Levin Theodor Reichel, NB.VII.R.2.48c; permission Unity Archives, Herrnhut)

new heels into old stockings, which, as it seemed, she understood well, as she is generally quite capable of knitting and doing needlework.

The evening passed quickly with different conversations until, after having said the evening blessing, we went to bed, where we received the very neatly arranged bed of Robert and Lea, who slept on the floor.

The next morning we went outside several times into different directions, first to a small island, ¼ of an hour distance from the house, where during the summer usually several families from here [Hopedale] stay. Then we went onwards to visit a forest, where large birch and mountain ash trees are standing, as I have so far not yet seen in Labrador, not even presumed to be there. Many of the birches I was hardly (and some not at all) able to encompass. But it pained me that many die without being used, since Eskimos, as far as they could reach, had stripped the bark all around to get the material for their houses and huts. Robert said that in Uksuktok Bay even nicer trees can be found, also tall poplars, of whose presence in Labrador I had not heard until then [Reichel 1861/69:52–53].

Robert Mitchell died on August 1, 1871, at Allatôk Bay after suffering from stomach troubles and was buried at Hopedale (Figure 8; KB Hoffenthal, Zweiter Theil, Heimgegangene:no.500, 471; Annual Letter 1871:3). The missionaries had found in him a knowledgeable and supportive congregant. "His steady and humble behaviour," the obituary read, "gained him the affection and friendship of the missionaries, who were always glad to see him in Hopedale, and frequently consulted him on a variety of subjects, for he possessed a very extensive knowledge both of persons and places on this coast" (Labrador 1873:399). Leah survived her husband by 15 years, dying also at Allatôk, on November 9, 1886, presumably of an "acute stomach illness" (KB Hoffenthal, Zweiter Theil, Heimgegangene:no.792, 505–506). She was buried on November 13 by Brother Peder Dam (1838–1914)

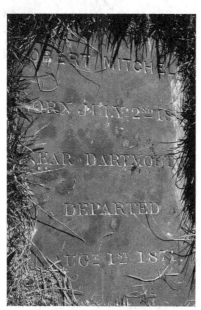

Figure 8. Grave marker of Robert Mitchell (1812–1871), Hopedale. (Courtesy of Hans Rollmann)

in Hopedale. The obituary entry in the Moravian Church Book of Hopedale on the occasion of Leah's death states that she:

> died at her place of habitation Allatôk on 9 November 1886, likely of an acute stomach illness. Lea was since 1846 the wife of the Englishman Robert Mitchell until he died in 1871. Lea was with her husband closely attached to the missionaries, and, even as a widow, she visited here [in Hopedale] as often as possible and usually came to her [widow] choir festival and quite frequently to the Lord's Supper since she and her husband had become communicants in 1868.
>
> Lea was a capable and energetic woman and remained the head of the family even as a widow, since her only surviving son [Edward; Figure 6] is of a quiet, obedient manner. With him and his wife she lived in peace and happiness, and she cared for and advised her adopted son Jonathan Pardy with true motherly love and devotion and was still able to rejoice with true grandmotherly joy over his firstborn child.
>
> But in addition to her protracted leg trouble, which for several months made it impossible for her to stand or walk, came her last illness and ended her earthly life after two days of suffering. We are, however, joyously certain that death will be for her the greatest victory and that she was united with her Lord in life and death [KB Hoffenthal, Zweiter Theil, Heimgegangene:no.792, 505–506].

Conclusion

In the 1850s, Moravians on Labrador's north coast were faced with a growing presence of a Settler population who trapped, hunted, and fished near their settlement of Hopedale. Up to this point, the church had seen its exclusive mission in the evangelization of Inuit, with whom they also engaged in trade. The English settlers who had married Inuit women came to recognize in the Moravian Church an institution similar to their own church while their Inuit wives sought to re-establish the broken ties with the Moravian Church that their unions with European settlers had caused. Both churches were episcopal in polity and had a sacramental and devotional life with which Settlers and Inuit could identify. Accepting a normative religious world view, the Settlers had a special desire to see their children baptized and integrated into a church body, which established meaningful social relations that their parents also could embrace and facilitated a rudimentary education for their children.

The original church mandate of serving only the Inuit of Labrador had to be extended to accommodate these Settlers, and the church rules governing membership and baptismal practice needed to be changed. The case that served as a transition and impetus for further change was the baptism of John and Johanne Reed in 1853, whose Aboriginal pedigree first seems to have eased the transition of accepting Settlers as members. This baptism, however, also revealed to other Settlers the kinship in church practice between the Moravian Church and the Church of England, and encouraged efforts to extend membership and the sacramental life in the Moravian Church to others, notably the Mitchell, Voisey, and Lane families. Labrador missionaries who petitioned their church authorities in Germany on behalf of the Settlers saw in the Settler population a welcome extension of their mission that might have ethical, religious, and financial benefits, notwithstanding the challenges they would face in meeting the cultural expectations that these Settlers had in the areas of education and ministry as well as the need to regulate their special relationship to the Moravian stores. The building of housing for Settlers at Hopedale intensified their contact with the church. The case of the Mitchell family of Allatôk Bay vindicated the expectation of the missionaries about a beneficial relationship with the growing Settler population.

Appendix: Settlers and Merchants

Contracts governing the relations of Settlers with the Moravian stores and their living on Moravian land, as well as correspondence from missionaries with church authorities in Germany and England, attest to a significant change in the 1850s and 1860s in attitude and policy on the part of the church towards so-called "Southlanders," including European Settlers, who had previously been perceived largely in negative terms. The changed outlook towards European Settlers and southern Inuit finds expression in several assessments of the Settlers by the Moravian superintendent Theodor Bourquin in Nain, notably in his report to the General Synod of the Moravian Church that covers the years 1857–1868 (Bourquin 1869:10786). Another document, likely written by Bourquin, from the mid-1860s deserves translation in full since it describes the church's new relationship with the Settlers, as well as the presence of European trading companies in the Moravian sphere of activity and influence. The untitled document, dated on page one as 1866, can be found in the Moravian Archives at Bethlehem, Pennsylvania, on pages 13897–13912 and is here published in translation with the permission of the archive. The author of the document wrote:

> In our reports the so-called "Southlanders" and outside traders are often mentioned, who in part have permanently settled here, but in part visit our coast only during summer for a short time. The influence of said people upon our Eskimo is presented in many ways as being disadvantageous; and thus it happens that our Brethren and friends in Europe, whenever a Southlander is mentioned, think of him as an enemy of our mission or a subject harmful towards our missionary work. In doing so, an injustice is done to some individuals and in particular to the inhabitants or settlers; for, even if it is unfortunately true that some lead an immoral life and are thus a bad example to the Eskimo, but the majority can be for our Eskimo an example,

as far as industry, thriftiness, etc., are concerned; for if the same are much more comfortable in their dwellings and their entire accommodation than our Eskimo, they have accomplished it after all with nothing else than with what is also available to the Eskimo, namely fishing, sealing and fox hunt.

Since here we are mainly concerned with those who have a great influence upon the Eskimo, in that they are trading with them, the settlers are therefore less the object; but we will say here briefly something about them. Most of them are former sailors or also such who were people in the service of the Hudson's Bay Company or other traders, who partly have married Eskimo women, partly have taken their life's partners from Newfoundland or from elsewhere. Others were already born on this coast and form a totally mixed race [Mischrace]; a few have Indian blood; still others are entirely Eskimo, who have never been attached closely with our church and live entirely like other settlers.

For a few years, such a settler family lived north of Kiglapeit in the area of Okak, but then moved south again; since then there are no longer settlers north of Nain, instead there are ca. 12 families south of Hopedale up to Maggovik (not counting John Ford and the trading place Ukkusiktalik), who nearly all occasionally visit Hopedale or Nain, especially during the festive periods. The entire southern coast is settled in a similar way only that our stations are no longer in touch with them. That among all of these people who live without spiritual care a field of labour is available, everyone can readily see, and it would be very desirable that either we would be able to take care of them even more or that a special (English) teacher were employed for them. Due to the great dispersion of these people, their care and especially the instruction of their adolescent children would, however, remain very imperfect and attended with many difficulties.

As far as the external circumstances are concerned, all settlers are more or less committed to one or the other trading company (which are named under a., b. and c. below). From them they receive all their supplies and trade with them what they acquire in fur and fish.

Besides the settlers, the following live on our coast or come here temporarily:

a. Firstly the establishments of the Hudson's Bay Company, none, however, lies on our coast north of Hopedale. Kippokak and the connected Ailik (ca. 50 English miles south of Hopedale) are its northernmost trading places, while North West River or Esquimaux Bay is its main establishment, from where they maintain trade connections with 2 small Indian tribes (Mountaineer and Naskopie Indians) that roam the interior of the Labrador peninsula.

   It is well known that this powerful company is still further trying to extend itself, and, e.g., has now again renewed a trade establishment in Ungava Bay that it had given up some years ago. It also seeks to secure the entire trade that until now has been carried out by us in the name of the S.F.G. in London, to which it will hopefully never come, since this would be for our Eskimo to their greatest detriment, since it is obvious that in this company trade interests outweigh by far any other interest.

   But to remain in the present, currently only the Hopedale church is in touch with the H.B.C., and the present trader at Kippokak and Ailik has a good relationship with us so that we hardly have reason to complain. That the Hopedale Eskimo are tempted to trade their goods there, while letting their debts made with us remain, has to be, among those who do it, more attributable to the dishonest character of the Eskimo than one could blame the trading company for buying the goods taken to them, provided, however, that the Eskimo are given harmless things, namely no liquor. However the situation is, whether or not everyone who comes to them to trade is given something free of charge, we have no satisfactory way of answering.

b. Our Eskimo come closer than to the H.B.C. with another trading house, Hunt & Henley (in London), which has its main trading place in Sandwich Bay, south of Eskimo Bay, and whose northernmost place, Ukkusiksalik, lies in the middle between Nain and Hopedale, but where also the sub-trader John Ford near Nain is situated. As far as the latter is concerned, he, together with his family, appears to be interested more than was the case earlier to be our friend, also seeking here occasionally edification, and we have no reason at all to complain on his part about harmful influence upon our Eskimo; as far as we know, he also does not give them liquor. That as far as trade is concerned we have a competitor in him should be no basis for enmity towards him.

As far as the large trading place Ukkusiksalik is concerned, what was just said pertains to it as well, also what was said earlier about the temptation for our Eskimo to trade there. What is most corrupting about that place is the character of the trader there, who is an unchristian and totally immoral man, and who through his bad example causes only damage for Eskimo, in that he attempts to attract them to him in many ways, leading them astray to drink, dance, and immorality. Because of its location, Ukkusiksalik is easily accessible for the Nain and Hopedale Eskimo, and also

Okak and Hebron experience his influence since nearly every summer a vehicle leaves Ukkusiksalik to go as
far as Saglek to engage in trade and fishery.

The establishment of Zoar [in 1865] is for that man
(Adams) a true thorn in his side since he truly has to
fear that because of it he will lose quite a bit; and, no
doubt, he will do what is in his power to diminish
trade at Zoar by settling good net- and fishing places.
As long as our mission is on a foundation of carrying
out trade at the same time, it should certainly be permitted and be an obligation to do in that regard whatever is possible and try to preserve for our Eskimo
good places of subsistence. But the Lord Himself may
guide us in how far we have to go so that we are not
enmeshed in subsistence activities and the actual missionary work suffers by it.

c. Besides H.B.C. and Hunt, also a Newfoundland trader, Captain Norman, has a firm trade establishment,
namely in Cross Water at the entrance into the great
Eskimo Bay or Aivektok Bay; from there comes each
summer a schooner (Samuel McNeill) as far as our
area to pick up pelts, fish, etc., from a part of the settlers who are obligated to Norman and equip them in
return with necessary provisions, etc. This trader is for
our Eskimo perhaps the least harmful of all.

d. Finally, such traders are to be mentioned that visit our
coast only during the summer months, in fact in part
as far as Hebron. Several such schooners only came for
one or a few years and then remained entirely absent;
but for several years now especially 3 schooners come
regularly, 2 from St. John's in Newfoundland (Jenkin
and Antoni [wooden leg]) and the third from Halifax
(Dikson).[2] The first one mentioned carries at least no

liquor, which is the case with the two latter, who altogether are for our Eskimo in moral regard of considerable harm, thus we can in no way see their annual appearance as something desirable, not to mention, that through their trade they cause our Eskimo in manifold ways to engage in disloyalty and dishonesty and hypocrisy towards us. For these schooners appear at a time where our Eskimo as a rule do not suffer any deprivation, and where they can and should acquire something to first of all pay off the debts accumulated during the long winter and secondly gather provisions for the coming winter. The situation of the country here is such that it is hardly possible for an Eskimo to survive without receiving at times the necessary supply in hunting gear and groceries without credit; but these are the times where the schooners are far from us. With them, the Eskimo have therefore never any debts and thus can also more easily trade against cash payment than where it is expected that they should pay off the old debts. Others who perhaps have no debts with us waste their goods quickly by trading for several things that are of little use or even harmful. But when the winter comes again and also generally hard times for subsistence, then each one still expects support and help from us. This remains always a very difficult point, which sometimes begs the question or wish, whether it might not be good if trade and mission were more separated from each other than has been the case so far.

Notes

1. Editor's note. While not disputing Moravian opinions of Reed, this appears to be the same John Reed (also spelled Reid and Read) mentioned in Hudson's Bay Company (HBC) correspondence in 1850 between Richard Hardisty at North West River (see Stopp, chapter 8) and William Cameron at Kaipokok. Hardisty writes, "I am sorry to learn that John Reid, the man from [whom] you expected 30 tierces of Salmon, has gone and sold them all to the Captain of an American vessel. . . . I find by our accounts that he has Debt at Kipokok amounting to nearly £60. You should not let him have anything more until he clear off some of the Debt that he already owes us" (B/153a/12/NWR 1850-51, p. 26). Assuming this is the same John Reed, it appears that the HBC and the Moravians had different opinions of the man.
2. The likely defective spelling may refer to Jenkins, Anthony, and Dickson.

References Cited

Abbreviations
CNS, MUN: Centre for Newfoundland Studies, Memorial University of Newfoundland.
KB: Kirchen-Buch (Church Book).
MAB: Moravian Archives, Bethlehem, Pennsylvania, U.S.A.
MCH: Moravian Church House, London.
UAH: Unity Archives, Herrnhut, Saxony, Germany.

1. Unpublished Sources

Dated
1780s Haven, Jens. Auszug aus Br. Jens Havens Aufsaz [*sic*] von seiner recognosci-rungs Reise u[nd] Aufenthalt unter den Eskimoern in Terra Labrador von Ao. 1770 bis 1784, Erster Theil, R15.K.a.5.4., UAH.
1796 Diarium des Hauss-Gemeinleins in Hoffenthal von den Monathen September, October, November, u[nd] December 1796 [Diary of the house congregation in Hopedale for the months September, October, November, and December 1796], R.15.K.b.2b, UAH.
1850a Hopedale Mission Conference to Brother Johann Lundberg in Nain, 23 January 1850, MAB.
1850b Lundberg, Johann, to the Brethren in Hopedale, 17 February 1850, MAB.
1851 Freitag, C. F. August, to Eugen Reichel of the Mission Department of the Unity Elders Conference, 8 July 1851, R15K.b.17.e, UAH.
1852–1853 Hopedale German Diary August 1852–1853, R.15.Kb.2.e, UAH.
1852 Freitag, C. F. August, to E. Reichel, 27 August 1852, R.15.K.b.17.e, UAH.
1853a Elsner, August, to Brother Reichel, Hopedale, 1 July 1853, R.15.K.b.17.e, UAH.

1853b Freitag, C. F. August, to E. Reichel, 30 June 1853, R.15.K.b.17.e, UAH.

1853c Mission Conference at Hopedale to Unity Elders Conference, 26 August 1853, R.15.K.b.17.e, UAH.

1854 Freitag, C. F. August, to Brother Reichel, 12 August 1854, R.15.K.b.17.e, UAH.

1854–1855 Hopedale German Diary August 1854–August 1855, R.15.Kb.2.e, UAH.

1855a Elsner, August Ferdinand. Einige Notizen von einer im Missions[dienst] unternommenen Reise zu den nördlich von Hoffenthal wohnenden Ansiedlern, 227–238, R.15.Ka.10.a.10, UAH.

1855b Freitag, C. F. August, to Ferdinand Kruth in Hopedale, Nain, 11 February 1855, MAB.

1855c Gemeinordnungen für auswärtige Mitglieder der Missionsplätze der Brüdergemeine in Labrador. Church orders, drafted by Moravian missionaries in Labrador and sent to Brother E[rnst Friedrich] Reichel, Mission Department of the Moravian Church, Berthelsdorf, Saxony, November 1855, R.15.K.a.7.a.1, 562–568, UAH.

1855–1856 Hopedale German Diary August 1855–August 1856, R.15.Kb.2.e, UAH.

1858–1859 Hopedale German Diary August 1858–August 1859, R.15.Kb.2.e, UAH.

1861–1869 Reichel, Levin Theodor. Labrador: 1861–1869, NB.VII.R.2.48c, UAH.

1866 Bourquin, Theodor. Untitled document, 13897–13912, MAB.

1867–1868 Hopedale German Diary July 1867–July 1868, R.15.Kb.2.e, UAH.

1868a Letter of the Hopedale Brethren for 1868 to the Unity Elders Conference in Berthelsdorf, Saxony, MAB.

1868b Ribbach, August, to Levin Theodor Reichel, 16 August 1868, Kb17g, UAH.

1869 Bourquin, Theodor. Bericht von der Labrador Mission 1857–1868 vor der Synode 1869, 10748–10788, MAB.

1870 Instructions of Ernst Friedrich Reichel and the Mission Department of the Moravian Church, Berthelsdorf, 2 April 1870, 38791–38796, MAB.

1871 Annual Letter of 1871 of the Mission Conference Hopedale to the Mission Department, Berthelsdorf, R.15.Kb17g, UAH.

1894 German Diary of Hopedale for 14–26 August 1894, 35798–35799, MAB.

Moravian Church Books

Catalogus der Südlaender oder solcher die als Getaufte unserer Gemeinschaft beigetreten, Moravian Church, Nain.

Erwachsen Getaufte Männer u[nd] Weiber Nain [1776–1906], Microfilm, CNS, MUN, unpaginated.

Kirchen-Buch der Evangelischen Brueder-Mission zu Hoffenthal in Labrador: Abendmahls-Candidaten, MAB.

Kirchen-Buch der Evangelischen Brueder-Mission zu Hoffenthal in Labrador: Abendmahls-Geschwister, MAB.

Kirchen-Buch der Evangelischen Brueder-Mission zu Hoffenthal in Labrador: Aufgenommene, MAB.

Kirchen-Buch der Evangelischen Brueder-Mission zu Hoffenthal in Labrador: Erwachsene Getaufte, MAB.

Kirchen-Buch der Evangelischen Brueder-Mission zu Hoffenthal in Labrador: Getraute, MAB.

Kirchen-Buch der Evangelischen Brueder-Mission zu Hoffenthal in Labrador: Heimgegangene, MAB.

Kirchen-Buch der Evangelischen Brueder-Mission zu Hoffenthal in Labrador: Tauf-Candidaten, MAB.

Kirchen-Buch der Evangelischen Brueder-Mission zu Hoffenthal in Labrador: Zweiter Theil, Eskimoische Kinder, Moravian Church, Hopedale.

Kirchen-Buch der Evangelischen Brueder-Mission zu Hoffenthal in Labrador: Zweiter Theil, Heimgegangene, Moravian Church, Hopedale.

Kirchenbuch der Gemeine in Zoar, Zum erstmaligen Genuss des hl. Abendmahls Gelangte, Moravian Church, Nain.

Moravian Policy Documents Governing the Settler Presence in Labrador, 13845–13921, MAB.

Nain Duplicate Church Book, Adult Baptisms 1776–1906, Microfilm, CNS, MUN, unpaginated.

Nain Duplicate Church Book, Baptisms 1778–1893, Microfilm, CNS, MUN, unpaginated.

2. Secondary Literature

Andersen, Joan
  1996 *Makkovik 100 Years Plus*. Self-published, Makkovik.

Brice-Bennett, Carol
  1981 Two Opinions: Inuit and Moravian Missionaries in Labrador, 1804–1860. Unpublished Master's thesis, Department of Anthropology, Memorial University of Newfoundland, St. John's.
  2003 *Hopedale: Three Ages of a Community in Northern Labrador*. Historic Sites Association of Newfoundland and Labrador, St. John's.

Grant, Dianne S.
  2003 Nain's Silenced Majority: An Anthropological Examination of Schooling in Northern Labrador. Unpublished Master's thesis, Department of Anthropology, Memorial University of Newfoundland, St. John's.

Kennedy, John C.
  2015 *Encounters: An Anthropological History of Southeastern Labrador*. McGill-Queen's University Press, Montreal and Kingston.

Kleivan, Helge
  1966 *The Eskimos of Northeast Labrador: A History of Eskimo–White Relations 1771–1955*. Norsk Polarinstitutt, Oslo.

Labrador
  1873 Labrador: Extract of the Diary of Hopedale, from August 1871 to July 1872. *Periodical Accounts* 28/298:399.
  1881 Labrador, *Missionsblatt* 45(12):242–247.

Rollmann, Hans

2008 Moravian Education in Labrador: A Legacy of Literacy. In *Conference Proceedings: Symposium 2008: Post-Confederation Education Reform: From Rhetoric to Reality*, edited by Gerald Galway and David Dibbon, pp. 227–236. Memorial University of Newfoundland, St. John's.

2009a Johann Christian Erhardt and the First Moravian Exploration of Labrador in 1752. In *Moravian Beginnings in Labrador: Papers from a Symposium held in Makkovik and Hopedale*, edited by Hans Rollmann, pp. 52–68. An Occasional Publication of Newfoundland and Labrador Studies, No. 2. Faculty of Arts Publications, St. John's.

2009b The Labrador Land Grants of 1769 and 1774. In *Moravian Beginnings in Labrador: Papers from a Symposium held in Makkovik and Hopedale*, edited by Hans Rollmann, pp. 104–131. An Occasional Publication of Newfoundland and Labrador Studies, No. 2. Faculty of Arts Publications, St. John's.

Schulze, Adolf

1901 *Abriss einer Geschichte der Brüdermission*. Verlage der Missionsbuchhandlung, Herrnhut.

Them Days

1997 Life in Voisey's Bay. Special issue, 22(2), Winter.

Treude, Erhard

1974 *Nordlabrador: Entwicklung und Struktur von Siedlung und Wirtschaft in einem polaren Grenzraum der Ökumene mit 37 Tabellen und 30 Abbildungen*. Selbstverlag des Instituts für Geographie und Länderkunde und der Geographischen Kommission für Westfalen, Münster.

Troeltsch, Ernst

1931 *The Social Teaching of the Christian Churches*. George Allen & Unwin, London.

Weber, Max

1969 *Die Protestantische Ethik I*. Siebenstern Taschenbuch Verlag, München & Hamburg.

CHAPTER 10

"We Don't Have Any Klick or Spam in the House—How About a Piece of Boiled Salmon for Lunch?": Country Food in NunatuKavut

Gregory E. Mitchell

Twentieth-century developments and events ranging from reset-tlement to the closure of the cod fishery have changed the location and timing of land and sea resource use but have not ended the relationship between Inuit-Métis and their environment. This chapter summarizes a larger document (Mitchell 2011) that presents the results of research conducted in relationship to a proposed 1,100–km-long transmission line that would transmit electricity from the Lower Churchill hydroelectric development to Soldiers Pond, near St. John's, Newfoundland (Labrador–Island Transmission Link [LITL]).

The information presented here was entered into the NunatuKavut Community Council (NCC) Cumulative Data Base, which is based on seven other limited studies conducted since 1979 (Mitchell 2013, Clarke and Mitchell 2010). A comprehensive land and sea use study has never been carried out in south/central Labrador that could be considered both representative of the population and scientifically acceptable (within statistically accepted parameters).

Historically, large-scale developments ignored the concerns of Labrador residents, but in the past few decades developments such as the massive nickel mine at Voisey's Bay and the Lower Churchill project have seen proponents consult with Labrador Aboriginal groups and hasten the resolution of long-standing land claims. The approximately 6,000 Inuit-Métis members of NunatuKavut Community Council (NCC) have been less fortunate. However, on January 20, 2011, Nalcor Energy, the proponent of the LITL, and the NunatuKavut Community Council signed a Community Consultation Agreement designed to discuss the project in south/central Labrador communities and to obtain land use information and concerns from NCC members. The two most important components of the 2011 agreement would be the gathering of 150 surveys and the collection of 30 in-depth map biographies from the regions. These extensive data are summarized below.

General Methodology

The study area included the Strait of Belle Isle zone, the Atlantic coastal zone as far north as Cartwright, and the Upper Lake Melville zone. In the 150 random sample surveys conducted for this study, of the 118 people in the workforce, 11.8 per cent were unemployed. Of the remaining respondents, six were students and 26 people in the "other" category were retired.

Three local people were hired as community consultation officers (CCOs) and trained in conducting surveys and map biographies. The surveys were administered in a random fashion and the CCOs helped participants to complete them. From the 1,050 pages of survey results, the CCOs segregated the survey answers for ease of compilation and reporting. This resulted in 114 pages of segregated answers to be tabulated and analyzed. The minimum returned sample size for categorical data falls below the number needed for a 95 per cent confidence level (approximately 475 surveys).[1]

Map Biography Methods

Map biographies or land use and occupancy mapping (Tobias 2000) are stories of land use and occupancy and are presented below in a visual map format. The methodology involves recording oral traditions and transferring them to paper for multiple purposes.

The study employed methods from a number of previously successful projects.[2] Four basic steps were involved in the process of collecting data:

1. CCOs identified individual land users and elders for the project based on land use frequency and availability for the interviews.
2. Written consent was obtained.
3. Two researchers participated in each interview.
4. The respondent was then asked to show places and locations of tilts, cabins, tenting locations, the harvesting of wildlife and plant resources, travel routes, etc., and encouraged to recall traditional stories, etc.

Respondent anonymity was ensured using methodologies developed by the Ethics Committee of the NCC. Respondents were primarily male (29 males and one female) and the average age was 57 years. Occupations were mostly listed as fishermen, equipment operators, and fish plant workers.

The collection of the 30 map biographies, stories, and answers to specific project-related questions were transcribed from the voice recordings and notes. In addition, 230 pages of interview notes from the various note-takers were reviewed and analyzed.

Differences among the approaches of researchers could lead to observer bias and respondent variances. Local interviewers were sometimes apt to overlook items due to the narrative style of the interview or because some knowledge is assumed to be "common" and remains unspoken, but respondents would more easily share information with the local interviewers, especially in cases where harvesting was "off limits" due to provincial and federal regulations.

Other issues with regard to research method variability occurred in the logistics of conducting the map biographies and other sources of bias. These included: (1) interviews taking place in a range of venues, from kitchens to boardrooms; (2) respondent anxiety, as some interviewees were either on breaks from shift work or were called to work during the interviews; (3) gender bias, since men are primarily the ones who are out on the land and the study was targeted at this group; and (4) variance in map scales causing some confusion.

Since respondents were asked to recall resource uses since their teenage years and their average age was 57, the information given covers a time period, on average, from approximately 45 years ago to the present time.

Results and Discussion

The 150 surveys originate from three zones (equally distributed): Zone 1, Strait of Belle Isle to Mary's Harbour; Zone 2, Port Hope Simpson to Cartwright (inclusive); and Zone 3, Upper Lake Melville area. There were 86 male respondents and 64 female respondents, so that a gender ratio of 1.3:1 favoured male participants. There appears to have been a good mix of age classes in the sample, which included only adults over 19 years of age. Results relevant to species harvested and activities on the land are given below.[3]

When asked about potential barriers to getting on the land, the 69 respondents in this category cited work (time limitations) (53 per cent), laws and regulations (18 per cent), medical problems (7 per cent), lack of finances (6 per cent), and other reasons (16 per cent). Under the category of "laws and regulations" people indicated that provincial laws and regulations restricted them, and in one case a person cited direct harassment by officials enforcing regulations as a barrier. The "other reasons" category included various barriers to people getting out on the land: fear of boats and planes (one person); pollution and development (two people); no snow/weather (two people); tired (two people); age (two people); and don't have time (two people).

Unlike the solitary trappers of their grandparents' era, only 19 per cent of the respondents went out on the land alone. Thirty per cent travelled with family, 26 per cent with extended family, and 26 per cent with friends. When asked whether people wanted to eat traditional foods more often, 71 per cent said "yes." Forty-three per cent of those respondents indicated that their major restrictions to eating more country food were regulations and game laws.

Table 1. Answers to General Questions on Land Use.

Question	Yes	No	Other
In this past year, did you go out on the land?[1]	87%	11%	2%
Does your immediate family participate in the traditional salmon harvest?[2]	76%	24%	-
Do you currently hunt, fish, and/or trap?	87%	13%	-
Does someone in your immediate family hunt, fish, and/or trap?	82%	18%	-
Does your family own a tilt or cabin inland from where you live?[3]	69%	31%	-
Are there barriers (obstacles) preventing you from going on the land more often?	45%	52%	3%
Do you eat traditional foods (wild game, fish, fowl, etc.)?	100%	-	-

1. An additional question was asked concerning activities on the land. The activities included hunting, fishing, berry picking, trapping, camping, snowmobiling, meditating, snowshoeing, boil-ups, cutting firewood, and enjoying the beauty of the land.
2. Of the 31 respondents who did not participate in the salmon fishery, most are from the Upper Lake Melville area where no quota was allotted for this activity at the time. Almost all coastal people participated.
3. In hindsight, this question may have seemed invalid for people in Upper Lake Melville, since many of them have cabins either in outer Lake Melville or on the Atlantic coast, which may have caused some ambiguity in the question.

To better understand the travel habits of people while resource harvesting, we asked how many days/weeks people spent away from home in an average year and during which seasons. The results show that the average number of weeks spent away from the primary residence in resource harvesting pursuits is 7.1 weeks per person, annually. In other words, an average of 14 per cent of a person's year is spent on the land, away from a primary residence and in search of country food.

Eighty per cent of respondents hunted, fished, or trapped. Most resource harvesting occurs during summer. Fall activities include migratory bird hunting and berry picking, and winter activities include snaring rabbits and caribou hunting. Labrador's Inuit-Métis are constantly "on the move."

Table 2. The Frequency of Country Food Consumption (149 responses).

Area/Zone	Weekly	Monthly	Special Occasions	Don't Know
Zone # 1 (Mary's Harbour to Forteau)	50	0	0	0
Zone # 2 (Port Hope to Cartwright)	46	1	3	0
Zone # 3 (Upper Lake Melville area)	42	5	2	1
Total	138	6	5	1
Per cent of total	92%	4%	3%	1%

When respondents were asked if they eat traditional foods, 100 per cent answered "yes" and 92 per cent eat traditional foods on a weekly basis. Given the relatively urban setting of Upper Lake Melville (one-third of the respondents) it is interesting that so many people find some way to acquire traditional foods such as wild game, fish, fowl, berries, etc.

Tables 3 and 4 indicate the taxa of country foods consumed by respondents and identified to the species level. An attempt was made to extrapolate from both the notes during the surveys and the map biography inquiries as to the quantity of each species consumed per household.[4] The tables divide country foods into the categories of Primary and Secondary foods which are hunted, fished, gathered, and consumed.

Table 3. Quantities of the Various Species Comprising Primary Country Foods Consumed by Respondents in NunatuKavut.

Common Name	Species Name	Quantity Consumed per Household
Rabbit	*Lepus americanus*	30
Caribou	*Rangifer tarandus*	2
Porcupine	*Erethizon dorsatum*	opportunistic
Moose	*Alces alces*	1 per 3 households
Beaver	*Castor canadensis*	opportunistic
Harp seal	*Pagophilus groenlandicus*	3
Ring seal	*Pusa hispida*	2
White partridge	*Lagopus lagopus*	20–30
Canada goose	*Branta canadensis*	2
Turr	*Uria aalge*	10–20
Divers/scoter	*Melanitta fusca*	opportunistic
Eider ducks	*Someraria mollisima*	15
Shellbirds/mergansers	*Mergus merganser*	opportunistic
Spruce partridge	*Dendragapus canadensis*	10-15
Salmon	*Salmo salar*	12
Codfish	*Gadus morhua*	30–40
Trout	*Salvilinus fontinalis*	40
Herring	*Clupea herengus*	opportunistic
Capelin	*Mallotus villosus*	opportunistic
Smelt	*Osmerus mordax*	100–120
Shrimp	*Pandalus borealis*	4.5 kg
Snow crab	*Chionoecetes opilio*	9 kg/on coast
Scallops	*Chlamysis landica*	opportunistic
Mussels	*Mytilus edulus*	4.5 kg/spring
Bakeapple	*Rubus chamaemorus*	19–26.5 litres
Blackberries	*Empetrum nigrum*	3.5–7.5 litres
Red/partridge berries	*Vaccinium vitis-idaea*	15–19 litres
Squash berries	*Viburnum edule*	7.5 litres
Dandelion	*Taraxacum spp.*	opportunistic
Alexander/Scotch lovage	*Ligusticum scothicum*	becoming rare

Table 4. Species List of Country Foods Consumed on a Secondary Basis ("Rarely" or "Occasionally") in NunatuKavut.

1. Black bear/*Ursus americanus*	17. Whelks/*Baccinum undatum*
2. Dolphin/family: Delphinidae	18. Sea urchins/*Strongylocentrotus droebachiensis*
3. Bearded seal/*Erignathus barbatus*	19. Toad crab/*Hyas araneus*
4. Polar bear/*Ursus maritimus*	20. Clams/*Mya arenaria*
5. Mountain cat/lynx/*Lynx canadensis*	21. Blueberries/sweet hearts/*Vaccinium angustifolium and V. uliginosum*
6. Muskrat/*Ondatrazi bethicus*	22. Marsh berries/*Vaccinium macrocarpon/V. oxycoccus*
7. Black duck/*Anas rubripes*	23. Raspberries/*Rubus idaeus*
8. Bull bird/*Plautus alle*	24. Currants/*Ribes lacustre*
9. Pigeon/guillemot/*Cepphus grylle*	25. Juniper/*Juniperus communis*
10. Green-winged teal/*Anas crecca*	26. Wild pears/*Amelanchier spp.*
11. Arctic char/*Salvilinus alpinus*	27. Mushrooms/*Boletus spp.*
12. Halibut/*Hippoglossus hippoglossus*	28. Wild chives/*Alliums spp.*
13. Mackerel/*Scomber scombrus*	29. Mint berries/*Gaultheria hispidula*
14. Turbot/*Reinhardtius hippoglossoides*	30. Strawberries/*Fragaria virginiana*
15. Flounder/*Pseudopleuronectes americanus*	31. Rhubarb/*Rheum spp. (vestigial cultivars)*
16. Rock cod/*Gadus ogac*	

Seventy-six per cent of the surveyed individuals participated in the Aboriginal communal salmon fishery. Sixty per cent of the respondents who did not participate are located in the Upper Lake Melville area, where until 2013 there was no salmon fishery open near them. However, in 2013, the NCC negotiated an Aboriginal food fishery in the Upper Lake Melville area and residents there now take full advantage of this food source.

Respondents recorded 63 species that could be brought to a positive binomial identification. Virtually everything that grows, swims, walks, and flies in Labrador is consumed by Inuit-Métis. With a few exceptions these tables, showing species consumption, are almost comprehensive species lists for south/central Labrador.

The vast majority of respondents did not give further details. For example, only three species of seals are recorded, but from previous work we know that all six endemic species of seals are harvested. Other categories, such as "fish" or "ducks," can also be expanded given a higher level of inquiry. At least a dozen or more respondents replied that they eat "whatever [species] they can get."

Map Biography Results

The random surveys showed a very high percentage of land users in the project area. Since this map biography study canvassed only 30 land users and the adult population of the membership is greater than 3,000, the representative sample is 1 per cent of the total population. From several questions in the random survey results, it can be stated that 87 per cent of the population are current land and sea users. In numerical terms and for the adult population, more than 2,610 people (within acceptable error limits) have gone out on the land and sea over the past year to harvest resources and therefore can be considered potential candidates for map biography recording. The present study recorded approximately only 1.1 per cent of the potential candidates.

During the map biography-sessions, respondents were questioned about all species harvested during their lives. For report writing and ease of viewing, the results of those queries were divided into class groupings of species harvested. The class groupings included: (1) large land mammals, (2) small land mammals and inland birds, (3) sea mammals, (4) migratory and sea birds, (5) fur bearers (trapping), (6) fish, (7) shellfish, and (8) plants. Eight maps for each of the 30 respondents were produced for these various species categories, digitized, and added to the NCC cumulative land use and occupancy data base.

The 30 map biography respondents held an average of 4.5 cabins and tilts per person for the various rounds of harvesting (range: two to nine per respondent). Respondents were also encouraged to recount stories about important places and local toponyms.

The Labrador–Island Transmission Link project described above provides information on people's habits and species harvested and shows a degree of depth to the geographic information given in the NCC Cumulative Data Base.

Sea Mammals

This category includes the various seals, porpoise/dolphin (family: Delphinidae), and polar bear (*Ursus maritimus*). The three species of seals primarily harvested are the harp seal (*Pagophilus groenlandicus*), ring seal (*Pusa hispida*), and bearded seal (*Erignathus barbatus*). Depending on season and species, seals may be shot from open boats using a flat trajectory rifle, shot on the ice, or harpooned through the ice. The meat is brought back to the community and shared among family and community members, providing a rich protein for people's diets.

The seal, in general, has always been a traditional and highly valued food of NunatuKavut members and in the past skins were made into traditional skin boots. The bearded seal is especially valued for its tough hide for the use in boot bottoms (Rita Stevens, interviewed by Eva Luther on June 28, 2009). A number of other customs have survived regarding seals, especially the bearded seal:

> an old tradition that I was told and I actually seen this myself, as a young boy growing up on the coast. One of the, I guess, biggest events for any young boy was to kill an old square flipper [bearded seal] and you know back then there was no motors you basically rowed out. Whenever the square flipper[s] were taken they [hunters] came back with a flag flying on the boat somewhere, and rowing and towing the seals back in [*sic*]. If this was a young man who killed his first one [bearded seal], one of the traditions was that, the young fella' had to lie down and you have to imagine now these seals were not small, I mean they're probably 400- to 600-pound seals and they'd lie down on the ice and let the other hunters . . . drag that seal over him, go over . . . right over his body, and then he had to skin the seal himself, and depending on what he wanted the skin for,

had to skin the seal himself and deliver a piece or meal to ev-
erybody in the community . . . there's not a lot of people re-
member it [this custom], but I actually saw my older brother
had to do this [Interview with Jim Holwell, 2012, videotaped
session available at The Rooms, fourth floor, St. John's].

A number of respondents were reluctant to divulge information on
the killing of "jumpers" (dolphins) because of their protection under
game laws and for fear of reprisals. However, several people still kill
one or two a year and shared the following information with researchers. Jumpers are usually taken from an open boat with a rifle and are
sometimes hard to recover because they sink when not shot at the proper instant (with a lungful of air). Jumpers are also sometimes taken acci-
dentally by nets and, if fresh, are consumed. Several respondents
claimed that they killed jumpers in the past but now thought that killing
them was unnecessary. One respondent said that their habits and ac-
tions were too "human" and could not kill them any more. Whales have
not been taken in recent years. Several respondents have taken polar
bears, or were with parties that killed polar bears. This meat is consumed and the skins are highly prized.

Large Land Mammals

This category included caribou (*Rangifer tarandus*), moose (*Alces alces*),
and black bear (*Ursus americanus*). Caribou is especially important to the
diet of the people of NunatuKavut. Southerly ranging barren ground
caribou and the more sedentary woodland caribou have been mostly
absent from southern Labrador since the 1960s. Prior to the 1960s the
interior was accessed by dog teams and caribou were killed and brought
home where they were shared with the community.

Hunting for woodland caribou from the Mealy Mountain and Red
Wine herds is currently prohibited. Until recently, hunters from the
south coast (Cartwright and further south) have travelled great distances from southern Labrador to obtain caribou in the George River herd.

Caribou is used primarily for food. Hides are often used for camp bedding, filling snowshoes, and other purposes. Other parts of the caribou, such as one of the leg bones, are used to scrape sealskins, and sinews are used as threads for binding various tools and a number of other uses. On occasion, antlers are used for various crafts and tools.

With the advent of snowmobiles (1960s) people could travel as far north as the Nain area and as far west as the Churchill Falls Reservoir. In the past, groups of four to six snowmobiles, each towing a komatik,[5] would travel to the hunting grounds, in many cases making a round trip of 1,000 km over several weeks. Caribou were killed and individual komatiks were loaded with as many as eight or ten caribou at a time. The meat was shared with the community upon return of the hunting party. With the opening of the Trans Labrador Highway Phase III in 2009, hunters from the south coast have relatively easy road access to this herd. However, the current reduction in the George River herd explains present restrictions against hunting.

Labrador's moose population is low as compared to further south, as a result of low habitat availability. Consequently, only a few moose are taken in Labrador; in recent years many hunters apply for licences and harvest moose on the island portion of the province. Black bear populations are high and the animals are killed for food and hides. In recent years, access to black bear has been made relatively easy and many NunatuKavut hunters take black bear along the Trans Labrador Highway. Health concerns make people wary of killing black bears for food near communities, as bears forage in local dumps.

Small Land Mammals and Inland Birds

The most important small inland mammal harvested is the varying hare, or rabbit (*Lepus americanus*). Rabbits are mostly snared and sometimes shot when an opportunity presents itself. Trappers and hunters commonly set snares for rabbits near camping sites for immediate use at the camp. Snare lines are set near habitations and rabbits are common winter meals. In the case of respondents for the LITL study, many

Figure 1. An image of Archie Goudie getting ready for the country. (Photograph from the Grenfell Collection, compliments of The Rooms Provincial Archives)

households were made up of only two residents and the average number of rabbits consumed ranged from 20 to 30 per year.

All respondents consistently claimed that rabbits, all partridge (*Lagopus lagopus, Bonasa umbellus,* and *Dendragapus canadensis*), and porcupine (*Erethizon dorsatum*) were taken along all travel routes on an opportunistic basis. Species were harvested "everywhere" along these travel routes (see Figure 4) but some respondents had very specific places where snares were set or partridges were killed. Along travel routes anywhere within 1 km, on either side of the route, is where rabbits, partridge, or porcupine would be harvested. The numerous individual kill sites were impossible for respondents to recall and it would take a greater degree of topographic detail than 1:250,000 maps and much more time in order to gain this knowledge. Consequently, general areas were selected for recording along travel routes as well as "favoured" areas.

Partridges are generally shot or, less commonly, snared. In terms of numbers, an average of about 30 per year per household are harvested. Porcupine may be characterized as the "greatest of survival foods" because they can be secured without any special kind of tool or weapon and are, once again, taken opportunistically. Many residents relish porcupine; some consider it a delicacy.

Migratory Birds and Sea Birds
This category includes the migratory sea birds, ducks, and geese, as well as resident sea birds. Tables 3 and 4 include all the species harvested, excepting gulls. Very few gulls are now taken for food since the advent of community dumps. However, gulls' eggs are taken by about one-third of the respondents for food. The primary species for eggs is the eider duck, followed by shellbirds (mergansers) and sometimes terns. Eggs are harvested very early in the year before the eggs are "addled" (young birds developed inside). Many respondents only take a few eggs per year for their general consumption, because hens' eggs are readily available now in stores throughout the area. For the most part, harvesters and consumers of duck and gull eggs are the older people.

Ducks and geese are shot during open season and usually in an opportunistic fashion while seal hunting or engaged in fishing pursuits. Birds are hunted in an open boat in the salt water or are shot from the land. Migratory birds, such as Canada geese, are hunted with shotguns in ponds and lakes. Inuit-Métis hunters will often bring back birds to people in the community who cannot access the food, such as people who are engaged in other pursuits or the elderly. Numbers of birds taken varies with the family but will average between 20 and 30 per year.

All species of ducks are taken for food, along with geese, which makes a primary spring hunt in a number of locations.

Fur Bearers — Trapping

The numerous stone "fell" traps at historical Inuit sites in southern Labrador (Stopp 2002) bear witness to the long history of trapping. The Inuit ancestors of Inuit-Métis trapped foxes and other animals for their hides and later for trade. Since the late eighteenth century, trapping has been a mainstay of some Inuit-Métis people in south/central Labrador. Trappers in the more northern regions of the study area (Cartwright and Upper Lake Melville) would normally leave their homes in November and go "on the country" until the spring breakup, when they would return to trading posts, sell their furs, and move to the headlands for their rounds of fishing and hunting of other species.

The importance and techniques of trapping changed during the nineteenth century as this activity became part of the mercantile economy. Trappers expanded their traplines further inland along river systems such as the Paradise River and the Churchill River. Trapping still supplements south/central Labrador incomes. The most prized species trapped in recent years have been the American marten (*Martes americana*), followed by the mountain cat (lynx, *Lynx canadensis*), the fox (*Vulpe vulpes*), the otter (*Lontra canadensis*), and the beaver (*Castor canadensis*). To a lesser extent the Arctic fox (*Alopex lagopus*), the muskrat (*Ondata zibethicus*), the weasel (*Mustela ermine*), and the red squirrel (*Tamiasciurus hudsonicus*) are trapped using Conibear traps.

Traplines were inherited patrilineally, passed down from generation to generation (personal communication with Woodrow Lethbridge and other trappers, 2011). A large number of respondents in the present study made reference to continuing with traplines used by their fathers, grandfathers, and more distant ancestors. Many references were made to the traditions of respecting everyone else's traplines in the country and everyone knowing exactly where others are, or should be, during the trapping season. Knowing where another trapper should be, at any point in time, could save your life if an accident were to occur. Consequently, trapping traditions dictated respect and help for each other. In a number of interviews respondents discussed conservation methodologies that dictated that not all areas should be trapped at one time but that each area should be left to replenish itself on a three- to four-year basis.

Figure 5 combines travel routes and traplines. Traplines can mostly be distinguished by the webbed or branched lines showing where trappers would travel up and down brooks in search of fur and game. Singular lines often denote dog team/snowmobile routes or roads that have very recently been built in Labrador. Some respondents preferred to show "trapping areas" because they would travel all over an area in setting traps and not just on the waterways.

With the increased access to prime trapping areas as a result of the Trans Labrador Highway, many respondents questioned whether trapping would soon become a thing of the past due to overharvesting. Trappers also expressed the concern that the increased access caused by

Figure 2. A community sea duck hunt also means a community who comes together to scald, pick, and process the attained food, followed by a distribution of the ducks within the community. (NCC image from Sampson Photography)

the Labrador–Island Transmission Link would further degrade the habitats and reduce populations, especially in marten and lynx numbers (Mitchell 2011). Trapping is arguably the most important incentive that motivates people to use the interior of Labrador, providing greater opportunities to obtain "country food" than around home communities.

Some species of fur bearers are consumed (for example, beaver and lynx) and all skins are either sold or used for domestic purposes, such as handicraft production. Many respondents set between 200 and 400 traps per year over a vast range of territory. This large number of traps and the problems respondents had in recalling on this type of map where they set all their traps imply that another study would be required to pinpoint all areas trapped. Part of the problem here relates to the large scale of maps (approximately 1:250,000) we used, making it nearly impossible for respondents to follow all tributaries of brooks and streams on which traps were set. Suffice it to say, trapping continues to play an important role in the harvesting economy.

Fish as Food

Many respondents in the present study were fishermen and were asked not to include any activities of a commercial nature in their map biographies (Figure 4). They were asked only for their fishing activities for traditional and family uses. The two primary fish species for harvest are cod (*Gadus morhua*) and Atlantic salmon (*Salmo salar*).

Cod caught through the food fishery is a cornerstone of Inuit-Métis diet. With the recent Aboriginal Fishery Agreement that allows a total quota of 10 tons of salmon in the food fishery, one of the primary objectives is to conduct a community fishery whereby salmon are caught and shared with elders and people who may be infirm and cannot catch their own fish. According to Hanrahan (2002), the salmon holds a special place in Inuit-Métis culture, with the first salmon of the year shared among community members. However, Labrador people interviewed by Kennedy (chapter 11) consider such sharing to be a more generic, Labrador custom than one unique to Inuit-Métis.

The 10-ton quota of salmon under the agreement with NCC is caught by individuals within NCC using nets in the early summer. The catch is then either eaten fresh, frozen, dried, smoked, or bottled. Atlantic salmon commonly return only once to their natal rivers from the ocean; however, a small number may return as much larger salmon up to three or four years following their initial migration to the sea as smolts. The net fishery is set up using a small mesh net to prevent the catch of these large multi-sea-run salmon, unlike years gone by when all fish were caught. The excitement of families to move to traditional salmon berths in early summer to harvest this highly valued and culturally significant species is palpable.

Trout (*Salvilinus fontinalis*) and Arctic char (*Salvilinus alpines*) are also important staples in the diet. Trout are caught in nets during the summer and through the ice in winter. Smelt (*Osmerus mordax*) are also caught through the ice in spring. This food source is important to people living near river estuaries where smelt are easily obtained. Other oceanic species such as capelin (*Mallotus villotus*), herring (*Clupea herengus*), mackerel *(Scomber scombrus)*, and halibut (*Hippoglossus hippoglossus*) are also important items in the diets.

Shellfish Harvested

Mussels (*Mytilus edulus*), whelks *(Baccinum undatum)*, and scallops (*Chlamys islandica*) are the primary shellfish harvested. Mussels can be harvested at low tide at any time of the year when ice does not prevent such activity. In recent years, other shellfish such as shrimp (*Pandalus borealis*) and snow crab (*Chionoecetes opilio*) are consumed as a result of offshore commercial fishing for these species.

Plants Harvested

Of primary importance in this category are berries for food and wood for home heating and construction. Bakeapples (*Rubus chamaemorus*), redberries (*Vaccinium vitis-idaea*), blueberries (*Vaccinium angistifolium and V. uliginosum*), and blackberries (*Empetrum nigrum*) are the most common berries consumed in season. Generally, families will pick several litres of each and the berries are consumed fresh, are frozen, or are bottled for later use. Other species such as marshberries (*Vaccinium macrocarpon*), raspberries (*Rubus idaeus*), and squashberries (*Viburnum edule*) are consumed in smaller quantities.

One plant that is customarily consumed on the Labrador coast is Scotch lovage or Alexander (*Ligusticum scothicum*). It is harvested in the early summer as a green augmenting "boiled dinners" and other meals. Mushrooms (*Boletus spp.*) and dandelions (*Taraxicum spp.*) are also harvested in some locations.

Medicinal plants include the sap of balsam fir (*Abies balsamea*), which is used to heal and stitch fresh wounds. Of particular importance are the sap and boiled essences of the ground juniper (*Juniperis communis*). Twigs from this plant are collected in summer and boiled down, then either consumed immediately or bottled for later use. The use of juniper on the coast is ubiquitous and almost all respondents use it as a "tonic" for ailments.

Wood species harvested are primarily black spruce (*Picea mariana*), balsam fir (*Abies balsamea*), and white birch (*Betula papyrifera*). Wood is used as firewood, in house and shed construction, for building boats and komatiks, and for many other purposes. Very little firewood is available in the exposed "outside" locations where people once spent their summers, requiring transport of wood to these locations by boat in the spring for summer and fall use.

Figure 4 shows locations where berries, medicinal plants, firewood, and saw logs are harvested, and where sawmills are located. A number of "outside" communities, such as Williams Harbour and Black Tickle, have little access to firewood, especially during winters when poor ice conditions prevent travel to the mainland. Wood is the most commonly used fuel and is generally hauled directly to houses by snowmobile for drying and consumption. Today, the Trans Labrador Highway provides access to woodlots by truck and much wood is harvested in this manner.

Camping Places, Tilts, and Travel Routes

In harvesting the many species in Labrador the hunter/fisher/harvester often travels days away from the major winter or summer residence. In the past, the pattern of living was to move to the sheltered inner bays during the winter for wood harvesting, hunting, and trapping. The spring brought a round of harvest activities that included moving to the headlands for the various species during the summer and fall to follow a pattern of seasonal transhumance (Jackson 1982; Kennedy 1995). Since the cod moratorium, people increasingly use their former winter homes as a base for their economic and resource harvesting pursuits.

Geographic locations were obtained in the map biographies (30 respondents) for a total of 136 "occupation sites" that have been described as cabins, cottages, or tilts. The average number of tilts/cabins owned by respondents for resource harvesting was 4.5 per person.

Figure 3. Children smelt fishing through the ice and making their contribution to acquiring country food, Port Hope Simpson, Labrador. (Cindy Penney collection)

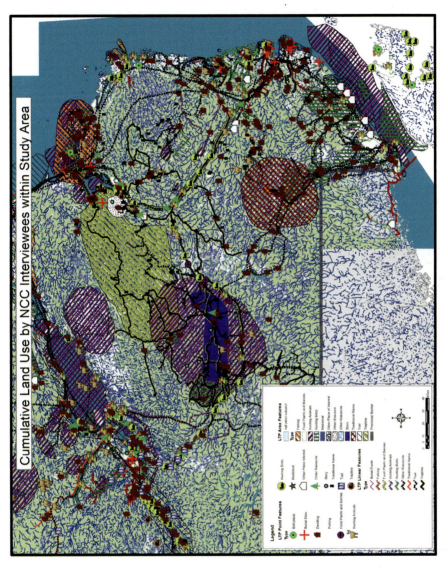

Figure 4. Map of all harvesting activities recorded spatially and digitized during the map biography interviews. This image is of the type that has been described as the "hodgepodge" map, which was used with the 30 NCC informants.

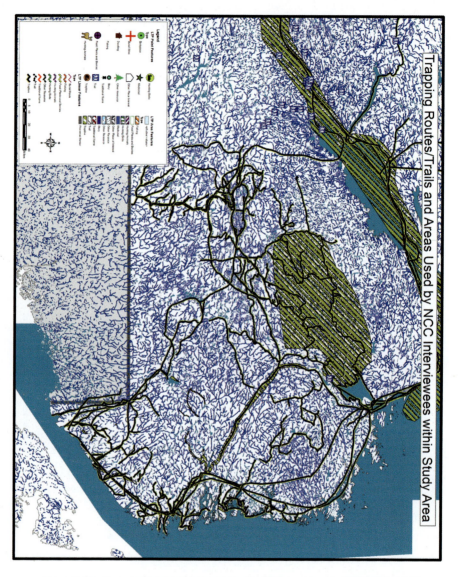

Figure 5. Traplines and travel routes used by the 30 interviewees obtained during the map biography sessions for the LITL assessment.

These cabins/tilts were maintained for the various harvested species and were usually visited at least once a year; some sites were frequented more than others.

Figure 4 shows dwellings and tilts, spiritual sites, and birth and burial places. For the most part, respondents were asked to identify only houses/cabins that were not their "chief" residence. In many instances respondents have houses in places from where their family have resettled to which they return for part of the spring, summer, and fall seasons. In many instances it is difficult to determine the prime residence since half the year may be spent at each site. As one respondent replied, "Cartwright is only our mailing address."

Many respondents, when asked where they had camped in a canvas tent on the land, just said "almost everywhere at the end of a day's travel." Respondents tried to recall specific places and their favourite spots to camp, which ideally would include shelter from winds, access to dry firewood, and a source of water. Walled canvas tents, usually with some kind of a fly covering, heated by a small portable wood stove and carpeted with balsam fir boughs are used. Formerly, travel to harvest sites was accomplished by dog team and komatik. Today, dogs are kept primarily for traditional competitive races and for nostalgia, rather than for necessity. Almost all winter travel to harvest sites now is accomplished by snowmobile or foot travel.

Special Places

Respondents were asked to point out any marriage sites, burial sites, special meeting places, or places where such things as spring water or minerals could be obtained. Some respondents pointed out burial sites previously unknown to the archaeological database and this will warrant further work. Several locations for spring water were obtained and a number of meeting places on the inside country were also documented.

Country Food

> "That's the kind of stuff we was born and reared on
> and we enjoyed it." —Jack Holwell, 1979

In conducting map biographies it is almost impossible to capture the stories associated with each place and report them in a textual script. It does not do justice to the individual telling of the story, which links the storyteller to the land in a way that often cannot be explained in words or even visual images. Our research shows that despite globalization, 92 per cent of Inuit-Métis eat "country foods" at least once a week. They are a part of the land and their stories live on in oral traditions.

Labrador is fraught with "boom and bust" fluctuations in the abundance of the various species due to the cyclic patterns over many years, such as those found in populations of caribou, snowshoe hare, etc. (Jackson 1982). The reliance on neighbours during times of hardship leads to strong ties that bind the community. When unpredictability of resources is the norm (fluctuations in abundance and fecundity), sharing among people becomes integral to the culture and ensures reciprocity in hard times (Renouf 1999).

Historic Inuit on this coast consumed similar species to what is being consumed by their descendants today. Faunal analyses of archaeological sites from Hamilton Inlet (Wollett 2003), Snack Cove (Brewster 2005), and Seal Island (Auger 1991) show a wide range of taxa consumed, with the primary consumption of *Phocidae* (seal species), sea ducks, and caribou, depending on the location of the sites. On the very southern portion, sea ducks made up a substantial portion of the diet. Near polynyas or on the outer coast, seals were the primary focus, and further inland sites showed caribou (but always as a secondary species to the various species of *Phocidae*).

Country foods are consumed fresh or stored in various ways: frozen, salted, dried, smoked, and bottled. A typical yearly larder for a family, then, includes: two caribou, at least one-quarter of moose, 30 rabbits, 5 seals, 45 partridges, 20 ducks and geese, 20 turrs (murres), 52 salmon/trout (approx-imately 50 kilograms), 35 cod (80 kilograms), 10 kilograms of other fish and shellfish, and 50 litres of the various berries. In addition to these primary foods, 39 other species (from porcupine and lynx to Scotch lovage and mushrooms) are consumed on an "occasional" or "opportunistic" basis.

Given the closure of resource-based industries in the past century (netting seals, commercial salmon fishing, and the cod moratorium), the Inuit-Métis of south/central Labrador continue to hunt, fish, and gather foods from the sea and the land. The "country food," the landscape, and the seascape are a tapestry of life, survival, and identity for these Ab-original people on the northern edge of the American continent into the twenty-first century.

Notes

1. See www.surveysystem.com/sscalc.htm.
2. During 2003 and 2004 the senior researcher conducted similar studies in the project area to add Aboriginal traditional knowledge to the forest management plans in Districts 19A, 20, and 21. See Mitchell (2004).
3. For the complete set of results from the work, which includes questions relevant to the environmental assessment, see Mitchell (2011).
4. The methodology of the study did not specifically include consistent questions regarding consumed quantities, but such information was recorded as relevant by researchers on an individual basis.
5. A komatik is a traditional Inuit sled hauled by an external power source. In the past, that source was sled dogs, but today snowmobiles are widely used.

References Cited

Auger, Reginald
> 1991 *Labrador Inuit and Europeans in the Strait of Belle Isle: From the Written Sources to the Archaeological Evidence.* Collection Nordica, No. 55. Université Laval, Québec.

Brewster, Natalie
> 2005 The Inuit in Southern Labrador: A View from Snack Cove. Unpublished Master's thesis, Department of Anthropology, Memorial University of New-foundland, St. John's.

Clarke, Bruce D., and Gregory E. Mitchell

2010 *Unveiling NunatuKavut: Describing the Lands and People of South/Central Labrador*. Electronic document, http://www.nunatukavut.ca/home/files/governance/unveiling_nunatukavut.pdf, accessed December 10, 2013.

Hanrahan, Maura

2002 Salmon at the Center: Ritual, Identity and the Negotiation of Life Space in Labrador Metis Society. Comprehensive Land Claim Supplemental Research Submission. Unpublished manuscript filed in NunatuKavut Community Council Library, Happy Valley-Goose Bay, Labrador.

Jackson, Lawrence

1982 *Bounty of a Barren Coast: Resource Harvest and Settlement in Southern Labrador—Phase One*. Labrador Institute of Northern Studies, Memorial University for Petro Canada Explorations Ltd., St. John's, Newfoundland.

Kennedy, John C.

1995 *People of the Bays and Headlands: Anthropological History and Fate of the Communities in the Unknown Labrador*. University of Toronto Press, Toronto

Mitchell, Greg

2004 Final Forest Management Report. Unpublished report, submitted to the Department of Forest Resources and Agrifoods.

2011 Contemporary Land and Sea Uses from NunatuKavut. Research conducted as part of the Labrador–Island Transmission Link Environmental Assessment. Manuscript on file in NunatuKavut Community Council Library, Happy Valley-Goose Bay, Labrador.

2013 An Inventory of Studies on Land and Sea Uses in NunatuKavut since 1979. Manuscript on file in NunatuKavut Community Council Library, Happy Valley-Goose Bay, Labrador.

Renouf, M.A.P.

1999 Prehistory of Newfoundland Hunter-Gatherers: Extinctions or Adaptations? *World Archaeology* 30(3):403–420.

Stopp, Marianne P.

2002 Reconsidering Inuit Presence in Southern Labrador. *Études/Inuit/Studies* 26(2):71–106.

Tobias, Terry

2000 *Chief Kerry's Moose, A Guidebook to Land Use and Occupancy Mapping, Research Design and Data Collection*. Ecotrust Canada. Electronic document, http://www.ubcic.bc.ca/Resources/tus.htm#axzz2egSqUxsU, accessed on September 12, 2013.

Woollett, James

2003 An Historical Ecology of Labrador Inuit Culture Change. Unpublished Ph.D. dissertation, City University of New York, New York.

CHAPTER 11

Identity Politics

John C. Kennedy

Identity politics has had as great an impact on the people of Labrador as anything since Confederation in 1949. While I have no intention in this short chapter of proving this claim to every reader's satisfaction, I will use some examples drawn from my 2013 field research on stigma, culture, and identity to show how identity politics is affecting the way one group of Labrador people view themselves, their past, and their future. In addition, my research revealed some of the unintended consequences of identity politics, both within southeastern Labrador and between most people there and their counterparts further north, within the Nunatsiavut self-government.

As used here, the concept of identity politics refers to political mobilization on the basis of racialized identities, gender, sexual orientation, ethnicity, or some other characteristic shared by a group of people. The characteristic shared here is Aboriginality or ethnicity, a factor that has mobilized various Labrador Aboriginal peoples and was explained in the introduction to this book.[1] As Rankin and Crompton's (2013) archaeological findings reported earlier in this book show, new knowledge is informing Inuit-Métis about their history and enhancing their chances for a better future. In the spring and fall of 2013 I returned to 10 of the 11 permanent communities in southeastern Labrador to learn how people were managing identity politics.[2] What I found surprised me, but first, a little background.

Stigma

Many years ago, sociologist Irving Goffman (1963:1) wrote that the original Greek meaning of "stigma" referred to marks or other visual signs cut or burned onto the bodies of criminals or traitors to publicize their failed moral status.[3] Like identity, the concept of stigma is most obvious in "mixed" social environments, where "normal" and "stigmatized" persons interact. Depending on context, persons with stigmatized social identities adapt to, or cope with, their unequal social burden by various strategies, including denying the traits that led them to be stigmatized.

People now embracing an identity as Inuit-Métis have not always been aware and/or proud of their Inuit roots. Many of the parents and grandparents of today's Inuit-Métis were ashamed of their Inuit ancestors and favoured the European side of their dual ancestry, especially when around outsiders. Indeed, before the era of identity politics that began in the 1970s, most people of mixed European–Inuit ancestry along the Labrador coast preferred the European side of their ancestry, as is reported, for example, in northern Labrador by Kleivan (1966:101). As noted in the introduction, the era of identity politics that saw Aboriginal people mobilize in pursuit of rights began in 1973 with the Native Association of Newfoundland and Labrador. My understanding of how peoples of mixed ancestry gravitated towards the European side of their ancestry began in northern Labrador in 1971–1972, just prior to the formation of the Labrador Inuit Association (Kennedy 1982:81–86, 90–97).[4] In one community, home to people then called by the problematic term "Settlers" *and* to Inuit relocated there from further north, I observed that Settlers with the strongest Inuit ancestries were often the most disparaging towards relocated Inuit, and they were reluctant to discuss their own Inuit or part-Inuit ancestors. "Settlers" was one of several terms used by Moravian missionaries in northern Labrador to refer to essentially the same hybrid or mixed peoples referred to here as Inuit-Métis (Rollmann, chapter 9). Some years later, during fieldwork in southeastern Labrador, and prior to the formation of the Labrador Metis Association, I observed a variation of the same phenomenon. Once again, individuals with the strongest Inuit ancestries evaded questions about their fore-bears, while other community members scorned recent marriages be-tween youths from their community and those from a nearby commu-nity known to have a strong Inuit heritage (Kennedy 1996).

The stigma of association with everything "Skimo" that I initially recorded in the south reminded me of the way Settlers in the north who had either grown up in or had close connections to Inuit settle-ments in the era prior to identity politics seemed to want to distance themselves from that part of their past. What I witnessed was related to power. Both in the north and south, persons of mixed ancestry sided with the more powerful local group, which at the time was most cer-tainly *not* the Inuit. Back then, referring to persons of mixed ancestry as "Native" was insulting. Shame or stigma tarnished those closest to Inuit.[5] Was southeastern Labrador more similar to northern Labrador than people thought?

For present purposes I limit my discussion of stigma to two points. First, historically, the stigma of appearing "dark," "Skimo," or "Native" may have prevented Inuit-Métis from acknowledging their roots and organizing. One 60-year-old woman recalled both stigma and its impli-cations. In her words, "it's hard to convince government that you have entitlement when you denied it for years." When the province's first Aboriginal association, the Native Association of Newfoundland and Labrador (NANL), was formed in February 1973, the member of the House of Assembly for the old riding of Labrador South, Cartwright native Mike Martin, spoke to the organizational meeting of NANL. Martin said that no more than 10 per cent of people in his southeastern Labrador riding lacked mixed ancestry. However, Martin wondered if the people of Paradise River (a community he chose at random) would accept being called "Native people." Martin was referring to stigma and he was well aware of how, at the time, it stalled any expression of Ab-originality in southeastern Labrador. The situation is completely differ-ent today, and many people estimated that around 100 people in

Sandwich Bay have applied for and become citizens of the Nunatsiavut government in northern Labrador.[6]

My second point about stigma is contemporary. As we shall see in the section on identity below, perhaps the greatest achievement of identity politics is that the stigma about one's roots is slowly being replaced by pride and acknowledgement of one's real social origins. However, one informant suggested that stigma persists. In his words:

> There's still some of them that got that outlook today. They don't want to be called that [Aboriginal] or they're ashamed of it. If someone said to me, "you look like you've got Native blood," I'd be proud of it. But some people thinks that's another breed, another tribe, not part of them. They knows they is [Aboriginal] but they don't want to say it. They're members of the Métis, some even have their LIA card, 'cause [their ancestors] moved up here [that is, from central to southeastern Labrador] years ago, settled down, and have families up here. They don't want to be called [Aboriginal]. It's like a Black person, they don't want to be called a "Nigger." They don't want to be called an Indian, a Mountaineer, Eskimo, or something like that. No, there's still people like that, but I don't know why.

Culture

The concept of culture has many meanings. Historically, anthropologists appropriated, defined, and guarded the concept of culture, but today they share at least the word with other academic disciplines and with media commentators who write about various "cultures": popular culture, gay culture, national culture, and others. For our purposes, let's assume a more traditional, anthropological definition of the term, that is, culture as learned behaviour, beliefs, and assumptions shared by a social group or a people at a particular place and time.

Before addressing the culture of Labrador's Inuit-Métis, it is important to reiterate two facts about coastal Labrador. First, not all people living in south/central Labrador have mixed ancestry and/or are members of the NunatuKavut Community Council (NCC). The NCC was only able to provide membership numbers for some communities, such as Mary's Harbour. There, 180 of the town's 350 (2013) residents are NCC members. On the other hand, local estimates put the Cartwright population at 562 (2013), of which around 100 are Nunatsiavut beneficiaries and most of the rest are NCC members. "Whitemen" and "Whitewomen," the terms currently being used, have no Aboriginal ancestry but have for generations lived alongside their Inuit-Métis neighbours. Consistent with the continuum of Inuitness my research reports, there are more Whitemen in the south, and their numbers generally decline as we move north along the coast. Indeed, I heard little about Whitemen in Black Tickle/Domino or Sandwich Bay, although the term is commonly heard further south.

Second (as noted in the introduction), historically and today, the amount of what I call "Inuitness" also occurs along a continuum that increases as we go north along the Labrador coast. My admittedly cumbersome neologism "Inuitness" refers to knowledge and use of Inuttitut and to other cultural practices and beliefs that people of Inuit ancestry consider their own. A similar gradient of Inuitness occurs along the southeastern coast where the Inuit origins of Inuit-Métis culture generally increase as we move north from the Lodge Bay–Mary's Harbour area. One exception to this generalization is St. Lewis (or Fox Harbour), historically recorded as an Inuit settlement.

During the 2013 research, local informants answered the question: Why were historic Inuit and Inuit-Métis coastal communities located where they were? In many cases, the answer involves seals, which Hawkes (1916:19) called the "chief food" of Labrador Inuit. The harp, ringed, bearded, and harbour seals are the most important of Labrador's six species. Black Tickle/Domino informants describe nearby Domino Run as "black" with harp seals each fall. Large concentrations of migrating harps congregate on the north side of Spotted Islands during their spring migration northward. Quite simply, then, Inuit spent much of each year on Spotted Islands to be as near as possible to a "refrigerator" filled with seals. Spotted Islands lies within the archipelago called Kikertet, Mille Isles, or Esquimaux Isles, where historic visitors (e.g., Jolliet, Fornel, Captain Atkins, the Moravians, Cartwright, Leiber, and others) commonly encountered Inuit (Kennedy 2015). Much as Woollett (1999:376) described some years ago for the Narrows of Lake Melville, Inuit chose locations along the southeastern coast where seals were most numerous or easily hunted.

"Annie" exemplifies the most Inuit end of the "Inuitness" continuum. In her childhood on Spotted Islands Annie heard and used Inuttitut words within a social milieu where, because of stigma, their origins were denied. During her early years, Annie and her playmates snacked on edible plants, referring to them only by their Inuttitut names, *Kuannik* (kelp) and *Tulligunnait* (rose wort). Annie loved *kuak* (frozen caribou meat) and *nipko* (dried seal meat).[7] Annie's grandfather would cut out the hard-textured pupils of fish eyes as a treat for children. The way Annie described her youth suggested that she and others raised in a community with a rich Inuit legacy gave little thought to their local vocabulary: these words were simply those used to describe foods and other local customs. However, encounters with visitors caused reflection. Annie recalled that local women commonly smoked pipes but quickly hid them when the "Shouthooks," (Newfoundlanders), who fished at nearby Griffins Harbour, occasionally came to visit. Annie's mother and grandmother told her nothing about her Inuit ancestry, and even claimed they had none. Physically, Annie and others on Spotted Islands appeared Inuit. When the Americans came ashore at Spotted Islands in the 1950s to begin work on a Cold War radar base, they asked the local children assembled on the beach, including Annie's sister, "are you Chinese?" As a university student years later, Annie remembered being approached by Chinese or Japanese students speaking to her in their respective languages, assuming she was one of them.

"Joseph" also grew up on Spotted Islands and said that the term "Shouthooks" referred to visiting Newfoundland fishers.[8] Joseph added details to Inuttitut concepts (such as *kuak, nipko, Kuannik*, and others) used by Annie and remembered that in his grandfather's time (i.e., the early twentieth century), two or three Spotted Islands families spoke Inuttitut. Once an active fisherman, Joseph's mobility is now reduced, requiring costly trips "outside" for care. Joseph does not complain. Ironically, although raised in a cultural environment with a rich Inuit legacy, he lacks kinship roots within the Labrador Inuit land claims area and is thus ineligible to become a Nunatsiavut beneficiary with access to benefits enjoyed by beneficiaries, many of whom lack his Inuit cultural heritage.

"Harry," a middle-aged man with roots to Spotted Islands, remembered "when the Shouthooks came down [to Spotted Islands] in the spring" to fish at places like Farmers Cove and Sandbank. "Sam" and "Mildred," a Domino couple in their eighties, also knew about the Shouthooks but during our interview the conversation moved to the process of making *wussen*, strands of stretched, dried, and separated membranes from seal throats that comprised one of two threads (the other was No. 10 cotton thread) used for sewing the sealskin boots everyone wore (Hussey 1981:54).

"Wilson," an Inuit-Métis man with strong Inuit roots, lived much of his life at North River, Sandwich Bay. Some years ago Wilson and I talked about how North River Inuit-Métis hunted seals in winter. Wilson and others used harpoons to retrieve seals. Excited by our conversation, he hurried to his shed to show me his harpoon.

At the more southern end of the cultural continuum are Inuit-Métis whose culture resembles that of their "Whiteman" neighbours lacking Inuit ancestry. People at this end of the continuum commonly explain their heritage with statements like: "grandmother was part-Inuit and came from Sandwich Bay." I asked "Tom" (originally from Port Hope Simpson) about his way of life, his culture. He responded:

> When I was growing up, we could go get a meal of fish or go in the woods and get a bit of wood for your fire. If you wanted to get a trout or to hunt, that's the only thing I could see, what we

always had to do. We couldn't run to the store. . . . We had to live off the land. I see that's the difference in culture. [Kennedy: Did people with no Aboriginal ancestry practise a similar way of life?] Yes they did, same thing. We was never against nobody for getting something to eat. If they was here, I mean, they had the same rights as we did. But we was born here. That's what makes the difference. And probably some of the white ones was born here, but some was implanted. We was always here. That makes the difference in Aboriginal. Really, they [Whitemen] had a choice, but we never had no choice, eh boy.

Another NCC member characterized "NunatuKavut culture" as:

Traditionally based around providing for our needs like the fishery, providing firewood. I mean you never hear people in St. John's say, "I'm going to fish for my food today or I'm going to chop wood." I mean it's all electric heat or oil furnace. Even simple necessities [of life] were so different back then. I believe it was a closer-connected community back in the day.

Today the central ingredient in Inuit-Métis culture at this end of the continuum is the realization of their part-Inuit ancestry, a fact either unknown or closeted during my earlier fieldwork. For these Inuit-Métis, then, identity rather than culture separates them from their "Whiteman" neighbours.

Identity

The word "identity" originates from the Latin word *idem* meaning "the same," and refers to a state of being, a consciousness or sense of "belonging" in common with others. Perhaps the most positive implication of identity politics for Inuit-Métis has been a rethinking of identity. Personal sensitivities about being dark-skinned or "Skimo," which were common years ago, are beginning to be replaced by an acknowledgement of Inuit ancestry and a new curiosity about family roots. This new awareness is emergent, sometimes equivocal, sometimes political and even emotional, as the following examples suggest.

One man with strong Inuit ancestry described his identity this way:

> Well I don't know. I knows all my life that I was Aboriginal, but I didn't know what it was all about. A lot of people, a good many first when the Métis was starting up, didn't want to hear talk of it. But I know myself, growing up, that I was Aboriginal. On Mother's side, they come from [a Newfoundland community], see, they got no trace of Métis. But on my father's side, come down Inuit . . . Inuit means Eskimo. [Kennedy: Did your family consider itself Inuit or Métis?]. No, there was never very much of that on the go when I was growing up, it was only after I got old enough. There was never much done or we never realized nothing, it was only after Todd Russell [current NCC president] got into it. That's when I got on the Board. [Kennedy: Why were people reluctant to talk about Métis?]. Well, I don't know. I signed up people. People came here; I had applications to fill out for them to get their Métis card. I knows one person in particular, well I knows she was Métis. Well, she looked Métis. And she said to me: "I don't know if I wants to be Métis or no." See, they didn't want to say they was. [Kennedy: Has the Métis organization been a good thing or a bad thing?] I'd say it's been a good thing, letting people know who they is and trying to get our rights. We've been robbed for years. Mining, the hydro. The land is rich. We have to fight and fight for what we're getting. We got to fight. It's getting better than it was. I was on the protest for the salmon [food] fishery. We had to fight for what we got. I've been in the boat when the DFO [Department of Fisheries and Oceans] come and tear the net right out of your hands.

Another man recalled how Inuit-Métis became conscious about their Aboriginality:

> We was a different breed. They say, they tell you that the old people, the ancestors, great-grandfather, he come across [from Europe] and got in with a Native woman, Indians, we used to call 'em Mountaineers, they had all kinds of names them times. But research and looking at it, and people digging up stuff here and there, they finds out more about it. We knows more about it. We knows we're part of it [Aboriginal].

A woman put it this way:

> When I define myself now, I simply say I am a person of Aboriginal ancestry. I don't say Inuit-Métis, and I don't say Inuit. I just say my ancestry is Inuit. Because you've got to be comfortable as well. Because I can't stand with someone from Nain, and say I'm on the same calibre. You can't do that.

My interview with three sisters, all over age 60 and NCC members, revealed a range of responses. All self-identify as Métis, a word they first heard 25–30 years ago. One preferred Métis to NunatuKavut, a word she said she could not pronounce. Two said that non-Métis and Métis should be "treated alike" with no special privileges. The sisters were well aware of their Inuit roots and when growing up were often called "Eskimos" or "Skimos" by their late brother, who used the term in a jocular fashion.[9] All remembered the times when anything Inuit was stigmatized but said that there is "more respect now."

A St. Lewis Inuit-Métis man explained his identity this way:

> I'm no different than I always was but I'm a Métis, I knows that. I didn't join. This just come from the ancestors, when they traced it all up, my mother was a Métis and that's how I come

to be one. We all got a card, a Métis card. My wife is not Métis. [Kennedy: Do you get advantages for being Métis?] No, I don't but they help young people get through school. We can set our salmon nets a week before other people can. The white person's got to wait for a week after. [Kennedy: Is this a good policy?] No I don't think so.

An NCC member in his twenties who works with younger people explained how younger people consider their identity:

> I think now more of the younger generation would identify themselves as NunatuKavut. I think just a few years back we were known as Métis or the Labrador Métis Nation. I went through that phase too. Okay, are we Métis, Southern Inuit, Inuit-Métis, and I think now probably a lot of the younger generation would identify as NunatuKavut, because of the services that's offered, and programs along the coast. Now they identify as NunatuKavut but do they really know what that means? Do they really know who they are?

Three Points from the 2013 Fieldwork

First, I have argued for a continuum of "Inuitness" that grows stronger the further north one goes, rather than the arbitrary boundary codified in the 2003 land claim that fixed the southern boundary of Inuit occupation just north of Sandwich Bay. As the archaeological, genealogical, and ethnohistorical work in this volume reports, Inuit lived south of that boundary. Yet, within a social environment dominated each summer by visiting fishers, Inuit-Métis suppressed or denied associations with all that might be seen as "Skimo" or Aboriginal and both these points emerge from the example of Annie. Her curious combination of suppression and unconscious use of an Inuit-derived culture characterized the way of life of some Inuit-Métis living in communities with a strong Inuit heritage, mainly in the northern portion of southeastern Labrador.

So what, then, is Inuit-Métis culture? Those growing up in communities where Inuit customs survived, people like Annie, practised a culture just as Inuit as that of many beneficiaries of the Nunatsiavut self-government in northern Labrador. But the culture of many other Inuit-Métis resembles that of their "Whiteman" neighbours, that is, an Inuit-derived culture of komatiks, ulus, and other practices of Inuit or Innu origin that are necessary to survive. Thus, the Inuit origins of what people do and think occurs somewhere along the continuum between these two extremes. However, even for Inuit-Métis whose culture is at the opposite end of the continuum from that of Annie, their new willingness to embrace and discuss their part-Inuit ancestry constitutes a significant social change since my earlier fieldwork. So, excepting Inuit-Métis like Annie, the culture of NCC members lies less in what they do than in who they know they are, that is, their identity.

Second, the 2013 research suggests that historically, the ancestors of contemporary Inuit-Métis developed a group consciousness much as we know happened with "Settlers" in northern Labrador. This amends what I presented in an earlier paper (Kennedy 1997), when I equated Métis ethnogenesis with their mobilization through identity politics in the 1980s, as explained in the introduction to this volume. In northern Labrador (thanks to Moravian scribes), we have known for many years that mixed "Settlers" had developed an ethnic consciousness by 1873. That year, the Moravian Periodical Accounts at Zoar record that the "English settlers . . . were not a little gratified that . . . the first infant baptized in the new church was the child of people of their own class" (Kleivan 1966:103). Noteworthy about this 1873 report is that it is one of very few references to Settler ethnogenesis in the massive corpus of Moravian documentation. One assumes that Zoar was not unique and that a similar ethnic consciousness arose in other northern settlements. In 1908, Moravian Bishop Martin recorded for the first time the Inuttitut word for "half-breeds," Kablunangajuit (now Kablunângajuit), and this word would figure prominently in the history of the LIA and contemporary Nunatsiavut, as discussed in the introductory chapter.

As is well known, in southeastern Labrador there were no outside observers equal to the Moravians. Instead, visitors used a plethora of confusing ethnic labels to refer to the ancestors of today's Inuit-Métis, including Anglo-Esquimaux, Liveyeres, planters, Labradorians, halfbreeds. We know relatively little about how early Inuit-Métis viewed their identity. Stopp (chapter 8) mentions Lydia Campbell's awareness of her own "half-breed" identity, an awareness that Stopp believes was already "a well-established part of the social landscape of central and southern Labrador." Describing Batteau during the period from 1923 to 1947, Newfoundland fisher Gretta Hussey (1981) recalls calling local Inuit-Métis "natives" and not Newfoundlanders.

At the very least, the term "Shouthooks" suggests that the Aboriginal people of Spotted Islands considered themselves distinct from visiting Newfoundland fishers. Relations between locals and visiting Newfoundland fishers were generally good, but Annie's reference to women hiding their pipes suggests some sensitivity towards how "they" would perceive "us" smoking pipes. While the term "Shouthooks" was localized and not recorded until now, it suggests that Spotted Islands people appear to have previously undergone an initial ethnogenesis.[10] My findings are tentative but amend what I summarized in 1997 (p. 13), suggesting that Inuit-Métis in communities like Spotted Islands developed a sense of distinctiveness, probably similar to that the Moravians recorded at Zoar. Given the larger numbers of Inuit in northern Labrador during the nineteenth century, "Settlers" in the north contrasted their "class" or group with local Inuit whereas in southeastern Labrador, where there were already fewer Inuit in places like Sandwich Bay, Spotted Islands, or Fox Harbour, Inuit-Métis contrasted themselves with visiting Newfoundland fishers. In Labrador, then, these new findings suggest that the ethnogenesis occurring through identity politics in the 1980s was more accurately the "'reformulation' of an existing ethnic identity" (Sawchuck 1978:72) than the creation of a brand new identity.

Third and finally, the 2013 fieldwork suggests that, like all change, identity politics has caused some unexpected consequences, both within southeastern Labrador and interregionally.

At present, one such consequence along the southeastern coast involves unequal rights to salmon. The recent history of this began in 1999, when the Department of Fisheries and Oceans closed the centuries-old commercial salmon fishery. This sparked protests by the Labrador Métis Nation (LMN; since 2010, the NCC) and an eventual agreement with DFO in 2004 that permitted Inuit-Métis an Aboriginal communal fishing licence for the coastal zone between Fish Cove Point and Cape Charles. As of 2013, members of NCC are allowed to net a maximum of six salmon per household per year while non-members, or "Whitemen," have a quota of only three. Most people I interviewed in 2013 in seven of the eight southernmost communities claimed that interest in joining the LMN spiked with the news that membership entitled members to six salmon tags, three more than "White" residents. As noted, I heard little about this issue in Sandwich Bay and Black Tickle. But in the seven southernmost communities visited, many NCC members are uncomfortable with the local burden of this hard-won Aboriginal right, claiming instead that all should receive four salmon. People are equivocal, applauding the fruits of difficult protests, but on the other hand they were remorseful that their "White" neighbours are allowed less.

When I asked one NCC member and his "Whiteman" wife about his culture, he spoke of salmon:

> I don't know what to tell you there. I suppose there's not much difference into it. The only difference into it is I can get six salmon and she can't get ne'er one. So it's rights. The government hasn't recognized the Métis. [The man's wife interjected angrily, saying:] I cannot put my hand on his net. Not allowed to touch it. He [a Métis] can get six salmon and I can only get three. Métis got to haul their own nets. And if you go out and get 30 salmon in your nets you got to throw away all but six.

In another community, an Inuit-Métis wife and her "Whiteman" husband spoke of the inequities generated by membership. They first described salmon. The wife continued, noting that she joined the LMN reluctantly, mainly because they had children who might benefit from educational programs. She quickly added, "I don't go to meetings or anything like that." Meanwhile, her husband, an experienced fisher, trapper, and hunter, stared silently at the floor as she spoke. I felt both her discomfort and his disenfranchisement. Once at home on the land and sea, he was now, by ancestry, second-class. Indeed, the situation today is the opposite of what I observed years ago. Then, one might say that the "Whitemen" were in charge, while people of mixed ancestry denied their Aboriginality or attempted to pass as whites. Nowadays, in some contexts, "Whitemen" have less capacity to access some resources than Inuit-Métis, a remarkable transformation that many find uncomfortable.[11] Possibly because of the new burden of inequity flowing from membership, most NCC members say little about it, not wanting to upset the delicate balance of harmony essential to community well-being.

Identity politics has also led to inequities between NCC members and Nunatsiavut beneficiaries. Identity politics and the 1993 discovery of nickel at Voisey's Bay led to the Nunatsiavut land claim in 2003. Geographically based eligibility criteria require that potential beneficiaries have a "connection" (residence, birth, birth of parent) to the Labrador Inuit land claims area and this has allowed some Inuit-Métis living in southeastern Labrador to become beneficiaries (LIA 2003:37).

Southeastern Labrador people apply mainly because of the Inuit government's generous Non-Insured Health Benefits program.[12] Those I interviewed in 2013 gave a few examples. One southeastern Labrador man needing medical attention applied for and was accepted as a Nunatsiavut beneficiary because his grandfather was born within the Labrador Inuit land claims area. However, when the man's sisters, who share the same social background, applied they were rejected, ostensibly because their brother was recognized to be more involved politically. One St.

Lewis woman of strong Inuit ancestry applied to become a Nunatsiavut beneficiary but her application was rejected, although two Port Hope Simpson families and roughly 100 Sandwich Bay people have become beneficiaries. A Black Tickle man explained what he believes are these new inequities:

> Now they [Nunatsiavut] got a land claim and we haven't. Yet we've been here, I'd say my generation, and my father, grandfather, and great-grandfather, all belonged to this land, the same as them guys there [Nunatsiavut beneficiaries]. I think a lot of it is unfair, unfair from the government. I'm not against nobody. I knows people [Nunatsiavut beneficiaries] who can go to St. John's and stay there for whatever appointment is required, and come back and it won't cost them nothing. That's paid for by the Nunatsiavut government. I went to St. John's a few years ago, my wife had this trouble, we went there and it cost me $1,800. I had to come with $1,800 to pay my way, although my buddies [friends who are Nunatsiavut beneficiaries] they're able to go out there and back and it won't cost them nothing. I knows another guy, well, my buddy, you might say, he went out there [St. John's] taking treatment for prostate cancer, stayed in a hotel for two or three months, whatever time it took to get his treatments, come back and it didn't cost him nothing. Now that's what I calls pretty unfair.

Those working on various NunatuKavut Community Council programs work on term contracts, in projects funded for varying periods of time by either the provincial or federal government. This contrasts dramatically with the more permanent services offered through the seven departments and extensive governmental infrastructure of the Nunatsiavut government. One Inuit-Métis woman who works in the health sector on the southeastern coast put it this way, "In Nunatsiavut, in their health and social development department, you know they do

Figure 1. NCC members protest Lower Churchill project, 2013. (Greg Mitchell photo, courtesy of Greg Mitchell)

some one-on-one with their clientele but in a lot of their health promotion sector they have 50 to 100 staff and we got two."

NCC members interviewed realize that these new, interregional inequities result from the Nunatsiavut land claim, which they, like me, applaud. On the other hand, Inuit-Métis remain unrecognized, excluded both by birthplace and by their historic denial of being Aboriginal. More positively, since mobilizing in the mid-1980s, identity politics provides Inuit-Métis with a community in which to examine and celebrate an identity that had been closeted previously. The voices aired above suggest that this examination is continuing. A momentum that is part cultural, part political is growing, not only in the NCC offices in Goose Bay, but in the small communities along the southeastern Labrador coast. I sensed in 2013 a growing concern that the same provincial government that terminates local programs and doggedly opposes their claim to be Aboriginal people is busily developing Labrador, often on lands long used by Inuit-Métis hunters and trappers, such as along the

Churchill River. Although the NCC protests in 2013 to gain a seat at discussions on the Lower Churchill hydro project were unsuccessful, identity politics is slowly building capacity and providing Inuit-Métis with an organization to ensure that their voices will not be silenced.

Notes

1. Relevant theoretical and/or comparative examples of identity politics, written from different perspectives, include Sawchuck (2001), Kuper (2003), and Cairns (2011).

2. My fieldwork in southeastern Labrador began with seven months in 1979 and 1980, primarily in the communities of Lodge Bay and Mary's Harbour. I then lived for three months in 1982 in Port Hope Simpson, and for another three months in Cartwright in 1983. Following this, I returned for more fieldwork in the fall of 2000, with several shorter visits after that. The 2013 fieldwork under the CURA project occurred in two phases. In April and May, I visited seven of the eight permanent communities between Lodge Bay and Port Hope Simpson. Williams Harbour, the sole community not visited, had at the time just 17 people living in seven households. Then, in September and October, I visited Cartwright, Paradise River, and Black Tickle/Domino. Local estimation in 2013 of the total population of southeastern Labrador's 11 communities is 2,217, down 12 per cent from the population reported by Martin et al. (2012:197–225), which was based on the 2006 census. I interviewed 49 men and 31 women, ranging in age from mid-twenties to 88 years. Local people suggested some informants. I contacted others through personal contacts or networking. My approach was qualitative and my questions open-ended. Participation was informed, voluntary, and unpaid. I explained the project and my research to all informants, and that the data could be used in two books. My questions covered a diverse range of topics, from identity to community history. Interviews lasted from around 40 minutes to several hours. Because of the brevity of my research and small number (80 of 2,217) of people interviewed, my findings must be considered preliminary; long-term qualitative and quantitative research in all communities would confirm or refute my findings. Before engaging in fieldwork, my research proposal was assessed and approved both by the Tri-Council Ethics Review committee (Interdisciplinary Committee on Ethics in Human Research or ICEHR) at Memorial University (Dr. Larry Felt, Chair), and a similar committee of the NunatuKavut Community Council. To protect the dignity, confidentiality, and privacy of informants, real names are not used and informants are not linked to their communities when informants are discussing potentially sensitive issues. As "professional strangers" who attempt to grasp complex realities, anthropologists

invariably misunderstand what locals know, getting some things wrong; I accept responsibility for any/all errors of fact or interpretation.

3.   Following Goffman (1963), many studies have explored various stigmas, such as those experienced by individuals with various medical conditions, including mental illness or those who have AIDS or are HIV-positive; other foci of research on stigma include work on discrimination related to sexual orientation, obesity, and poverty. Link and Phelan (2001) and Major and O'Brien (2005) provide good overviews of recent research.

4.   It is important to emphasize that I have long supported the successful LIA land claim in northern Labrador. Land claims offer the best way for Aboriginal peoples to control their future. My concern is solely with the inequities created by the claim, especially with Inuit-descendant peoples south of Nunatsiavut who were left out. This said, LIA acted on the knowledge available at the time, prior to our findings.

5.   My CURA colleague, Evelyn Plaice, observed the same phenomenon in North West River, where the offspring of mixed Settler–Innu marriages showed their allegiance to their Settler rather than to their Innu category. Plaice writes, "it seems the closer a person is to direct association with Indians and Indianness, the harder it becomes to manage an ethnic identity which shares traits with Indians and Indianness" (1990:95).

6.   Sandwich Bay is only about 30 km south of the southern boundary of Nunatsiavut. Most Nunatsiavut communities are further north, in central and northern Labrador.

7.   For a longer list of Inuttitut words from Spotted Islands, see NCC (2010:241).

8.   While its reference to Newfoundland fishers is the most common meaning, curiously, Joseph also associated the word "Shouthooks" (spelled here phonetically) with a scraper used to remove fat from sealskins so that it wouldn't get on socks worn inside sealskin boots. Former Spotted Islands residents older than about age 50 are more familiar with the term than younger people. "Shouthooks" is not listed in the vernacular or dialectal Labrador word lists or dictionaries that I examined, including Carleton (1924), Evans (1930), Strong (1931), Story et al. (1982), Kennedy (1996:123–129), and NCC (2010:241). Locals I interviewed are unaware of the origins of "Shouthooks," or its relationship, if any, to the Island of Ponds topoynm Pennyhook's Cove. Further research might resolve whether "Shouthooks" was simply a jocular vernacularism, an anglicized corruption of an Inuttitut word, or something else altogether.

9.   My informant readily agreed that "Skimo" was most commonly used as a derogatory term. Her description led me to conclude that her brother inverted the term from denigration to empowerment. Although the context is very different, this kind of strategic reappropriation of highly offensive terminology can be

seen among some African Americans (cf. e.g., Kennedy 2002).

10. In her recent memoir, Inuit-Métis Josie [Curl] Penny (2010:31), who wintered at Roaches Brook and summered on Spotted Islands, contrasted her own people as "we Liveyeres" as distinct from visiting Newfoundlanders. I acknowledge that, alternatively, the local sensitivity to *women* smoking pipes may have been a gendered distinction, rather than one based on ethnicity, as Annie seemed to suggest. Or it could be a gendered and/or Newfoundland–Labrador distinction.

11. The situation is more complicated than this sentence suggests, especially as many Inuit-Métis feel uncomfortable having rights exceeding those of their neighbours. For a description of social relations prior to identity politics, see Kennedy (1996).

12. According to the Nunatsiavut website, the national Non-Insured Health Beneifts (NIHB) program supplements provincial health plans or private insurance; NIHB pays for some or all medical, dental, and pharmaceutical costs not covered by other plans for eligible First Nations or Inuit.

References Cited

Cairns, A.
    2011 *Citizens Plus: Aboriginal Peoples and the Canadian State*. University of British Columbia, Vancouver.

Carleton, Fred P.
    1924 Notes on the Labrador Dialect. *ASDF* January 1924:138–139.

Evans, Mary S.
    1930 Terms from the Labrador Coast. *American Speech* 6(1):56–58.

Goffman, Erving
    1963 *Stigma: Notes on the Management of Spoiled Identity*. Prentice-Hall, Englewood Cliffs, New Jersey.

Hawkes, E. W.
    1916 *The Labrador Eskimo*. Anthropological Series, Memoir 91. Government Printing Bureau, Ottawa.

Hussey, Greta
    1981 *Our Life on Lear's Room Labrador*. Robinson-Blackmore, St. John's.

Kelvin, Laura
    2011 The Inuit-Métis of Sandwich Bay: Oral histories and Archaeology. Unpublished Master's thesis, Department of Archaeology, Memorial University of Newfoundland, St. John's.

Kennedy, John C.
    1982 *Holding the Line: Ethnic Boundaries in a Northern Labrador Community*.

Social and Economic Studies, No. 27. ISER, Memorial University of Newfoundland, St. John's.

1995 *Peoples of the Bays and Headlands: Anthropological History and the Fate of Communities in the Unknown Labrador.* University of Toronto Press, Toronto.

1996 *Labrador Village.* Waveland Press, Prospect Heights, Illinois.

1997 Labrador Metis Ethnogenesis. *Ethnos* 63(3–4):5–23.

2015 *Encounters: An Anthropological History of Southeastern Labrador.* McGill-Queen's University Press, Montreal and Kingston.

Kennedy, Randall L.

2002 *Nigger: The Strange Career of a Troublesome Word.* Pantheon, New York.

Kleivan, Helge

1966 *The Eskimos of Northeast Labrador: A History of Eskimo–White Relations, 1771–1955.* Norsk Polarinstitutt, Oslo.

Kuper, Adam

2003 The Return of the Native. *Current Anthropology* 44(3):389–402.

Labrador Inuit Association (LIA)

2003 Labrador Inuit Land Claims Agreement. Initialled 29 August 2003. St. John's.

Link, Bruce G., and Jo C. Phelan

2001 Conceptualizing Stigma. *Annual Review of Sociology* 27:363–385.

Major, Brenda, and Laurie T. O'Brien

2005 The Social Psychology of Stigma. *Annual Review of Psychology* 56:393–421.

Martin, Debbie H., James E. Valcour, Julie R. Bull, John R. Graham, Melita Paul, and Darlene Wall

2012 *NunatuKavut Community: Health Needs Assessment.* Final Report. NunatuKavut Community Council, Happy Valley-Goose Bay.

NunatuKavut Community Council (NCC)

2010 Unveiling NunatuKavut: Document in Pursuit of Reclaiming a Homeland. Document on file with NCC, Goose Bay. Electronic document, http://www.nunatukavut.ca/home/files/governance/unveiling_nunatukavut.pdf, accessed December 10, 2013.

Pace, Jessica E.

2008 There Is Where We Live, But It's Not My Home: Archaeology and Identity in Sandwich Bay, Labrador. Unpublished Master's thesis, Department of Archaeology, Memorial University of Newfoundland, St. John's.

Penny, Josie

2010 *So Few on Earth: A Labrador Métis Woman Remembers.* Dundurn Press, Toronto.

Plaice, Evelyn

1990 *The Native Game.* Newfoundland and Economic Studies, No. 40. ISER Books, Memorial University of Newfoundland, St. John's.

Rankin, Lisa, and Amanda Crompton

2013 The Labrador Métis and the Politics of Identity: Understanding the Archaeological Past to Negotiate a Sustainable Future. *International Journal of Heritage and Sustainable Development* 3(1):71–79.

Sawchuck, Joe

1978 *The Metis of Manitoba: Reformulation of an Ethnic Identity.* Peter Martin Associates, Toronto.

2001 Negotiating an Identity: Métis Political Organizations, the Canadian Government, and Competing Concepts of Aboriginality. *American Indian Quarterly* 25(1):73–91.

Story, G. M., W. J. Kirwin, and J. D. A. Widdowson (editors)

1982 *The Dictionary of Newfoundland English.* University of Toronto Press, Toronto.

Strong, William Duncan

1931 More Labrador Survivals. *American Speech* 6(4):290–291.

Woollett, James M.

1999 Living in the Narrows: Subsistence Economy and Culture Change in Labrador Inuit Society during the Contact Period. *World Archaeology* 30(3):370–387.

CHAPTER 12

Conclusions

John C. Kennedy

In the 1970s the Newfoundland government, scientists, and New-foundlanders believed that oil would be discovered off the Labra-dor coast. Although the consortium Eastcan and other companies would discover several impressive natural gas fields, the expectation had been that Labrador, Newfoundland's "Awakening Giant" to the north, would be the site of offshore oil discovery, just as Labrador had long been the source of cod, hydro power, iron ore, uranium, and more. Thus the surprise in 1979 when the Hibernia oil field was discovered 300 km off St. John's.

Prior to this book, academics and governments have long associat-ed Aboriginal peoples with Labrador, and more specifically, Inuit with northern Labrador. Just as it was assumed that oil must be off Labrador, all assumed that Inuit were only in northern Labrador and that the Lab-rador people along the coast further south lacked Aboriginal heritage.

Empirical research trumps such assumptions. Our five-year multi-disciplinary Community–University Research Alliance (CURA) project discovered definitive proof of an Inuit legacy in central and southeastern Labrador. Among other research methodologies and discoveries, our team's archaeologists excavated Inuit sod houses that are essentially the same as those excavated in northern Labrador; we excavated several In-uit communal houses near Cartwright; we worked on a method to de-termine the distinguishing characteristics of Inuit-Métis houses and settlements; we conducted new and very detailed genealogical work on several Inuit-Métis families that document historic *métissage* and traced successive generations through time; we translated German correspondence providing our best window yet as to why the Moravians of northern Labrador invited Settlers (essentially Inuit-Métis) to join their church, with implications that continue; we gathered data showing that even after the devastating closure of the commercial cod and salmon fisheries, southeastern Labrador Inuit-Métis have continued to harvest resources of the land and sea; we gathered concrete evidence of the region's Inuit legacy with new implications for historic ethnogenesis; and we discovered some of the unexpected consequences of identity politics.

Although regional in focus, our work provides detailed empirical findings that may be useful for those participating in the broader discourse on Inuit, Métis, *métisssage*, and hybridity. As mentioned in the introduction, the adaptation and historical influences affecting various Métis groups are best understood regionally, and in Canada, the conceptual category of "Métis" unites distinct Métis communities largely because they were included as Aboriginal peoples in the 1982 Constitution Act. Nevertheless, despite regional differences, there are similarities in the history of Canada's Métis, as illustrated here by notions of stigma, which in the Labrador case might have led to assimilation were it not for identity politics. At a deeply personal level, the lives of many Canadian Métis have been journeys of discovery. For Métis women like Heather Devine (2010) and Annie (Kennedy, chapter 11) and for their male counterparts, childhood questions about ancestors were often met with silence or denial. Now and finally come answers. Answers bring certainty and build confidence, and when shared with others through political mobilization, they can help Canadian Métis to see themselves not as marginal to our nation's story but as the descendants of those who built Canada.

While our work breaks new ground, we consider our findings as much a call for further research as they are anything approximating the final statement on any of the topics presented. For example, while the long-term research of Rankin and her students in Sandwich Bay has greatly increased what we know about that area, we realize that other portions of the coast further south remain relatively unstudied. The same can be said about our ethnographic and ethnohistorical work, where many questions have not received the attention they warrant. Thus, the families traced through our genealogical and historical work live primarily on the northern edge of Inuit-Métis country and similar examinations of *métissage* might well have occurred in the Battle Harbour, St. Lewis, or Seal Islands areas. Similarly, archaeological work in old merchant centres like St. Francis Harbour or Venison Tickle might improve our understanding of Europeans or Inuit-Métis who worked for companies located there. If my short stints in Black Tickle/Domino and St. Lewis are any indication of the potential, new long-term research could revise older understandings about the histories and contemporary adaptations of people living in these small communities. We lament that in recent decades there has been very little long-term ethnographic research in most communities south of Sandwich Bay. Long-term ethnographic work within specific communities or sub-regions such as St. Michael's Bay could prove very rewarding. Thus, the research reported in this book is really an appeal for further research that could fill in details of the general picture our book presents.

In presenting the archaeology and ethnohistory of Labrador's Inuit-Métis, our hope is that this volume will stimulate conversations in the fish plants, kitchens, and retail stores of Inuit-Métis communities. As our work shows, it is really only through research that facts begin to replace assumptions about the peoples and histories of regions. Scientific evidence about the past provides present and future generations with some of the tools needed to build new futures. Along with our NCC partners, then, our goal continues to be as our project is titled: to understand the past to build the future.

Reference Cited

Devine, Heather

2010 Being and Becoming Métis. In *Gathering Places: Aboriginal and Fur Trade Histories*, edited by Carolyn Podruchny and Laura Peers, pp. 181–210. University of British Columbia Press, Vancouver.

Index